Proactive Law in a Business Environment

Gerlinde Berger-Walliser & Kim Østergaard (Eds.)

Proactive Law in a Business Environment

DJØF Publishing

Gerlinde Berger-Walliser & Kim Østergaard (eds.)
Proactive Law in a Business Environment

1. edition

Cover: Bo Helsted
Print & Binding: AKA-Print, Tilst
Printed in Denmark 2012

ISBN 978-87-574-2759-3

Sold and distributed in Scandinavia by:
DJØF Publishing
Email: forlag@djoef.dk
www.djoef-forlag.dk

Sold and distributed in North America by:
International Specialized Book Services (ISBS)
Email: orders@isbs.com
www.isbs.com

Sold in all other countries by:
The Oxford Publicity Partnership Ltd
Email: djof@oppuk.co.uk
www.oppuk.co.uk

Distributed in all other countries by:
Marston Book Services
Email: trade.orders@marston.co.uk
www.marston.co.uk

Content

Preface

According to definitions found in common English language dictionaries, the word proactive implies "acting in anticipation of future problems, needs, or changes". This definition and variations of it go back to experimental psychology from the 1930s. Today the term is used and sometimes misused in many different contexts. Proactive behavior is increasingly sought for in various areas of human, social and business life. Companies search for proactive employees, develop proactive processes and look for proactive business strategies. Politicians and the media call for proactive solutions to deal with social and environmental problems. In IT, fault-tolerant chips can operate under a proactive mode, and proactive medicine prevents health problems before symptoms manifest.

The law, in contrast, focuses on problems and litigation and in so far continues to be predominantly past-directed and reactive. Traditional legal research and practice mainly deal with failure to respect private and state regulation and the consequences of this non-compliance. It addresses rights, obligations and broken relationships instead of anticipating future problems, stakeholder expectations, and possible needs or changes in a relationship. In business or personnel relationships the lawyer much too often only gets involved in order to prevent economic loss, or when the legal problem has already occurred. Not always but typically, companies see the law as a constraint, a cost factor, something they have to comply with, instead of embracing it as an opportunity, a success factor, or a management tool. Only recently the law has been discovered as a resource that companies can use to create value and competitive advantage, and that it can be used proactively to manage risk and relationship.

Though obviously many lawyers counsel their clients in order for them to stay out of court, proactivity in law requires more than dispute prevention. In addition to preventing legal problems from arising, a proactive approach to law develops and promotes good legal behavior, prevents undesirable behavior and minimizes risk.

This book assembles articles on what could be called an alternative way of legal thinking, known in Scandinavia as the proactive approach to law. It features contributions presented at the second European Proactive Law Conference, hosted by the Law Department at Copenhagen Business School on December 1 and 2, 2011 in Frederiksberg, Denmark. The conference followed a series of previous conferences and subsequently published books in Scandinavia as well as the first European Proactive Law Symposium held in Nancy, France. It is our goal to continue the tradition of bi-annual conferences in different geographic regions in order to bring the proactive approach to law to the attention of a broader international audience.

This year's conference focused on Proactive Law as it relates to various business areas. It brought together European researchers from the developing field of proactive law with their counterparts from the United States where similar issues of problem prevention and value creation through the proactive use of law have been discussed for many years in the comprehensive law movement, especially preventive law, and more recently in the growing area of law and strategy.

Besides a general overview of proactive law, the contributions in this book include topics such as legal risk management, strategic contracting, pre-contractual negotiation, collaborative contracts, iterative contracts, and selective distribution. One of the central concerns in proactive law is to include legal considerations in the managerial process by bringing in business-oriented legal advice, and generally speaking engage in cross-professional and interdisciplinary collaboration. Consequently one of the core objectives of this year's conference and the submitted papers was to foster an interdisciplinary approach between proactive law and economics, as well as various management disciplines, in order to further develop an economic theory of proactive law. Examples of such interdisciplinary research are the articles on how proactive law affects transaction costs, relational contract theory, and the brand value of a company.

As you will notice by reading the articles, the objective of interdisciplinary collaboration has been achieved to a great extent during this conference, either through the interdisciplinary topic of many of the contributions or the diverse background of the presenters from disciplines such as law, economics and management. Nevertheless, future research needs to further develop a general legal theory of proactive law. Future contributions hopefully will design additional proactive legal tools, such as the Manager's Legal PlanTM presented in DiMatteo, Seidel and Haapio's contribution to this book. Additional research will be needed to prove the economic value which a proactive approach to the law can provide for businesses and society as a whole.

Special thanks goes to Helena Haapio, who as far as we know was the first to publicly use the term "proactive contracting" in the 1990s and since then she has inspired many of the conference participants in their work on proactive law. We would also like to thank her for her encouragement and active support in organizing this proactive law conference and editing the present book. Moreover, we would like to honor Louis Brown, who since the publication of his book in 1950 has been known as the "father of preventive law" and without whose ground laying work on preventive law, the proactive law movement probably never would have emerged.

We are grateful to Dreyers Foundation for its financial support to publish this book and to the law department of Copenhagen Business School. We would like to thank Trine Buch, Vinni von Benzon, and Sandie Nøhr Nielsen for all their assistance before and during the conference and with the preparation of the submitted papers for publication in this book.

Last but not least, we would like to thank all authors for their contributions which have made this book possible.

Frederiksberg, March 2012
Gerlinde Berger-Walliser & Kim Østergaard

The Past and Future of Proactive Law: An Overview of the Development of the Proactive Law Movement

By

Gerlinde Berger-Walliser
Dr.jur., Associate Professor, CEREFIGE-ICN Business School Nancy-Metz[1]

1. Introduction

Over the recent years, a growing body of literature, conferences, books and other publications has contributed to the definition and further development of *proactive law* following its introduction in the late 1990s.[2] Since then the idea of a *proactive approach to law* has been developed further, enriched, refined,[3] and extended into new areas, thereby enlarging the concept of proactive law and its fields of application. Recently, academic courses on proactive law and management have been established in European law and business schools[4], and the concept has been

1. I thank Helena Haapio for her insights and comments on an earlier draft of this chapter.
2. The approach specifically called proactive law emerged in Finland in the late 1990s. *See* the first publication relating to the approach: Helena Haapio: Quality Improvement through Proactive Contracting: Contracts Are Too Important to Be Left to Lawyers!, American Society for Quality, Proceedings of Annual Quality Congress (AQC), Philadelphia, PA, Vol. 52, May 1998, pp. 243-248.
3. See e.g. Henrik Lando, Determinants of the Optimal Degree of Pro-activeness in Contracting, in A PROACTIVE APPROACH 255 (Scandinavian Studies in Law vol. 49, Peter Wahlgren ed. 2006) [hereinafter A PROACTIVE APPROACH]., *available at* http://www.scandinavianlaw.se/pdf/49-14.pdf.
4. *See* ERASMUS curriculum development project on Proactive Management and Proactive Business Law (PAM PAL) funded by the Lifelong Learning Programme of the European Commission. See ProActive Management and ProAc-

taken up by the European Economic and Social Committee in the form of its own-initiative opinion on "The proactive law approach: a further step towards better regulation at EU level" published in the Official Journal of the European Union in 2009.[5] The proactive approach to law, sometimes also called *proactive law movement*, has triggered interest not only by people working in the field of law and regulation but also in other academic and professional areas such as information technology, economics, strategy, marketing and communication, commercial and contract management, thereby fostering its interdisciplinary scope.

Without pretention to be exhaustive, this chapter is a modest attempt to synthesize some of the existing literature on proactive law. Hopefully it can make a small contribution to the definition and the development of a comprehensive theory of proactive law by providing a framework for future research in the area of proactive law and the development and application of proactive legal and management tools in academia and practice.

In the following I will explain the concept of proactive law, summarize the history of the proactive law movement, and reflect on some of the reasons for the emergence of the approach. I will describe its origins in and contrast it from preventive law, identify the basic principles of proactive law, and finally conclude with perspectives on future research.

2. History of the proactive law movement

The approach specifically called proactive law emerged in Finland in the late 1990s. The first publication relating to the approach was a paper entitled "Quality Improvement through Proactive Contracting" that Helena Haapio presented at the Annual Quality Congress of the American Society for Quality in Philadelphia in 1998. This paper was followed

tive Business Law, TURKU UNIVERSITY OF APPLIED SCIENCES, http://pampal.turkuamk.fi/index.php.

5. See Opinion of the European Economic and Social Committee on 'The proactive law approach: a further step towards better regulation at EU level', 2009 Official. J. Eur. Union, July 28, 2009, at C 175/26, available at http://eur-lex.europa.eu/LexUriServ/LexUriServ.do?uri=OJ:C:2009:175:0026:0033:EN:PDF.

by a series of publications and the first proactive law conference, which was held in Helsinki in 2003.

A central player in the field is the Nordic School of Proactive Law, a network of researchers and practitioners from Denmark, Finland, Iceland, Norway, and Sweden, each of whom has an interest in proactive law. The Nordic School was instrumental in the creation of the ProActive ThinkTank, led by a core team from Denmark, Finland, France, the Netherlands, and the United Kingdom. The mission of the ThinkTank is to provide a global forum for business leaders, lawyers, academics, and other professionals to discuss, develop, and promote the proactive management of relationships, contracts, and risks and the prevention of legal uncertainties and disputes.[6] Among the publications following conferences organized by the Nordic School are three English language books, A Proactive Approach[7], Corporate Contracting Capabilities[8], and A Proactive Approach to Contracting and Law.[9] Some of the early work of the Nordic School is available in Finnish or Swedish only.

After initial developments in the Nordic countries, the proactive approach started to awaken interest outside Scandinavia, first in Europe and later in other countries, leading to conferences and publications on a broader scale.[10] Through these and the International Association for Contract and Commercial Management (IACCM), information about the approach reached pioneers of *law and strategy*, and law for competitive advantage (LCAM),[11] an emerging field of legal scholarship in the United States.[12] This expanded the already existing close collaboration

6. *See* ProActive Think Tank Mission Statement, available at http://www.proactivelaw.org/. See also https://www.iaccm.com/gp/proactive/?java&preview.
7. A PROACTIVE APPROACH, Scandinavian Studies in Law vol. 49 (Peter Wahlgren ed. 2006).
8. CORPORATE CONTRACTING CAPABILITIES, University of Joensuu Publications in Law, No. 21 (Soili Nyste'n-Haarala ed. 2008).
9. A PROACTIVE APPROACH TO CONTRACTING AND LAW (Helena Haapio ed, 2008).
10. Proactive law conferences have taken place biannually in Helsinki, Stockholm, Turku, Nancy and Copenhagen.
11. *See* Larry A. DiMatteo, George J. Seidel & Helena Haapio, Strategic Contracting: Examining the Business-Legal Interface, in this book.
12. See generally Robert C. Bird, Pathways of Legal Strategy, 14 Stan. J. L. Bus. & Fin. 1, 3-4 (2008); Constance E. Bagley, Winning Legally: The Value of Legal Astuteness, 33 ACAD. MGMT. REV. 378, 383 (2008); Constance E. Bagley, What's

between the promoters of preventive law and proactive law to new fields and led to first attempts to trace the history of these parallel developments and to merge their common themes.[13]

3. Definition and nature

Proactive law seeks a new approach to legal issues in business and society. Instead of regarding law as a constraint that companies and people in general need to comply with, a cost factor, an administrative burden, or – at best – a means to protect one's own or somebody else's interests against harmful behaviour of others, proactive law considers law as an enabling instrument to create success and foster sustainable relationships. An objective of proactive law is to use the law as a lever to create value for the company, the individual or society in general.

According to definitions found in common English language dictionaries, the word *proactive* (also spelled *pro-active*) implies "acting in anticipation of future problems, needs, or changes."[14] According to Randy M. Page, "[t]he concept of proactivity emphasizes taking personal responsibility for behaviour" based on values rather than "blam[ing] circumstances, conditions or, conditioning for their behaviour." [15] These definitions go back to experimental psychology from the 1930s which define proactivity as "impairment or retardation of learning or of the

Law Got to Do with It?: Integrating Law and Strategy, 47 AM.BUS.L.J. 587 (2010); Robert C. Bird, Law, Strategy and Competitive Advantage, 44 U. CONN. L. REV. 61(2011), available at http://connecticutlawreview.org/documents/Bird.pdf.

13. See e.g. George J. Siedel & Helena Haapio, Using Proactive Law for Competitive Advantage, 47 AM. BUS. L.J. 641 (2010); Gerlinde Berger-Walliser, Robert C. Bird & Helena Haapio, Promoting Business Success Through Contract Visualization, 17 J.L., BUS. & ETHICS 55 (2011); Larry A. DiMatteo, George J. Seidel and Helena Haapio, Strategic Contracting: Examining the Business-Legal Interface in this book.
14. http://www.merriam-webster.com/dictionary/proactive.
15. Randy M. Page: Fostering Emotional Well-being in the Classroom. Chapter 2: Skills for Emotional Well-Being. Paragraph: Responsibility: Are We Proactive or Reactive? pp 50-52 Jones & Bartlett Publishers, 2003, citing Stephen R. Covey, The Seven Habits of Highly Effective People, 1992, 2004 and Viktor E. Frankl, Man's search for meaning: an introduction to legotherapy, 1959.

remembering of what is learned by effects that remain active from conditions prior to the learning".[16] Today, the word proactive or proactivity is commonly used (and sometimes misused) in different contexts, such as life sciences, business, information technologies and management literature.[17] The latter differentiates between *proactive thinking*[18] and *proactive behaviour* (proactivity).[19] The so-called *proactive thinking framework* developed by Alain Paul Martin, Herbert A. Shepard and Richard Beckhard "applies primarily to issues (threats and opportunities) and complex social systems such as communities and organizations (corporations, government, NGOs, World Bank),"[20] while *proactive behaviour* mostly applies to the individual, namely in the workplace.[21] Findings from the aforementioned literature show that professionals who are considered to be proactive typically engage in the following behaviors:[22]

1. Scan for change opportunities.
2. Set effective, change-oriented goals, and focus on accomplishment with real impact.
3. Anticipate and prevent problems.
4. Do different things, or do things differently.
5. Take action.
6. Persevere, persist in their efforts.
7. Achieve results.

16. Whiteley, Paul L.; Blankfort, Gerald (1933), „The Influence of Certain Prior Conditions Upon Learning", Journal of Experimental Psychology (APA) 16: 843-851.
17. *See* generally The Professional Development Institute, Proactive Thinking and Strategic Brainstorming, at http://www.executive.org/proactive/Default.asp.
18. Alain Paul Martin (1983). Think Proactive: New Insights into Decision-Making. The Professional Development Institute. 233 (1983).
19. *See* e.g. Bateman, T. S., & Crant, J. M. (1993). The proactive component of organizational-behavior: A measure and correlates. Journal of Organizational Behavior, 14(2), 103-118.
20. The Professional Development Institute, Proactive Thinking and Strategic Brainstorming, at http://www.executive.org/proactive/Default.asp.
21. Id.
22. Thomas S. Bateman, & J. Michel Crant, J. M., *Proactive Behavior: Meanings, Impact, and Recommendations*, Business Horizons 63 (1999).

In addition to the research on proactive thinking and proactivity at work, organizational research has identified design features which characterize a *proactive organization*. According to Jon M. Shepard, Michael Betz and Lenahan O'Connell the proactive organization adopts the following four features: cooperation, participation, negotiation, and direct anticipation.[23]

Some of these features are reflected in the already existing literature on proactive law; others could be developed further in the future. Proactive lawyering involves acting in anticipation of legal disputes, taking control of potential problems, providing solutions, and self-initiation, instead of reacting to failures and shortcomings as traditional law usually does. Literature and those practising proactive law try to develop concepts, theories and tools to use legal instruments proactively in order to achieve business goals. This includes drafting contracts that foster good relationship(s) and provide a roadmap for performance (instead of providing legal safeguard clauses in case something goes wrong), regulation that encourages good behaviour, or agile contracts that adapt to changing situations and help to create trust among business partners.

On the website of the Nordic School of Proactive Law, proactive law is defined as: "… a future-oriented approach to law placing an emphasis on legal knowledge to be applied before things go wrong. It comprises a way of legal thinking and a set of skills, practices and procedures that help to identify opportunities in time to take advantage of them – and to spot potential problems while preventive action is still possible. In addition to avoiding disputes, litigation and other hazards, Proactive Law seeks ways to use the law to create value, strengthen relationships and manage risk." This definition of proactive law builds the foundation for many publications on proactive law, and is reflected in the EESC opinion on the proactive approach.[24] While this initial definition of proactive law has lost nothing of its validity and well reflects the basic idea of proactive law, it is not static or graved in stone. The definition of proactive law will be subject to modification as the concept of proactive law evolves. Al-

23. Jon M. Shepard, Michael Betz and Lenahan O'Connell, *The Proactive Corporation: Its Nature and Causes*, 16 Journal of Business Ethics 10, 1001 at 1007 (1997).
24. http://eur-lex.europa.eu/LexUriServ/LexUriServ.do?uri=OJ:C:2009:175:0026:0033:EN:PDF.

ternative definitions which stress different aspects of proactive law, and concentrate more on the concept and methods than the "approach" or the "way of legal thinking" which characterizes the early work on proactive law, have already been developed.[25] The concept has been adapted to different areas such as contracting, ICT, management or regulation.

4. Origins and causes

The concept of proactive law has been developed based on a certain dissatisfaction with the current legal system, often called "traditional law" in opposition to the proactive approach to law. Proactive law could be classified among other emerging alternative legal approaches, which Susan Daicoff in her extensive study on the law as a *healing* profession calls *vectors* of the *comprehensive law movement*, and which approach law in a more comprehensive, integrated, humanistic, interdisciplinary, restorative way.[26] Some of these alternative approaches or processes (vectors) are also reflected in proactive law, such as collaborative law, restorative justice, procedural justice, transformative mediation, therapeutic jurisprudence, holistic justice, creative problem solving.[27] A common

25. *See* e.g. Salmi-Tolonen PAMPAL glossary (2011), on file with the author, who states that proactive law "is a comprehensive concept concerning civil and commercial matters which refers to any regulation measure/activity, undertaken by public or private actors, as well as its methods, instruments, and results, whose purpose is by imposing duties, conferring rights and creating competences enable and empower individuals concerned or private or public bodies in achieving their commonly defined goals. In practice, the forms this concept takes are rules, practices and/or processes."
26. See Susan Daicoff, Law as a Healing Profession: The "Comprehensive Law Movement", bepress Legal Series, Working Paper 1331 (July 22, 2005), available at: http://law.bepress.com/expresso/eps/1331.
27. It can be argued whether "creative problem solving" is a specific vector of the comprehensive law movement, see Susan Daicoff, Law as a Healing Profession: The "Comprehensive Law Movement" (July 22, 2005). bepress Legal Series. Working Paper 1331, at 22-25. available at: http://law.bepress.com/expresso/eps/1331, or a part of preventive law, see Thomas D. Barton and James M. Cooper, Preventive Law and Creative Problem Solving: Multi-Dimensional Lawyering, National Center for Preventive Law, available at http://www.preventivelawyer.org/content/pdfs/Multi_Dimensional_Lawyer.pdf.

feature for all these different forms of comprehensive legal approaches, and essential for proactive law, is that they seek to optimize human well-being and consider "extra-legal factors", whereas the prevailing European legal theory considers law as "a coherent conceptual system that creates legal cause and effects relationships"[28] in a framework of greatest possible neutrality.[29] The idea of proactive law has been born out of practical needs, in collaboration between academics and practitioners in order to "balance the prevailing legal logic".[30] It is not as the name proactive law *movement* could suggest a legal ideology, but deeply based on existing realities, practice-oriented, with the objective to reach real-life (especially business) goals. Insofar, and not surprising given its Finnish origins, proactive law is rooted in (Scandinavian) legal realism[31], and takes into account the economic dimension of legal decisions.[32]

4.1 From prevention to promotion

The idea of an *ex-ante* view or proactivity in law is not new in itself. It has been known for years that the sooner a dispute or a potential dispute is addressed, the better the chances of a fair and prompt solution. In the context of practicing law, the idea of prevention was first introduced by Louis M. Brown, himself an experienced practitioner as well as a law professor. In his ground-laying treatise *Preventive Law* published in 1950, he states a simple but profound truth that has not lost any of its value. Indeed, many attorneys and in-house-counsel actually act according to this motto: "It usually costs less to avoid getting into trouble than to pay for getting out of trouble."[33] The contribution of Louis M. Brown and other scholars in the field of preventive law consists in identifying preventive law with its own name, organizing it into a distinctive

28. Soile Pohjonen, Proactive Law in the Field of Law, in A PROACTIVE APPROACH 54 at 56 (2006).
29. Soile Pohjonen, Proactive Law in the Field of Law, in A PROACTIVE APPROACH 54 at 57 (2006).
30. Soile Pohjonen, Proactive Law in the Field of Law, in A PROACTIVE APPROACH 53, at 54 (2006).
31. Soile Pohjonen, Proactive Law in the Field of Law, in A PROACTIVE APPROACH 54 at 57 (2006).
32. See e.g. Henrik Lando, Determinants of the Optimal Degree of Pro-activeness in Contracting, in A PROACTIVE APPROACH 255 (2006).
33. Louis M. Brown, Preventive Law 3 (1950).

way of thinking, developing concepts, if not a comprehensive general theory of preventive law.[34] By doing so they made preventive law visible and recognizable for people with a similar mindset. They have created awareness, which is necessary to change people's mindset in order to use the law according to business goals, to become more creative, preventive – "better" lawyers.

Edward Dauer identifies four core principles of preventive law:[35]

1. Preventive law aims at predicting human behavior. A lawyer practising preventive law tries to predict human behaviour. He or she will search for a legal solution, which takes into account what the people will do, and by doing so helps anticipate and prevent litigation. Traditional law practice tries to predict what a court will decide. Insofar traditional law practice also seems to be preventive. It might prevent losing in court, but still not achieve what the people really need and want. Therefore traditional law practice remains backwards, and failure and litigation-oriented. It does not improve personal or business relationships, which is essential for preventive – and proactive – law.
2. Preventive law is based on the assumption that the most successful treatment is prevention, and seeks to transfer this idea from the medical to the legal context of conflict management.[36] Dauer sets forth a three-step strategy for managing legal risk, illustrated in Figure 1 (see page 22).
3. Adapted from: Edward A. Dauer in A Proactive Approach to Contracting and the Law 14, at 25 (Helena Haapio ed. 2008). Preventive law embraces risk. This means to deliberately embrace some risk as a way of reducing overall risk, rather than try to drive one element of risk to zero.
4. Make preventive legal services available to clients: According to the basic ideas of preventive law, lawyers must work with others in multi-disciplinary teams in the planning of clients' ventures. While the first three principles predominantly ask for a change in the at-

34. Edward A. Dauer, *Four Principles for a Theory of Preventive Law*, in, A Proactive Approach to Contracting and Law 14 (Helena Haapio Ed., 2008).
35. Id.
36. Tobias Mahler, The State of the Art of Contractual Risk Management Methodologies, in A Proactive Approach to Contracting and Law, at 63 (Helena Haapio, Ed. 2008).

titudes and practices of lawyers, this fourth principle is oriented towards the client – the business or private person. Not only do lawyers need to become more prevention-oriented, but clients need to bring in lawyers early enough, so they can together detect legal risk and prevent harm from occurring and engage in interdisciplinary collaboration, otherwise even the best preventive lawyer won't help.

Figure 1: A three-step strategy for managing legal risk. Source: Daver.

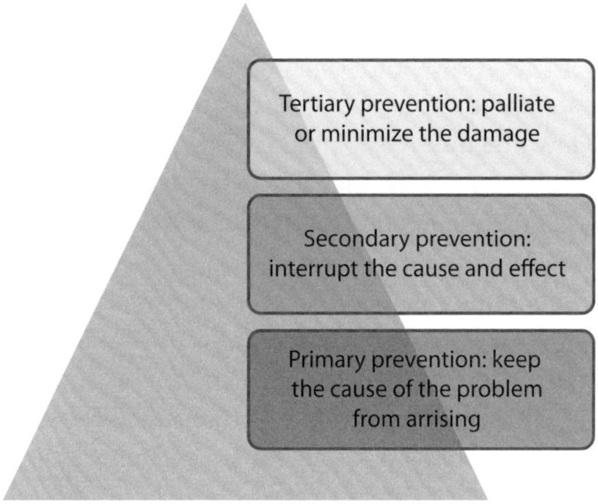

Proactive law encompasses the basic principles of preventive law described above, namely preventing what is not desirable, and keeping problems and risks from materializing. To the preventive dimension, proactive law adds a second aspect – the promotive (or positive, constructive) dimension that is promoting what is desirable, encouraging good behaviour. While preventive law prevents problems and ill-health, proactive law promotes "legal well-being" and clients' "self-care".[37] It has been stated that Louis M. Brown's work on preventive law was targeted toward lawyers. While influenced by his work, the proactive law approach emphasizes the importance of collaboration between legal professionals and other disciplines. Though – so far – mainly rooted in

37. See Helena Haapio, Introduction to Proactive Law: A Business Lawyer's View, in A Proactive Approach to Contracting and the Law 23, at 24 (Helena Haapio ed., 2008).

the legal paradigm, proactive law expressively addresses other fields of expertise. The practice of proactive law requires collaboration between lawyer and non-lawyer, therefore the client can't be a passive "patient", leaving the legal issues to the legal professional, but needs to take an active role in the law-making, contract drafting, or other law related processes.[38] In the words of Soile Pohjonen: "[preventive law] favors the lawyer's viewpoint, i.e., the prevention of legal risks and problems. In Proactive Law, the emphasis is on achieving the desired goal in particular circumstances where legal expertise works in collaboration with the other types of expertise involved. In Proactive Law, the need for dialogue between different understandings is emphasized." [39]

4.2 Development of proactive law

The concept of proactive law was first introduced and continues to be extensively used in connection with contracts.[40] From the perspective of proactive law, traditional contracts are often reactive, focusing on legal problems and litigation instead of serving as a management tool and to foster collaboration between business partners, though the latter is crucial for success in todays' global and networked economy.[41] In contrast to *contract law*, which is based on the interpretation of legal rules

38. Id.
39. Soile Pohjonen, Proactive Law in the Field of Law, in A PROACTIVE APPROACH, supra note 3, at 53; see also Soile Pohjonen, Law and Business – Successful Business Contracting, Corporate Social Responsibility and Legal Thinking, TIDSKRIFT UTGIVEN AV JURIDISKA FÖRENINGEN I FINLAND (JFT) 470, 477 (2009), available at http://www.helsinki.fi/oikeustiede/omasivu/pohjonen/Law%20and%20Business.pdf.
40. Helena Haapio: Quality Improvement through Proactive Contracting: Contracts Are Too Important to Be Left to Lawyers!, American Society for Quality, Proceedings of Annual Quality Congress (AQC), Philadelphia, PA, Vol. 52, May 1998, pp. 243-248.
41. See e.g. Gerlinde Berger-Walliser, Robert C. Bird & Helena Haapio, Promoting Business Success Through Contract Visualization, 17 J.L., BUS. & ETHICS 55 (2011); Vaula Haavisto, Contracting in Networks, in A PROACTIVE APPROACH, 49 SCANDINAVIAN STUD. L., in A PROACTIVE APPROACH 237 (2006); Soili Nystén-Haarala, Contract Law and Everyday Contracting, in A PROACTIVE APPROACH 263 (2006); Tim Cummins, Best Practices in Commercial Contracting: Key Initiatives That Are Driving Competitive Advantage, in A PROACTIVE APPROACH 132 (2006); Tobias Mahler, Faculty of Law University of Oslo, Legal Risk Management: Developing and Evaluating Elements

by a court, i.e. ex post, *proactive contracting* emphasizes the contracting process and tries to develop an adequate set of tools for building functioning collaboration in real life (business) relationships. When drafting a proactive contract, the focus is on capturing the goal of the business deal, assuring a shared understanding between the contract partners and developing structures, rules and procedures that ex ante enable the creation and achievement of desired goals and avoidance of future problems.[42]

Shortly after its emergence in contracting, the *proactive approach* has been extended to other areas[43] and a more comprehensive theory has started to evolve.[44] Legal scholars[45], business practitioners,[46] and the European Economic and Social Committee are calling for a paradigm shift. According to the latter: "[t]he time has come to give up the centuries-old reactive approach to law and to adopt a proactive approach. It is time to look at law in a different way: to look forward rather than back, to focus on how the law is used and operates in everyday life and how it is received in the community it seeks to regulate. While respond-

of a Method for Proactive Legal Analyses, With a Particular Focus on Contracts (2010).

42. *See* e.g. Soile Pohjonen, Proactive Law in the Field of Law, in A PROACTIVE APPROACH 53, at 55 (2006); Tobias Mahler, The State of The Art of Contractual Risk Management Methodologies, 57 in A PROACTIVE APPROACH TO CONTRACTING AND LAW, AT 63 (HELENA HAAPIO, ED. 2008); for an example of possible application *see* Soile Pohjonen and Katja Koskelainen, Empowering Contracting Parties, Proactive and dialogic contracting in public procurement, in this book.
43. See e.g. Dag Wiese Schartum, Introduction to A Government-based Perspective on Proactive Law, in A PROACTIVE APPROACH 35 (2006); Jarl S. Magnusson, Proactive Law – and the Importance of Data and Information Resources, in A PROACTIVE APPROACH 407 (2006).
44. See e.g. Soile Pohjonen, Proactive Law in the Field of Law, in A PROACTIVE APPROACH 54 (2006); Thomas D. Barton, A Paradigm Shift in Legal Thinking, in A Proactive Approach to Contracting and The Law 35 (Helena Haapio, Ed. 2008); Edward A. Dauer, The Role of Culture in Legal Risk Management, in A PROACTIVE APPROACH 93 (2006).
45. Thomas D. Barton, A Pradigm Shift in Legal Thinking, in A PROACTIVE APPROACH TO CONTRACTING AND THE LAW 35 (Helena Haapio, Ed. 2008).
46. Tim Cummins, Taking the Law Out of Contracts – And Putting Lawyers Into the Contracting Process, in A PROACTIVE APPROACH TO CONTRACTING AND THE LAW 97 (Helena Haapio, Ed. 2008).

ing to and resolving problems remain important, preventing causes of problems is vital, along with serving the needs and facilitating the productive interaction of citizens and businesses."[47] The claim for this legal paradigm shift is based on the observation of changing economic and social realities.[48] The scope of this chapter doesn't allow developing these sociological aspects in depth, leaving this to further research. In a nutshell one can say that society has changed, from a nationalistic, vertical structure, based on authority towards a globalized, horizontal, networked and individualistic social and economic system.[49] Or in the words of Thomas D. Barton, from a system of rules, separation, and power to one based on understanding, integration and accommodation.[50] According to proactive law researchers and some sociologists, these societal changes require a change in the role of lawyers. More than ever in Western societies, the law affects personal and business life. One of the reasons for the observed "colonization of personal life by the law"[51] could be the loss of traditional authorities in todays' society, thereby leading to increasing litigation. According to Eric van de Luijtgarden, lawyers in our contemporary western society are increasingly functioning as professional substitutes for lost authority. This implies that lawyers are asked to take over functions that go beyond their traditional role and classic legal theory. These functions require other than legal knowledge, skills that lawyers typically are not trained in. He proposes that proactive law, which as described above is inter-disciplinary

47. See Opinion of the European Economic and Social Committee on 'The proactive law approach: a further step towards better regulation at EU level', 2009 Official. J. Eur. Union, July 28, 2009, at C 175/26, § 1;4, available at http://eur-lex.europa.eu/LexUriServ/LexUriServ.do?uri=OJ:C:2009:175:0026:0033:EN:PDF.
48. E.g., Richard Susskind, The Future of Law at 292 (1998); Kaisa A.E. Sorsa & Tarja Salmi-Tolonen, Contracting in Transition (Apr. 16, 2008) (unpublished manuscript), available at http://ssrn.com/abstract=1120919; Soili Nysten-Haarala et. al., Contracting Capabilities in Industrial Life-Cycle and Service Business (research summary), at 3, available at http://wanda.uef.fi/oikeustieteet/siviili/CCC%20Research%20Report.pdf.
49. Eric van de Luijtgaarden, PAMPAL Handbook, on file with the author.
50. Thomas D. Barton, Preventive Law and Problem Solving, Lawyering for the Future at 8, Vandeplas Publishing (2009).
51. Lawrence M. Friedman, The republic of choice, law authority and culture, Cambridge Massachusetts/London at 15 (1990); Jürgen Habermas, *Legitimation crisis*, London at 356-373 (1976).

in nature and by definition takes into account social and economic realities, and its integration in law school curriculum, could help to fill this gap and enable lawyers to better fulfil their new role.[52]

5. Basic concepts of proactive law

Just like preventive law, proactive law is not new in itself;[53] there have always been proactive lawyers, or proactive elements in contracts or legislation. An area of law where the move towards "understanding, integration and accommodation" has already become clearly visible is the broad use of ADR (Alternative Dispute Resolution) mechanisms in todays' dispute resolution practice.[54]

The objective of the proactive law movement is to identify and generalize this shift in legal thinking, collect and evaluate practical experiences and develop theoretical studies and concepts which show what can be gained in developing further the proactive dimension of the legal domain and interdisciplinary collaboration between lawyers and managers, or subject-matter experts from other for example technical fields. Cecilia Magnusson Sjöberg clarifies that the notion of law in this context "is not equivalent to rules and regulations, but refers instead to law as an instrument that can be shaped in a whole variety of ways, e.g. a basis for risk analyses, legal system design and management."[55]

While preventive law originated in the US, in response to the adversary Common law system, proactive law has evolved in the European, less litigation-oriented, Civil law context, which explains its different focus. Also, the context in which proactive law has developed and continues to develop is very different from the preventive law movement in the US. While research on preventive law and the comprehensive law movement in general is predominantly located in US law schools, concerned with traditional legal topics such as litigation, criminal law,

52. See generally Eric van de Luijtgaarden, PAMPAL Handbook, on file with the author.
53. See Cecilia Magnusson Sjöberg, in A Proactive Approach, at 1.
54. Thomas D. Barton, Preventive Law and Problem Solving, Lawyering for the Future at 8, Vandeplas Publishing (2009).
55. Id.

constitutional law, corporate law, employment law etc., the proactive law movement from its early stages has been truly interdisciplinary and business-oriented. It pays particular attention to non-legal disciplines such as project management, quality management, contract and risk management, legal document management, and ICT. Referring to Figure 1, presented above, preventive law so far has focused on the secondary and tertiary level of legal care, while proactive law concentrates on the primary causes of legal disputes.

To the preventive aspects described above, proactive law adds a *promotive* dimension. The main objective of proactive law is helping the stakeholders – be it individuals, businesses or legislators, reach their objectives. For example contracts are designed as to enable the parties to reach their common goals and implement their business plans the way they want them to be. This implies tight collaboration between lawyers and those implementing the contract. The parties need to reach a common, unambiguous understanding of all clauses of the contract, leaving nothing to unexpected ex-post interpretation by a court, which might run counter the parties' true interests. For the legal profession this means a different type of legal counseling. Instead of making sure that the contract is "safe" in case of non-performance or legal dispute, the lawyer (or whoever is in charge of contract design and drafting) must work with those involved in the business relationship to identify, and translate into contractual language, the parties' goals and expectations regarding scope, intentions, requirements, etc. of the business deal. The person in charge of drafting the contract has to make sure that the business deal doesn't fail and the parties reach their objectives. This fundamentally changes the nature of the contract: it turns from a failure-oriented risk management tool into an instrument which assures performance, quality and success.[56]

The main differences between preventive law and proactive law can be identified as follows in Figure 2 (see page 28):

56. *See generally* Larry A. DiMatteo, George J. Seidel & Helena Haapio, Strategic Contracting: Examining the Business-Legal Interface, in this book.

Figure 2: Main differences between preventive law and proactive law.

Preventive law focuses on	Proactive law focuses on
Managing conflict and handling problems	Eliminating causes of problems, promote sustainable relationship
Avoiding litigation	Help stakeholders reach their common goals
Managing risks	Balancing risk and reward, achieving desired outcomes, i.e. success
Minimizing costs and losses	Creating value for all parties involved
Professional legal care	Shared care and team approach, lawyers supporting client's self-care

Recently more mutual influence between European and US researchers can be observed. On the one hand, the proactive and interdisciplinary dimension has been added to the preventive dimension of preventive law (see Dauer's principle 4 above), on the other hand common interests have been discovered between the European proactive law movement and the emergent discipline of *law and strategy* in the US which, similar to proactive law, aims at creating value through strategic use of law.[57]

Though proactive law has only developed recently, and literature, compared to other vectors of the comprehensive law movement (see above) is less abundant, at this stage the following principles of proactive law can be identified:

1. Proactive law is based on legal certainty, literacy, and cross-professional collaboration. In the words of Helena Haapio, for a lawyer helping business people navigate in unknown regions trying to find out where the safe routes run, proactive law is about "localizing the mines and preventing them from exploding."[58] Today's legal system evolves rapidly. Requirements for corporate compliance, environmental and safety standards, regulation of the information society etc. are constantly becoming more demanding. Therefore not only legal experts need to be informed about the law, but management and employees need to be aware of the legal "mines". Lawyers, in turn, need to be knowledgeable about the business processes and

57. George Siedel and Helena Haapio, Using Proactive Law for Competitive Advantage, 47 AM. BUS. L. J. 641-686; see alsoLarry A. DiMatteo, George J. Seidel & Helena Haapio, Strategic Contracting: Examining the Business-Legal Interface, in this book.
58. Helena Haapio, Introduction to Proactive Law: A Business Lawyer's View, in A Proactive Approach, at 21.

objectives of the company they are counseling. Recent scandals such as Enron or WorldCom have shown how integrated law and business are. It is not only about compliance with the law; ethical standards and the reputation of a company are at stake as well. Therefore, in addition to avoiding lawsuits through compliance with regulations, companies need to engage in cross-professional collaboration and group-learning. They need to manage their compliance with the law and align it to business objectives. In order to be able to do this, not only lawyers and regulators need to know the law, managers and other actors in society need to have at least a basic understanding of the legal "mines". They need a basic legal literacy[59], awareness, or legal astuteness,[60] which in the end can help them not only to avoid litigation and the costs related to it, but enable them to use the law for competitive advantage.[61]

2. Law and legal professionals should create economic value and therefore need to be outcome orientated. As the organizational behaviour research on proactivity cited above suggests, lawyers need to scan for change of opportunities, set effective, change-oriented goals, and focus on accomplishments with real impact and take action and achieve results. Preventing legal disputes may save costs and time wasted by legal proceedings, but from an economic standpoint this is not enough. In order to convince companies of the importance of the law, lawyers need to be able to show to their clients not only the negative side of law – constraints that are "in the way of business", but the economic value, the opportunities proactive use of the law can offer to build solid business foundations, roadmaps for performance, trust, and better, sustainable business relationships.

59. Helena Haapio, in A Proactive Approach, at 23.
60. Constance E. Bagley, *Winning Legally: The Value of Legal Astuteness*, 33 Acad. Mgmt. Rev. 378, 383 (2008).
61. See generally George J. Siedel & Helena Haapio, *Using Proactive Law for Competitive Advantage*, 47 Am. Bus. L.J. 641, 667-68 (2010); Larry A. DiMatteo, *Strategic Contracting: Contract Law as a Source of Competitive Advantage*, 47 Am. Bus. L.J. 727, 728 (2010); Constance E. Bagley, *Winning Legally: The Value of Legal Astuteness*, 33 Acad. Mgmt. Rev. 378, 383 (2008).

3. In proactive law the focus is on dispute pre-emption, legal risk management, rather than dispute resolution.[62] Though there is need for case studies to prove the following, the hypothesis in proactive law is that if practiced correctly, there would seldom be need for any dispute resolution. Many legal disputes are due to misunderstandings and disappointed expectations. The objective of proactive law is to avoid getting to the stage of dispute, through careful attention to legal clarity, early warning mechanism and enhanced collaboration between business partners.
4. For proactive law, cross-professional collaboration between lawyers, managers and subject matter experts, such as the engineers in charge of the execution of the goals set forth in a business contract, are essential to reach common goals and to avoid problems and legal disputes. A common understanding is necessary, which can be enhanced by the use of non-traditional legal communication tools such as visualization.[63]
5. Creative thinking: Because of the outcome orientation of proactive law, and as proactive law looks towards the future rather than the past, it requires from all actors the ability to develop new ideas and concepts in order to respond to needs, problems or challenges, sometimes by means of an original and previously non-existing approach.

6. Conclusion and perspectives

Some of the principles of proactive law enumerated above seem to be obvious factors for successful legal counseling. Therefore some lawyers, especially in-house or corporate counsel, when they are confronted with the ideas of proactive or preventive law for the first time, suggest that this is what they actually do. Though this might be true for some experienced business lawyers who possess extensive business knowledge and

62. *See also* Richard Susskind, *The Future of Law*, at 292 (1998).
63. *See generally* Gerlinde Berger-Walliser, Robert C. Bird and Helena Haapio, *Promoting Business Success through Contract Visualization*, 17 Journal of Law, Business and Ethics, pp. 55-75 (2011); Larry A. DiMatteo, George J. Seidel & Helena Haapio, *Strategic Contracting: Examining the Business-Legal Interface*, in this book.

anability for strategic legal thinking, traditional young law school graduates are not educated in the proactive use of the law. Interestingly, observations by the author in the PAMPAL curriculum development project[64] have shown that even students enrolled in double-degree programs such as law and economics or JD-MBA programs seem to quickly adapt to classic legal theory and "forget" about a truly integrated approach to law and management. There also seems to be some lack of knowledge or understanding related to the proactive and preventive approaches,[65] which need to be addressed in future work. Preventive and proactive law are not (only) about keeping clients out of court or making sure that one's client's interests will prevail in case of a legal dispute. Proactive law is about problem-solving, detecting real-life causes for potential misunderstandings and failures, but mostly about fostering sustainable relationship, enabling stakeholders to reach their goals, creating value for businesses, individuals and society as a whole. One of the reasons for the aforementioned lack of understanding could be that proactive law literature so far has extensively addressed the reasons and objectives of the paradigm shift it calls for, but to a lesser degree how to make it happen. What will be needed in the future are more case studies, identification of best practices, and more distinctive methods and tools to turn proactive law into practice.[66]

64. *See* ERASMUS curriculum development project on Proactive Management and Proactive Business Law (PAM PAL) funded by the Lifelong Learning Programme of the European Commission. See ProActive Management and ProActive Business Law, TURKU UNIVERSITY OF APPLIED SCIENCES, http://pampal.turkuamk.fi/index.php.
65. See Petri Mäntysaari, Theories of Commercial Law, Corporate Governance and Corporate Law at 35 (2012).
66. Some interesting examples already exist, e.g. the Managers Legal Plan™ in George J. Siedel and Helena Haapio, Using Proactive law for Competitive Advantage, Am. Bus. L. J. 641, 651-656 (2010); or Tobias Mahler, Legal Risk Management, Developing and Evaluating Elements of a Method for Proactive Legal Analyses, With a Particular Focus on Contracts, Faculty of Law, University of Oslo (2010); Soile Pohjonen and Kerttuli Visuri, Proactive Approach in Project Management and Contracting, in A PROACTIVE APPROACH TO CONTRACTING AND LAW, AT 75 (HELENA HAAPIO, ED. 2008); Antoni Brack, A Managerial Format for a Business Legal Audit, 12 European Business Law Review 34 (2001), *see* also Larry A. DiMatteo, George J. Seidel & Helena Haapio, Strategic Contracting: Examining the Business-Legal Interface, in this book.

Proactive Management and Proactive Business Law (PAM PAL) curriculum; Educating Professionals for the Future

By

Kaisa Sorsa
Turku University of Applied Sciences

1. Introduction

The aim of this paper is to contribute to aligning higher education towards the needs of future business society. The global economic system is rapidly changing and less predictable than before. Sustainability issues have set new challenges to be taken into account all over the world. In order to tackle environmental, social or economic challenges and rapidly changing business environments, *proactive (Goerdel 2005; Eisenhardt & Martin 2000), systemic and interdisciplinary approaches are required from all actors of society* (Sorsa 2011b; 2008a; 2008b; 2009a; 2009b; Compete&Collaborate 2008).

System level changes require changes in different sectors of the society. In the current academic environment, corporate responsibility and sustainability have entered but not yet become embedded in the mainstream of business-related or law-related education (PRME). As institutions of higher education involve themselves in the development of current and future managers, they are important drivers of change on the field of education. The PAM PAL project group seeks to establish a process of continuous improvement among institutions of business education and institutions of law education in order to develop a new generation of business leaders capable of managing the complex challenges faced by business and society in the 21st century.

The Proactive Management and Proactive Business Law curriculum development project started in 2009 and was finished in 2011[1]. A need for more proactive professionals became apparent during the research conducted in Finland in the project Corporate Contracting Capabilities (CCC) 2006 – 2009 and in the project Proactive law as a source of competitive advantage 2009 – 2011 (Sorsa 2011a; Sorsa 2009c; 2010a; 2010b; 2010c). It was discovered that business and law as well as corporate social responsibility are inseparably embedded in the global economic environment, but they are taught as separate entities in higher education. However, on the global scale, law and its implementation and monitoring are no longer the prerogative of the public lawmakers as private actors are taking an active role in rule making, implementation and monitoring phases.

This paper will focus on *the innovations proliferating in the field of higher education*. The aim of this paper is twofold:

- First, the aim is to describe *the concept of Proactive Business Law* which captures the *dynamic, enabling and empowering nature of law.*
- Second, the aim is to describe the Proactive Management and Proactive Business Law (PAM PAL, 24 ECTS) curriculum.

The proactive management and proactive law curriculum integrates business studies with legal studies in an interdisciplinary way while enlivening students' relationships through problem-based learning, case studies and student projects. PAM PAL plays a role by acting as a meeting point for students from different disciplines to study sustainability in an interdisciplinary and problem-based way.

1. The writer was the Project Manager in the PAM PAL project and Sub-Project Manager in the CCC project. The seven project partners of the PAM PAL project are from European law schools and business schools in four different countries. One SME company was also involved. The partner institutions are: Hogeschool Utrecht (NL), Florida Centre de Formacia (ES), Aarhus School of Business (DE), FerensLegal (NL), ICN Business School (FR), Universidade de Santiago de Compostela (ES) and the University of Turku (FI).

2. Proactive law as a regulatory innovation; challenges for education

2.1 Understanding regulatory issues through innovation

Innovation research typically analyses processes and phenomena that contribute to industrial and socio-economic renewal and growth[2]. The nature of innovation is continuously changing and broadening. The analytical lens in innovation studies has refocused from firm-level processes to wider, linked processes that improve systems of social and technological practice by which we satisfy our needs, e.g. the system for production, selling and consuming food. (Sorsa 2011b and footnotes; Goerdel 2005). Here the focus will be on linking proactive management and proactive business law in higher education and processes of globalized trade for the driver of change.

According to Potworowski's research, there are a large number of barriers of innovation and change. In the change toward a more sustainable society, the barriers of innovations reflect the habits of individual consumers, established practices and institutions, and they arise from the shortage of people with appropriate skills, or they reflect unsuitable structures of government regulation (Potworowski 2009; Van Dorp 2011). The barriers of innovations can be found both from the actors on the demanding side, from the supply side of economy and in the regulatory and educational institutions. In summary, to tackle the multi-dimensional problems and challenges of globalised trade, a multi-level understanding of the reality is needed (Hughes 2011) and changes need to take place at several levels of the economy.

New regulatory frameworks have already emerged and developed in the global value chain networks. Their role has been disputed, commended, underrated and encouraged depending on the role of the actor in the business environment. However, these new regulatory schemes exist and seem to fortify their position. Addressing this situation de-

2. The traditional definition of innovation (Schumpeter) "The introduction of new goods (...), new methods of production (...), the opening of new markets (...), the conquest of new sources of supply (...) and the carrying out of a new organization of any industry" highlights goods, services and methods. The project was funded by the EU Lifelong Learning, Curriculum development programme.

mands innovative approaches in teaching: new regulatory frameworks are created outside the field of public law making, which requires new ways of structuring and combining the fields of study and teaching materials.

In this curriculum development process, these concurrent phenomena have been taken as a real fact and their importance has awoken a need to specify, first, the concept of law, and secondly, its relationship with the business.

2.2 Proactive law notion

A proactive law is an enabling, empowering and dynamic law which is done by and with the actors of society (EU opinion). It has emerged in the field of global private regulation and in the field of proactive contracting in which new management tools for global value chains have been developed (Sorsa 2010b; Cafaggi 2010, 2011a and 2011b). These include self- and private regulation instruments and standards, looser relational networks as well as contractual arrangements (Pohjonen 2002; Haapio 2007; Nysten-Haarala 2008) which have been developed in different business sectors, with non-governmental-organisations and in public-private co-operation (See e.g. coffee sector, Manning & Hagen 2010). Private actors can be called "lawmakers" and not only "law takers" (Sorsa 2009c and 2010c[3]).

We call this phenomenon proactive law (Sorsa 2010e; Pohjonen 2005) and *an innovation* in the regulatory field. A concept of innovation in general comprises an idea of creation of *better or more effective* products, processes, services, technologies, or ideas that are accepted by markets, governments, and society. In the regulatory field, the production of private regulation in its different forms has shown to be evolving via very innovative processes. They seem to be more effective tools to deal with global sustainability challenges than their public counterparts like trade agreements between states or national statutory laws.

3. The research of CSR and private regulation consisted of analysis of 42 self and private regulation systems and their role in global value chain management (Sorsa 2009d, 2010b and 2010c).

The proactive law comprises the notion that the legal system itself has shown to be proactive (Sorsa 2011f, 20): first, the actors creating and monitoring the law are not only public lawmakers anymore; secondly, the law is born from the bottom-up reflecting the needs of the users and implementers of the law and finally, from the timing perspective, these private regulatory schemes often proceed hard law (proactive law's process perspective). Also the contents of these schemes are very flexible: The issues covered in the private standards include social issues like labour related rights, environmental issues like the use of pesticides or fertilizers, economic issues like fair-trade principles and safety aspects like food safety. The content of standards is ranging to cover both social and environmental issues which in public statutory law are normally kept in totally separate fields of law *(proactive law's contents perspective).*

An emergence of corporate social responsibility (CSR) in society has brought other stakeholder groups in addition to contracting parties and new legal tools (Sorsa 2008a and 2008b) to the business agenda. The importance of legal environment for businesses has grown continuously over the last two decades (CEO Survey 2008, 56-57). The role of self-regulation (standardisation, code of conducts, code of ethics, general terms and conditions etc.) has become an important part of daily business especially in international context. Private actors participate in all phases of the regulatory life cycle: in standard setting, implementation, in monitoring and in sanctioning. The big multinational companies may create their own standards (IKEA and IWAY Standards; McDonald and its purchasing standards) and implement them in their value chains but small and medium size companies' participation takes place via collective standards setting procedures or in implementing the standards developed by other value chain actors.

2.3 Challenges for higher education

In the multilevel, networked environment (Sorsa & Salmi-Tolonen 2009), companies need capabilities to manage these multilevel rule systems and the capability to use other tools in addition to contracts, for the management of all the relevant relationships with their different stakeholders. The need to broaden the perspective from contractual relationships to value chain management and from grass root level to multilayer bird's eye view calls for understanding the role of different regulatory systems. These systems include self- and private regulation, hard law and contracting as well as the softest, un-institutional relational aspects in managing the critical sustainability issues in global value chains (Sorsa 2008b; 2009d and 2010d; Barnett 2000).

According to our understanding in the PAM PAL project, there is a need for a new knowledge base for learning proactive law (Sorsa 2011f, 56-59). The topic of so-called proactive management and proactive business law has not been in the curricula of law faculties or business schools. The complexity of real-world sustainability challenges and desires to train students for the more sustainably driven society both suggest the need for developing the knowledge base, core competencies and new teaching materials and innovative educational practices.

The role of institutions of higher learning is especially crucial in that they educate a great number of professionals and leaders of tomorrow's society. In addition to the basic knowledge of law and business, future managers need to be more proactive in combining business and legal knowledge, tools and skills. This has already been acknowledged by some business law professors and professionals (Tolonen 2007; Rudanko 2004; Lampe 2006; Compete&Collaborate 2008). Our new curriculum, developed in concert among seven European higher education institutions, focuses on what business managers should know about the proactive law and how they should learn this (Lampe 2006; Barton et al. 2006).

Despite the academia's vital role in the success of any plan or strategy towards a sustainably developed society, there are still many barriers to the interaction inside the academia and between academia and the community in which it operates. Business and legal curricula have so far been isolated islands focusing on strictly specialised areas of subjects. Law degrees have also been focusing mainly on statutory law and court cases. The PAM PAL curriculum changes the focus to society and sustainability and establishes education for sustainable development through university research, teaching and learning.

3. Description of proactive management and proactive law curriculum

3.1 Competences

Two sets of competences, the general ones for proactive management and proactive law, and more specific ones for proactive contracting have been developed. During the PAM PAL project, we defined four general competences which characterise proactive behaviour in management and business law: 1) Multi-disciplinary analysis, 2) Cross-professional communication and networking, 3) Creative thinking and 4) Outcome orientation. Each of these competences is further divided into attitude, skills and knowledge elements and also into three performance levels.

Multi-disciplinary analysis

We define *multi-disciplinary analysis* as "an ability to identify the key factors for success and opportunities based on the necessary scientific analysis, including interdisciplinary analysis and best business practice analysis." It involves dealing with uncertainty since when faced with specific situations, people do not always have all the information necessary for decision-making. The use of scientific information-gathering methods and reasonable assumptions can be indispensable for progressing in the analysis process. If a person has the lowest level of this competence, he or she uses own skills and resources to achieve the objectives in common situations, following instructions. On the second best level, one is able to address new or complex situations with a specific approach that leads to designing and developing a plan with concrete actions to resolve them. At the highest level of competence, one addresses new or complex situations in collaboration with others to get to design a coherent action plan (Camacho et al. 2011, 34-36).

The mastery of multi-disciplinary analysis is reflected in the ability to faster identify steps to achieve the established objectives, and a better ability to argue why these are adequate. It is also reflected in the ability to critically assess the arguments of others, which facilitates the leadership, or at least plays a role of authority in groups.

Cross-professional communication and networking

Cross-professional communication and networking competence is defined as "an ability to act autonomously as well as to cooperate, communicate and solve disputes in interdisciplinary teams or diverse professional settings" (Camacho et al. 2011, 32; See also Barton et al. 2006; Pohjonen 2002).

This competence relates to the promotion of a communicative and constructive relational context in which the individual interacts with the rest of the team members, participates and shares ideas, encourages honesty and sincerity and contributes to reaching an inclusive consensus. If the student has the lowest level of this competence, he or she establishes dialoguing relationships with peers and supervisors, listening and speaking in a clear and assertive way. At the second best level, he or she is able to use dialogue and understanding to build partnerships. Mastering this competence, the student develops a sincere and empathetic communication aimed at constructive dialogue (Camacho et al. 2011, 32-34).

Creative thinking

Creative thinking is described as "an ability to develop new ideas and concepts in order to respond to needs, problems or challenges, by means of an original and previously non-existing result." The creative competence is associated with divergent thinking. Also, it requires some spontaneity and sense of wonder, and in turn can be influenced by self-esteem. Similarly, an individual who masters the creative competence will be able to generate and transmit new ideas or generate innovative alternatives to problems or situations that arise, these being quality and applicable ideas that affect nearby people and / or processes (Camacho et al. 2011, 29-32; see also Eisenhardt & Martin 2000).

At the lowest level of competence, the student generates and communicates new ideas or generates innovative alternatives to known problems. On the second best level, the student is able to generate original, quality ideas that can be translated in a formal way and defended when faced with known or unknown problems and/or situations. On the highest level, the student can contribute original, practical and implementable ideas and solutions, flexible and complex, involving both him/herself and processes s/he is involved in, as well as people and processes nearby known or unknown problems and/or situations (Camacho et al. 2011, 29-32).

Outcome orientation

Outcome orientation is defined as "an ability to establish goals and to take appropriate and sustainable decisions in order to implement the necessary strategies which secure success and new opportunities." This competence suggests that the individual is able to define clear and concise goals and objectives she/he strives to achieve, and organizes allocation of resources in time to do so, trying to optimise the time and effort in reaching the goals. It involves establishing a system which enables periodical monitoring showing the degree of progress achieved and facilitates the taking of measures to correct potential deviations. At the same time it clearly defines all the people involved, the final status to be achieved, and the means deemed necessary to pursue the path between the present situation and the desired goal (Camacho et al. 2011, 36-38; Sorsa 2009b).

At the lowest level of competence the student is able to establish goals and objectives, plan their implementation and control its progress. On the second best level she/ he is able to effectively pursue the objectives and goals, analysing and responding to the challenges and appropriate adjustments. On the highest level the student is able to set challenging goals and share them with others in order to achieve them as well as design a short-term oriented project with clear guidelines (Camacho et al. 2011, 38).

As an outcome from proactive behaviour connected to the proactive law substance, our students will be able to contribute in the development of legal environment, especially in the field of fast developing private regulation and standardization as well as in the field of contracting and management (Sorsa 2009b).

As an outcome of the CCC project, the competences 'contract contents', 'contract process', 'contractual relational capability' and 'contractual capability as organisational and personal proficiencies' were defined (Sorsa 2009b; Sorsa & Salmi-Tolonen 2009). Corporate contracting capability on contract contents is related to knowledge and information possessed and generated within the company. This capability includes various types of knowledge on how to manage the company's contracting, in respect of assigning roles and responsibilities to the parties, conferring control and decision rights, and understanding and managing future contingencies. This knowledge is not limited to any particular type of contracts (Salmi-Tolonen 2008).

Contract process capability is a capability of a company to manage the contract negotiations both internally (inter) and externally (intra). This capability is about the company's capacity of conducting business projects. Negotiating and bargaining generally involve a number of participants with vested interest. This is an interactive process that can be standardized only to a certain extent allocating the roles and responsibilities to the persons who take part in the negotiations. Contract process capability is conditional on the individual competences of technical experts, sales personnel, contract managers and legal counsels and, in addition, the company presence. It is manifest especially in the adoption of contracting process management tools such as contract process maps, checkpoint flowcharts, and contract document management software (Salmi-Tolonen 2008, 10; Sorsa 2009a).

The concept of personal competencies is quite broad, including not only technical skills or knowledge, but also those competencies that conform to the foundation and ruling principles of the professional activity. The professional activities in which our students will enter after passing our course might be in the field of general management, contract management, product management, CSR management, lawyering, marketing or accounting. One can see that the spectrum of the different professional activities is very wide. This means that we wanted to develop some general competences and some more specific ones for contracting.

3.2 Curriculum – 24 ECTS

The new curriculum involves the inter-disciplinary integration of knowledge, insights, skills and practices from the business management and legal sciences directed to generate the PAM PAL competences. Our curriculum emphasises interaction, reflexivity and the integration of theory and practice (Sorsa 2010e; Teece et al. 1997). It also aims to foster inter-disciplinary collaboration between engineering, social sciences and law through problem-based learning opportunities (Boud & Feletti 1999). An inter-disciplinary synthesis of concepts and praxis is more likely to generate innovative solutions to complex business challenges. Our curriculum development is concordant with the aims of the European Qualifications Framework (EQF) as well as the Principles of Responsible Management Education. EQF was created in 1999 with the adoption of the Bologna Declaration and it has defined a set of general descriptors indicating the learning outcomes relevant to qualifications at bachelor and master's level education. One of the key elements of the reform is the establishment of a new learning model, in which the acquisition of competencies by the student is recognised as especially relevant. Therefore, the idea is that the student becomes more proactive and engaged already in his/her own education. This way, this acquisition of competencies reaches a new dimension.

The new curriculum of 24 ECTS consists of three teaching modules (Sorsa 2011f, 13-21):

1. Proactive law and prevention and resolution of disputes (5 ECST + 3 ECTS)
   - Focuses on how companies can act as "private law makers" and not only "law takers". The role of non-governmental organisations in relation to companies will be discussed. Alternative dispute resolution mechanisms and conflict management methods are presented and promoted instead of court cases.

2. Proactive contracting and risk management (5 ECTS + 3 ECTS)
   - Gives insights into how contracting and private regulation can be used as an opportunity management and risk management tool in global value chain management. It also introduces concepts and tools for contract management.

3. The proactive management and business ethics module (5 ECTS + 3 ECTS)
   - Focuses on proactive management and practices on the company level. It aims at producing proactive management skills on the organisational level and on the personal level. This module concentrates on integrating sustainability to company practices as well as generating innovations.

4. Knowledge base: A multi-level perspective – systemic understanding

The knowledge base in our curriculum is based on a systemic view to the legal and business environments offering a synthesis of these for preparing students to face real-life challenges. The module of proactive law focuses on the systems of business environment and the systems of private and public regulation (Cafaggi 2010 and 2011a; Sorsa 2011f, 55-62). The theoretical model developed by Geels (2002) summarizes the systemic perspective. Firstly, we will open the theoretical model and after that apply it into a PAM PAL context.

The model distinguishes between three levels of heuristic, analytical concepts: niche-innovations, socio-technical regimes and socio-technical landscapes (Geels 2002; see also Harmes-Liedtke 2010). Socio-technical regimes are relatively stable configurations of institutions, techniques and artefacts, as well as *rules, practices and networks* that determine the 'normal' development and use of technologies. Regimes fulfil socially valued functions like food production, transportation or education, which they also help to constitute (Geels 2002; Smith et al. (2005),1493-1494). Despite, their relative stability, regimes change. Radical changes are likely to proceed through a complex and unique history of interrelated events. Less economically visible pressures emanating from institutional structures and conventions, include changes in broad political economic 'landscapes' (Figure 1), or wider socio-cultural attitudes and trends (Geels 2004).

4.1 Increasing structuration of activities in local practices

A socio-technical landscape contains a set of heterogeneous, slow-changing factors such as cultural and *normative values, broad political coalitions, long-term economic developments*, accumulating environmental problems growth. The main point is that the landscape is an external context for actors in niches and regimes. While regimes can be changed to some extent by actors in the regime, it is more difficult to change landscape factors. (Geels 2004, 35).

A socio-technical regime of food is used as the focal unit of analysis in 'The Proactive Management and Proactive Business Law Handbook', because it is a quite natural business context for all students. The notion

Figure 1. Multi-level perspective on transitions (adapted from Geels 2002, 1263).

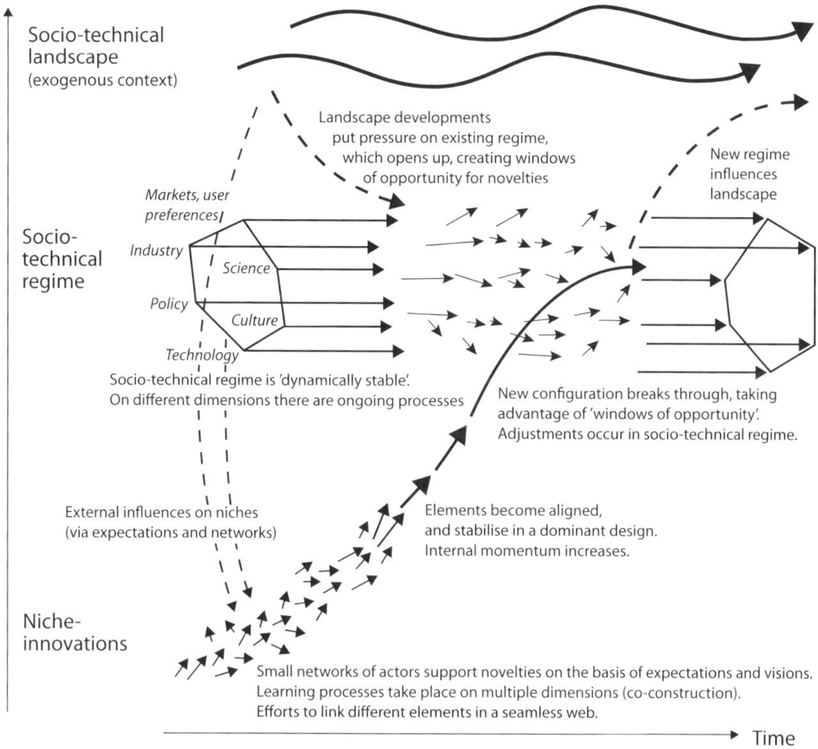

of a socio-technical system consists of a cluster of elements, including technology, regulation, user practices and markets, cultural meaning, infrastructure, maintenance networks and supply networks (Geels 2004, 19). It recognizes that firms and technologies are embedded within wider social and economic systems. A *socio-technical regime* refers to the semi-coherent set of rules carried by different social groups (Geels 2004, 33). In the PAM PAL Handbook, the elements of the socio-technical food regime are especially supply networks, private regulation networks as well as markets and user preferences. In the proactive law module the private regulation networks and their monitoring networks are explained and discussed in the context of the food industry. The focus is in the multi-level regulatory actor networks as well as different stakeholder groups of the companies. Some examples represent the IT sector but the main examples are focused on the food industry. The IT sector, however, will be more in our focus, because it is a very dynamic sector and it is also possible to find very good examples showing the development of proactive law in that context. (Sorsa 2011e, 39-84). Dispute prevention and a resolution topic, on the other hand, familiarize the students with different tools of conflict management. In the proactive contracting module, the value chain analysis opens to the student the broader view of contracting instead of bilateral contractual relationships. (Salmi-Tolonen 2011, 85-109).

Technological niches form the micro-level where radical novelties emerge. These novelties are initially unstable socio-technical configurations with low performance. Niches act as 'incubation rooms' protecting novelties against mainstream market selection. Niche innovations are carried and developed by small networks of dedicated actors, often outsiders or fringe actors. (Geels & Schot 2007,400).[4]

Micro-level analysis is used in the PAM PAL Handbook in several parts of the book, but especially in the proactive management and business ethics module[5] as well as in the module 'Proactive Business Law and the Prevention and Resolution of Disputes, Part II: Proactive Approaches to Law[6]. The innovation perspective is, however, broadened to system level innovations in the same chapter of the PAM PAL Teacher's guide in order to have the multi-level perspective through all of the modules[7]. The module 'Proactive Contracting and Risk Management' discusses

4. Technological niches and socio-technical regimes are similar *kinds* of structures, although different in size and stability. Both niches and regimes have the character of organisational fields (community of interacting groups). For regimes, these communities are large and stable, while for niches they are small and unstable. Both niche and regime communities share certain rules that coordinate action. For regimes these rules are stable and well articulated; for niche-innovations, they are unstable and 'in the making'. Following Scott's (1995) synthesis of institutional theory, we distinguish three kinds of rules: regulative, normative, and cognitive. Examples of *regulative* rules are regulations, standards and laws. Examples of *normative* rules are role relationships, values, behavioural norms. Examples of *cognitive* rules are belief systems, innovation agendas, problem definitions, guiding principles, search heuristics.
5. Camacho & García 2011, 277-338 and Santateresa 2011, 339-359.
6. Berger-Walliser 2011, 113-126; 158-170; van de Luytgaarden 2011, 127-142; Janssen 2011, 143-149; Jansma 2011, 150-157.
7. Sorsa 2011f, 157-160.

the topic both from the micro-level perspective[8] and from macro-level viewpoint[9].

The multi-level perspective going throughout the PAM PAL Handbook is an important element of the knowledgebase because without it our future professionals would not be change makers and they would not be able to see the complexity and the different nuances of the business environment. By practicing students to handle and discuss complex issues they will be better equipped in the future business.

Characteristics of system-level innovations

Due to the fact that systemic innovation processes frequently span beyond the boundaries of the firm they often entail the coordination of different parts of the value network (Chesbrough 2003b). In systemic innovation processes, firms need to coordinate as well with producers of complementary products and services and in many cases even with direct competitors to ensure the viability of the innovation, rather than coordinating solely with suppliers and customers as is frequently the case in closed innovation models (Maula et al. 2005, 2-3). However, systemic innovations also call for ever more discussions and co-operation between different professionals. This means that our students need to understand different professional vocabulary and they need qualifications for inter-professional communication.

System-level innovations take place *on the socio-technical system level.* The systemic nature of innovation *makes companies increasingly dependent on others.* Because in complex systemic innovations, vertical integration is rarely an option, the innovation processes increasingly become collaborative processes. Innovating companies or actors are dependent on *complementary innovators.* The move from internal innovation processes to collaborative open processes forces companies to take a wider perspective to resource allocation processes and *to adopt new governance modes to carry out activities related to the creation of systemic innovations.* In systemic innovations, companies need new tools for foresight and

8. Salmi-Tolonen & Sorsa 2011, 179-195; Henschel 2011, 243-254; Henschel et al. 255-262; Sorsa & Salmi-Tolonen 2011b, 263-273.
9. Sorsa & Salmi-Tolonen 2011a, 196-210; Sorsa 2011g, 211-242.

shaping to manage the business environment of the corporation *over different time horizons* (Maula et al. 2005, 8).

This increases the role of different tools. Maula et al. suggest tools like external venturing, research collaboration, and industry consortia. In this research the focus is on *regulatory tools like private regulation*[10] *(codes of conduct, guidelines, good agricultural/management/practices, co-regulation etc.) and network contracts.* Especially in the Proactive Contracting and Risk management module, the implementation of different regulatory tools is discussed from a value chain management and from a contract management perspective. Companies which have proactive contract content and contract process related competences will be better equipped for the future than their competitors who lack these kinds of competences.

System innovations are seldom about the breakthrough of one radical technology or the use of new production methodology or a new product, but come about by *the linking and clustering of multiple technologies/actors/methods or all of them.* The multi-perspective viewpoint can be seen as a conceptual combination of the following kinds of explanations: a) external circumstances and b) internal drivers (Geels 2004, 37).

External circumstances

Ongoing processes in socio-technical regimes and landscapes provide *windows of opportunity for novelties.* These windows emerge when tension occur between elements in the socio-technical regime, that is, when the activities of social groups are misaligned. Climate change, for instance, is now putting pressure on many different sectors. Broad cultural changes in values and ideologies, or change in legal environment[11] and political coalitions, may also create pressure. Also internal technical problems in

10. Transnational private regulation differs from international regulation (hard law) primarily because rule making is not based on states' legislation. It is rather centered around private actors, interacting with international organizations (IO) and intergovernmental organizations (IGO). A key focus of transnational rule-setting activities has lately been sustainability.
11. Legal environment is a quite stable contextual factor in socio-technical landscape. We live in a world in which the *national and private* law competes and cooperates with the ever growing set of national and transnational private regulation.

the existing technology can create opportunities for novelties. Changing preferences may lead to tensions when established systems have difficulties in meeting them (Sorsa 2009b). For instance, consumers' preferences towards sustainably produced food have been a source for innovation like varying eco-labelling and certification systems (Sorsa 2011b).

5. Pedagogical background

In terms of pedagogy, higher education (HE) needs to educate and train graduates capable of dealing with and thriving within complexity. Barnett and Hallam (1999, 152) argue that we need to see a shift from what they call 'Pedagogy I' – the established approaches to and conceptions of learning and teaching, to 'Pedagogy II' a "pedagogy for super complexity [which will] …enable graduates to purposively effect change in the world, and to have the enduring will to do so." Currently, knowledge is sourced, combined and disseminated in many parts of society, formally, informally and non-formally, with knowledge transfer and learning being facilitated by many of the new media-centred tools. Education is no longer the main supplier of knowledge. The impact on education is that it must redefine its role as a knowledge provider, and help teach students to effectively deal with societal change. They must be taught to exercise choice in the face of a far greater complexity. Students must be taught how to source, combine and judge knowledge (Van Dorp 2011, 7; Chau 2007).

Turku University of Applied Sciences (TUAS) has emphasized the innovation pedagogy approach in the TUAS education development (Lehto et al. 2011). Innovation pedagogy redefines how knowledge is absorbed, produced and used in order to create innovation. According to the rector of TUAS, "the philosophical foundations of innovation pedagogy are based on the humanistic way of understanding people as creators of their own future" (Kettunen 2009). This kind of teaching calls for applied research and development activities that support regional development, and the production of innovations in working life are integrated into multi-disciplinary teaching in accordance with the principles of innovation pedagogy. The education offered by the university promotes entrepreneurship and includes service activities while taking into account both the needs of the region as a whole as well as the constantly changing trends of working life. These guidelines have guided the research conducted by TUAS personnel also in this project. (Sorsa 2011f, 18-21).

For the PAM PAL curriculum, the above described pedagogical approaches have been found useful. Such pedagogy will need to attend to the domains of knowledge, action and self, such as in addition to learning about things, students will develop a capacity to act on that knowledge and will connect that knowledge and actions to their own lives and behaviour. (Sorsa 2011f, 18-21). The pedagogical challenge then, "is to produce a set of experiences that in turn encourage the formation of human qualities able to engage effectively with multiple frameworks, contesting value systems and open-ended action situations" (Barnett 2000, 263). In piloting PAM PAL modules we have used different pedagogical approaches depending on the audience. The different approaches and tools for teaching are discussed in the PAM PAL Teacher's Guide (Sorsa 2011f).

Several challenges accompany the efforts to implement an inter-disciplinary curriculum. The PAM PAL curriculum is aimed at both higher education organisations of business schools as well as law schools. Obstacles to incorporating private regulation, self-regulation and other soft-law concepts and business concepts into legal education are challenging. Students with social sciences background may be disinclined or lack the confidence to study normative issues. We also offer these modules to engineering students. More generally, there are also challenges associated with implementing collaborative learning (Chau 2007) designs among students who identify with different disciplines. On the other hand, the elements that characterise the goals of these approaches are positive interdependence, individual accountability, group processing, social skills, and face-to-face interaction (Rosca 2005).

As a result of the application of these kinds of pedagogical approaches, we will hopefully have proactive managers who will be the change makers of the future (See Figure 2). As law *per se* is not a permanent institution and as it is an output of individuals the idea in this curriculum is to develop the students' abilities and capabilities to enable them to participate and make change also in the field of regulation. We also suggest solutions as to how the legal system in itself can be a

Figure 2. Proactive actors can make the change

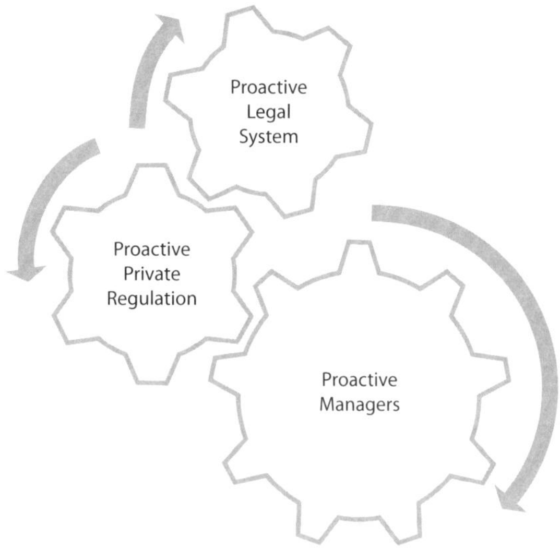

proactive and continuously self-correcting system (discussion of self and private regulation systems). It develops in time and it can have both permanent and dynamic elements. If our students become proactive actors in the society, they will be able to participate in the society's development more efficiently than those who are reactive. Our students may be working either in companies, non-governmental organizations, in the public sector and furthermore they are also consumers. Proactive skills are needed in all these roles. In order to reach these outcomes we need to develop our learning environments so that they also encourage students into action and taking initiative (Sorsa 2011f, 20).

Many educational institutions are moving towards problem-based learning as a solution to educating students who will be creative and can think critically and analytically, and solve problems. Knowledge is no longer an end but a means to making better problem solvers. Problem-based learning has become increasingly popular in educational institutions as a tool to address the inadequacies of traditional teaching. It encourages students to question what they have learnt and to associate with previously acquired knowledge. Problem-based learning is seen as an innovative measure to encourage students to learn via real-life problems (Boud & Feletti, 1999). Problem-based learning teaches students to solve problems and concretizes theoretical issues.

We aim at raising the student's proactive thinking and skills by using innovative teaching methods and techniques. As the possibilities to use different pedagogical techniques depend partly on the size of the group of students, it is the competence of the teacher to analyze which methods and techniques will be feasible in each case.

6. Discussion

Proactive law competences are needed in order to succeed in the future business environment. Developing proactive management and proactive business law competences in an organisation is particularly crucial in global business networks. After the first trials of implementing this curriculum and teaching materials developed for it, several questions arise: what approaches are the most effective strategies to develop problem-centred learning and the PAM PAL curriculum? What are the challenges and how can we overcome them?

Despite the efforts to develop an integrated PAM PAL curriculum, broader educational trends have emerged as persistent obstacles, and possibly stifling innovation. These trends include:

- increasing specialisation into narrowly defined academic disciplines e.g. a law degree, business studies, engineering;
- departmental and other institutional barriers to collaboration amongst faculty and students; and
- ivory-tower teaching traditions that externalise the outside world are hindering scientific literacy.

It seems to be quite difficult to get a new curriculum to be integrated into a narrowly defined curriculum (e.g. law degrees in universities). There also seems to be different understandings and foci between the researchers regarding the content of the proactive law concept, especially researchers having only the law degree seem to consider the concepts and ideas of private regulation rather odd. Different viewpoints, however, is the richness of the dynamic research and it will advance the theory development of the proactive law.

References

Barnett, R., and Hallam, S. (1999). Teaching for supercomplexity: A pedagogy for higher education. In Mortimore, P. (ed.), Understanding pedagogy and its impact on learning, London: Paul Chapman. 137-154.

Barnett, R. (2000). Supercomplexity and the curriculum. *Studies in Higher Education,* 25 (3), 255-265.

Barton, K. & Cunningham, C., D. & Jones, G.T. & Maharg, P. (2006). Valuing What Clients Think: Standardized Clients and the Assessment of Communicative Competence. Clinical Law Review, Vol. 13:1, 1-22.

Berger-Walliser, Gerlinde (2011). The development and History of a proactive Approach to Law. In: Proactive Management and Proactive Business Law; A Handbook. Course materials of the Turku University of Applied Sciences 66. Turku: University of Applied Sciences, 113-126.

Berger-Walliser, Gerlinde (2011). A Proactive Approach to Law for Business Professionals. In: Sorsa, Kaisa (ed.). Proactive Management and Proactive Business Law; A Handbook. Course materials of the Turku University of Applied Sciences 66. Turku: University of Applied Sciences, 113-126.

Boud, D. & Feletti, G. (1999). The Challenge of Problem-Based Learning, (2nd Ed.), London: Kogan Page.

Cafaggi, Fabrizio (2010). Private Regulation, Supply Chain and Contractual Networks: The Case of Food Safety. European University Institute, Florence. Robert Schuman Centre for Advanced Studies Private regulation series-03.

Cafaggi, Fabrizio (2011a). New Foundations of Transnational Private Regulation. Journal of Law and Society, Volume 38, Number 1, March 2011, 20-49.

Cafaggi, Fabrizio (2011b). Private Regulation in European Private Law. In: Hartkamp, Arthur S., Hesselink, Martijn W., Hondius, Ewoud H., Mak, Chantal & Perron, C. Edgar du Perron (2011). Towards a European Civil Code. Woplters & Kluwer, 91-129.

Camacho, Amparo & García, Enrique & Santateresa, Patricia (2011). The Common Frame of Reference. In: Sorsa, Kaisa (ed.). Proactive Management and Proactive Business Law. A Teacher's Guide. Reports from Turku University of Applied Sciences 65, 24-52.

Camacho, Amparo & García, Enrique (2011). Proactive Management and Business Ethics, Sections 1-3. In: Sorsa, Kaisa (ed.). Proactive Management and Proactive Business Law; A Handbook. Course materials of the Turku University of Applied Sciences 66. Turku: University of Applied Sciences, 277-322.

Chau, K.W. (2007). Incorporation of sustainability concepts into a civil engineering curriculum. Journal of Professional Issues in Engineering Education and Practice, Vol. 133, 188-199.

Crant, M. (2000). Proactive Behavior in Organizations. Journal of Management, Vol.26, No. 3, 435-462.

Compete&Collaborate. What is success in a connected world? 11th Annual Global CEO Survey. 2008, PriceWaterhouseCoopers, www.pwc.com/ceosurvey.

Eisenhardt, K. & Martin, J. (2000). Dynamic Capabilities: What are they? Strategic Management Journal 21, 1105-1121.

Geels, Frank W. (2002). Technological transitions as evolutionary reconfiguration processes: a multi-level perspective and a case-study. Research Policy, 31(2002), 1257-74.

Geels, Frank W. (2004). Understanding system innovations: a critical literature review and a conceptual synthesis, 19-47. In: Boelie et al. (2004). System Innovation and the Transition to Sustainability. Bodmin, Cornwall, MPG Books LTD.

Geels, Frank & Schot, Johan (2007). Typology of sociotechnical transition pathways. Research Policy 36 (2007), 399-417.

Goerdel, H. T. (2005). Taking Initiative: Proactive Management and Organizational Performance in Networked Environments. Journal of Public Administration Research and Theory, July 13, 351-367.

Haapio, H. (2007). An ounce of prevention… – Proactive legal care for corporate contracting success. Tidskrift utgiven av Juridiska Föreningen I Finland, häfte 1/2007, 39-68.

Harmes-Liedtke, Ulrich (2010). The Relevance of the Quality Infrastructure to Promote Innovation Systems in Developing Countries. Physikalisch-Technische Bundesanstalt.

Hughes, Peter (2011). Critical, Collaborative and Constructivist Pedagogy for the Social Science of Climate Change. In: Haslett, France & Gedye, Sharon (eds.) (2011). Pedagogy of Climate Change, 51-61.

Henschel, René Franz (2011). Applications: Proactive Risk Management. In: Sorsa, Kaisa (ed.). Proactive Management and Proactive Business Law; A Handbook. Course materials of the Turku University of Applied Sciences 66. Turku: University of Applied Sciences, 243-254.

Jansen, Jos (2011). Proactive lawyering. In: Sorsa, Kaisa (ed.). Proactive Management and Proactive Business Law; A Handbook. Course materials of the Turku University of Applied Sciences 66. Turku: University of Applied Sciences, 143-149.

Jansma, Meine (2011). Lawyers understanding the business environment. In: Sorsa, Kaisa (ed.). Proactive Management and Proactive Business Law; A Handbook. Course materials of the Turku University of Applied Sciences 66. Turku: University of Applied Sciences, 150-157.

Lampe, Marc (2006). A New Paradigm for the Teaching of Business Law and Legal Environment Classes. Journal of Legal Studies Education, Volume 23, Issue 1, 1-51.

Lehto, Anttoni & Kairisto-Mertanen, Liisa & Penttilä, Taru (eds.) (2011). Towards innovation pedagogy – A new approach to teaching and learning for universities of applied sciences. Reports from Turku University of Applied Sciences nr 100.

Manning, Stephan & von Hagen, Oliver (2010). Linking local experiments to global standards: How project networks promote global institution-building. Scandinavian Journal of Management (2010) 26, 398-416.

Maula, Markku V. & Keil, Thomas & Salmenkaita, Jukka-Pekka (2005). Open Innovation in Systemic Innovation Contexts.

Nysten-Haarala, S. (ed.). (2008). Corporate Contracting Capabilities. Conference proceedings and other writings. University of Joensuu, Publications in Law 21.

Pohjonen, S. (toim.). (2002). Ennakoiva sopiminen. Liiketoimien suunnittelu, toteuttaminen ja riskien hallinta. Vantaa, WSOY Lakitieto.

Pohjonen, S. (toim.). (2005). Ex ante – ennakoiva oikeus. Vaajakoski, Gummerus Kirjapaino Oy.

Rosca, D. (2005). Multidisciplinary and active/collaborative approaches in teaching requirements engineering. European Journal of Engineering Education. Vol. 30 No. 1, 121-128.

Rudanko, Matti (2004). Yritysjuridiikka – kauppaoikeutta vai liiketaloutta? Lakimies 7-8/2004, 1225-1243.

Salmi-Tolonen, T. (2005). Oikeus kielenä ja kommunikaationa. Teoksessa Pohjonen, S. (toim.) Ex ante – Ennakoiva oikeus (46-64). Helsinki, Talentum.

Salmi-Tolonen, T. (2008). A Multidimensional Topic Requires a Multidisciplinary Approach. In Nysten-Haarala, S. (ed.), Corporate Contracting Capabilities. Conference proceedings and other writings (pp. 1-17). Joensuu, University of Joensuu, Publications in Law 21.

Salmi-Tolonen, Tarja (2011). Proactive law and Alternative Dispute Resolution Mechanisms. In: Sorsa, Kaisa (ed.) Proactive Management and Proactive Business Law; A Handbook. Course materials of the Turku University of Applied Sciences 66. Turku: University of Applied Sciences, 85-109.

Salmi-Tolonen, Tarja & Sorsa, Kaisa (2011). Proactive Contracting. In: Sorsa, Kaisa (ed.) Proactive Management and Proactive Business Law; A Handbook. Course materials of the Turku University of Applied Sciences 66. Turku: University of Applied Sciences, 179-195.

Sandberg, B. (2007). Customer-related proactiveness in the radical innovation development process. European Journal of Innovation Management, Vol. 10 No. 2, 252-267.

Santateresa, Patricia (2011). Organizational skills: Proactive Business Culture. In: Sorsa, Kaisa (ed.). Proactive Management and Proactive Business Law. A Teacher's Guide. Reports from Turku University of Applied Sciences 65, 339-359.

Smith, A., & Stirling, A. & Berkhout, F., (2005). The governance of sustainable socio-technical transitions. Research Policy 34, 1491-1510.

Sorsa, K. (2008a). Responsible Business; Integrating the Legal Environment to Company Strategy by Proactive Approach.. In Lowe, D. (ed.), IACCM International Academic Symposium On Contract & Commercial Management. Bringing together academics and practitioners to promote research and best practice (pp. 139-162). USA.

Sorsa, K. (2008b). Ennakoivan oikeuden näkökulmia sopimustoiminnan itsesääntelyyn EU:ssa. Oikeus 2008 (37):1, 45-66.

Sorsa, K. (2009a). Towards a Contracting Capabilities Maturity Model for Projects. In Martinsuo, M. (ed.), Recipes for success in project-based management (187-212). Espoo, Project Management Association Finland.

Sorsa, K. (2009b). Elinkeinoelämä tarvitsee ennakoivaa sopimusosaamista. Defensor Legis 1/2009, 128-147.

Sorsa, K. (2009c). The Proactive Law Approach: A Further Step towards Better Regulation. In Tala, J. & Pakarinen, A. (eds.), Changing Forms of Legal and Non-Legal Institutions and New Challenges for the Legislator – International Conference on Legislative Studies in Helsinki (pp. 35-70). Helsinki, National Research Institute of Legal Policy. Research Communications 97.

Sorsa, K. (2009d). Itsesääntely- ja yhteissääntely arvoketjussa. Toimialakohtaista tarkastelua. Helsinki, Oikeuspoliittisen tutkimuslaitoksen julkaisuja 100.

Sorsa, K. (2010a). Proactive Law Approach and Consumer Protection – Comparing UK and Finnish Consumer Authorities Systems. Tidskrift utgiven av Juridiska Föreningen I Finland, häfte 3/2010, 211-231.

Sorsa, K. (2010b). Self-Regulation in Global Value Chain – A Trade Barrier or an Opportunity for Public-private Co-operation?. In: Tala, J. & Pakarinen A. (eds.), Better Regulation – A Critical Assesment. Helsinki, National Research Institute of Legal Policy. Research Communications 105/2010,81-110.

Sorsa, K. (2010c). Itsesääntely ja yhteiskuntavastuu. Yhteisjulkaisu: Työ- ja elinkeinoministeriön julkaisuja. Kilpailukyky 45/2010. Oikeuspoliittisen tutkimuslaitoksen verkkokatsauksia 14/2010.

Sorsa, K. (2010d). Yksityinen sääntely ohjaa merkittävästi kauppaa. Erilaiset standardit ja ohjeistot vaikuttavat yritysten toimintaan usein tehokkaammin kuin lait. Helsingin Sanomat, Vieraskynä 8.11.2010.

Sorsa, K. (2010e). Proactive Law. Insights to theory and practice. Course materials 55. Turku, Turku University of Applied sciences.

Sorsa, Kaisa (2011a). Kansainvälisen kaupan arvoketjujen sääntely. Yhteiskuntavastuun ja ennakoivan oikeuden tarkastelua. Annales Universitatit Turkuensis TOM 320. Turku 2011.

Sorsa, Kaisa (2011b). The Role of Proactive Law for System Level Innovations. In: Franz Henschel, René (ed.) 2011, Academic Forum for Innovative Research and Practice. Bringing together academics and practitioners to promote research and best practice in Contracts and Commercial Management. USA: The international Association For Contract and Commercial Management.

Sorsa, Kaisa (2011c). Yhteiskuntavastuu, yksityinen sääntely ja systeemiset innovaatiot. Edilex asiantuntijakirjoitukset 10.11.2011. www.edilex.fi

Sorsa, Kaisa (2011d). Standardit sääntelyinnovaatioina, 151-162. In: Pakarinen, Auri & Hyvärinen, Anna & Ervasti, Kaius (toim.) (2011). Lainvalmistelu, tutkimus, yhteiskunta. Jyrki Talan juhlakirja. Turun yliopisto, oikeustieteellinen tiedekunta 2011.

Sorsa, Kaisa (ed.) (2011e). Proactive Management and Proactive Business Law; A Handbook. Course materials of the Turku University of Applied Sciences 66. Turku: University of Applied Sciences.

Sorsa, Kaisa (ed.) (2011f). Proactive Management and Proactive Business Law; A Teacher's Guide. Course materials of the Turku University of Applied Sciences 65. Turku: University of Applied Sciences.

Sorsa, Kaisa (2011g). Applications: Proactive Contracting in Value Chain Management. In: Sorsa, Kaisa (ed.). Proactive Management and Proactive Business Law; A Handbook. Course materials of the Turku University of Applied Sciences 66. Turku: University of Applied Sciences, 211-242.

Sorsa, K. – Salmi-Tolonen, T. (2009). Contracting Capabilities in project Business – Proactive Management Approaches to Contracting. In Kähkönen, K. & Samad K. A. & Rekola, M. (eds.), The Human Side of Projects in Modern Business (pp. 221-236). Project Management Association Finland (PMAF) in collaboration with, VTT Technical Research Centre of Finland.

Sorsa, Kaisa & Salmi-Tolonen, Tarja (2011a). Proactive Contracting and the Legal Framework. In: Sorsa, Kaisa (ed.). Proactive Management and Proactive Business Law; A Handbook. Course materials of the Turku University of Applied Sciences 66. Turku: University of Applied Sciences, 196-210.

Sorsa, Kaisa & Salmi-Tolonen, Tarja (2011b). Contract Management Maturity. In: Sorsa, Kaisa (ed.). Proactive Management and Proactive Business Law; A Handbook. Course materials of the Turku University of Applied

Sciences 66. Turku: University of Applied Sciences, 263-273.

Teece, D.J., Pisano, G. and Shuen, A. (1997). Dynamic capabilities and strategic management. Strategic Management Journal, 18, 7, 509-533.

Tolonen, Juha (2007). Oikeus, talous ja yhteiskunta: kaksi oikeustieteen mallia. Lakimies 2/2007, 259-264.

Van de Luytgaarden, Eric (2011). A Proactive Approach to Law for Lawyers (2011). In: Sorsa, Kaisa (ed.). Proactive Management and Proactive Business Law; A Handbook. Course materials of the Turku University of Applied Sciences 66. Turku: University of Applied Sciences, 127-142.

Van Dorp, Cornelis Adrianus (2011). Systemic Innovation of Education: Forging Action, Gaining Momentum, Shifting Paradigm. *Journal for the Systemic Innovation of Education (JSIE).* Volume 1, Issue 1, 1-102. Available at: www.essie-society.org.

Strategic Contracting: Examining the Business-Legal Interface

By

Larry A. DiMatteo
Huber Hurst Professor of Contact Law

George J. Siedel
Williamson Family Professor of
Business Administration and
Thurnau Professor of Business Law

Helena Haapio
Master of Laws (LL.M.),
Master of Quality (MQ),
Contract Coach

"In transactions, lawyers are important players, but even when they are leaders it is almost always as part of a multi-disciplinary team."[1]

1. Introduction

Most of the American literature on the strategic use of the law is found in the management literature, namely, in organizational behavior and human resource management scholarship. This literature explores how managers and their companies may use law as a tool to create value and protect competitive advantages, as well as how best to deal with regulatory law in a strategic manner. However, the lawyer needs to be educated in business as well in order to recognize business opportunities that the law can advance. This chapter focuses on the importance of exploring how clients and lawyers can work together to use contracts proactively and the skill set that best allows them to serve the strategic

1. Jeffrey M. Lipshaw, *Contract as Meaning: An Introduction to 'Contract as Promise'* at 30, 31Pace L. Rev. (2011).

needs of business. Managers need to have a better understanding of law as not only a matter for lawyers or an ex-post necessity in cases of dispute resolution and regulatory compliance. On the other side, transactional lawyers need to explore the intricacies of their client's business in order to advance and protect the client's interests.

Section 2 of this chapter – "Contract Literacy" – draws from the basic theme that managers and their legal advisors need a framework for integrating legal astuteness into business practice. This section uses a Manager's Legal Plan™ that provides a four-step process for using contracts as competitive assets.[2] This process provides the framework for the integration of legal sources into day-to-day business practice. The four steps include: (1) Understanding the law, (2) Knowing how to react to legal problems, (3) Developing strategies to prevent future problems, and (4) Incorporating a proactive approach to the use of law in business. The final step equates to converting contracting from a post-negotiation exercise to strategic contracting that begins at the pre-negotiation stage and continues throughout the course of the contractual relationship.

The Manager's Legal Plan™ emphasizes the importance of legal astuteness and, specifically, contract literacy. Contract literacy includes understanding legal issues that arise in contract formation – such as, legal requirements for an agreement, legality, writing, and agency concerns. This section includes the use of a "decision tree" in deciding whether to enter into a contract. Another important part of contract literacy is understanding the interaction between express and implied terms. Obtaining a high level of legal astuteness and contract literacy will help minimize the chances of contract breach through strategic contracting. Nonetheless, there will be instances of dispute. The question then becomes: how should the business person react to such legal problems? There are generally two options – after re-negotiation and conciliation efforts have failed – either fight or move on. Emphasis here will be on practical tools that managers and their legal advisors can use in litigating and resolving disputes – decision tree analysis and alternative dispute resolution (ADR).

2. See George J. Siedel & Helena Haapio, Proactive Law for Managers: *A Hidden Source of Competitive Advantage* (2011); George J. Siedel, *Using the Law for Competitive Advantage* (2002).

This section also explores two areas often associated with each other: preventive law practices and proactive approaches. It explores the preventive notion of developing the perfect legal contract. International Association for Contract and Commercial Management (IACCM) surveys of most frequently negotiated terms and types of ADR clauses that can be included in contracts will be given special attention. The section concludes with an analysis of the proactive approach to using the law.

Section 3 of the chapter – "Tactical to Strategic: The Need for a Paradigm Shift" – draws from the areas of sales and procurement of works, services, solutions, plant and equipment – the kind of contracting that produces significant current revenue and where significant portions of the contract are technical, financial, and business terms (scope, service levels, performance/output requirements, and so forth). Most of this content is provided by business managers rather than lawyers. Here, lawyers are typically in charge of contract templates and Standard Terms and Conditions (STCs), but play little role during the contract implementation or performance stage. Additionally, existing templates and STCs suffer from status quo bias and relate only to failure-focused terms. The section argues that contract planning and drafting should involve a more holistic approach to increase the likelihood of business success rather than simply to minimize the consequences of failure. Legal autopsies are suggested as a way to learn from the past. In order to enable the negotiator-manager and contract drafter-lawyer to better understand and address strategic business needs and the changes necessary in existing contracting processes and documents, the use of visualization techniques – adding tables, charts, and images to supplement text – is recommended.

The final section of the chapter – "Proactive Contracting as Learning to Think Strategically" – reviews the limitations and efficiencies related to contract writing. The major function of contract law and contracts is to allow contracting parties to plan for the future.[3] Parties make promises of future performance, which allows them and other parties to plan business activities on the assumption that these promises will be fulfilled. Unfortunately, business persons and their lawyers often fail to use the planning function of contracts to best ensure future performance,

3. See Ian R. Macneil, *A Primer of Contract Planning*, 48 S. Cal L. Rev. 627 (1975).

minimize the costs of non-performance, and to provide alternatives for non-performance. This section will review a number of theories of contract drafting and contract interpretation. It will then analyze standard contract problems, such as, the incompleteness of contracts and the complexity of contracts. It also analyzes the flexibility of contracts as an opportunity to minimize the probability of breach and the costs of breach. The law and economics literature will be used to gain insight in contract design. Contract design should focus on deal-preserving norms and ways in which managers and their lawyers can better utilize the flexibility of contracts as a strategic device to create value and competitive advantages for the company. While the second section focuses on the manager's use of contracts as strategic devices, this section focuses on the other side of the business-legal interface – the transactional lawyer. The middle section acts as a bridge between Section 2's focus on the manager perspective and Section 4's focus on the transactional lawyer perspective. By introducing proactive methods and tools that can be incorporated into corporate contracting practice, the second (i.e., the bridge) part encourages a shift towards strategic contracting and explains how visualization can be used to change mindsets and enhance communication and decision making between the strategically-inclined lawyer and manager.

2. Contract Literacy

Contracting is a core business activity. As noted in a leading book on managerial responsibilities, "obtaining a contract is the primary goal of a business entity."[4] According to Tim Cummins, CEO of IACCM, "[c] ontracts lie at the heart of most business relationships, certainly within Western culture and economies, and increasingly among all companies or entities that seek to operate in an international market."[5]

4. O. Lee Reed et al., *The Role of Contracts in the Introductory and Only Law Course That Most Business Students Will Ever Take*, 9 J. Legal Stud. Educ. 1, 14 n.23 (1990) (quoting Am. Corporate Counsel Ass'n, Legal Responsibilities of Corporate Managers 45 (1985)).
5. Tim Cummins, *Best Practices in Commercial Contracting, in* A Proactive Approach 131, 132 (P. Wahlgren & Cecilia Magnusson Sjöberg eds., Scandinavian Studies

Because contracting is essential to business success, contract literacy is a necessity for managers. This section reviews the requirements for contract literacy. The section begins (2.1) with a discussion of the general importance of law as a source of competitive advantage, including a practical plan that is designed to enable managers to bring theory into action. This plan provides a framework (discussed in 2.2) for managers seeking to gain contract literacy. This section will conclude (2.3) with a review of key aspects of contract law that should receive greater attention in the legal education of managers.

2.1 Law as a Source of Competitive Advantage and the Manager's Legal Plan

In recent years, law has gained increased prominence as a source of competitive advantage. This prominence originated with the work of scholars and practitioners in the United States and Europe. In the United States, for example, a Law for Competitive Advantage Movement (LCAM) includes research by Robert Bird, who used a strategy framework to analyze the attributes of law that are necessary to achieve competitive advantage. He concluded that:

> Laws confer significant *value* to firms through the protection of innovation, the enabling of free labor markets, and the efficient regulation of contracts.Some legal resources are also *rare*, such as the benefits conferred through individual contracts between buyers and suppliers, manufacturers and customers, and labor and management. The competitive advantage of legal resources may be sustained by virtue of *their imperfect imitability*, their causal ambiguity, and their social complexity. Finally, *substitutes for laws* are rare and costly to obtain.[6]

Professor Bird also developed a model that incorporates five paths of legal strategy: avoidance, compliance, prevention, advantage, and transformation.[7] Another professor, Constance Bagley, has developed a

in Law, Vol. 49, 2006), *available at* http://www.scandinavianlaw.se/pdf/49-8.pdf.

6. Robert C. Bird, Law, *Strategy and Competitive Advantage* 5 (Working Paper Series 2009), *available at* http://ssrn.com/abstract=1327795 (emphasis added).
7. Robert C. Bird, *Pathways of Legal Strategy*, 14 Stan. J.L. Bus. & Fin. 1 (2008).

framework illustrating how law can increase a firm's chances for success[8] and a model for integrating law and strategy.[9]

In Europe, the Proactive Law Movement (PLM) parallels LCAM in the United States. PLM has been championed by the Nordic School of Proactive Law,[10] a network of practitioners and researchers who were instrumental in creating the ProActive ThinkTank. The ThinkTank provides a forum for discussion, development, and promotion of the proactive management of relationships, contracts and risks, and the prevention of legal uncertainties and disputes.[11]

Proactive Law has both preventive and promotive dimensions. The preventive dimension emphasizes collaboration between the law function and other company or business functions to prevent legal problems.[12] The goal of the promotive dimension "is to embed legal knowledge and skills in clients' business strategies and everyday actions to actively promote business success, ensure desired outcomes, and balance risk with reward."[13] PLM received a major boost when the European Economic and Social Committee (a consultative body created to advise the European Parliament, the European Council, and the European Commission) recognized the desirability of the proactive law approach in a 2009 Opinion directed towards improving regulation at the EU level.[14]

8. Constance E. Bagley, Winning Legally: *How To Use the Law to Create Value, Marshal Resources, and Manage Risk* 28 (2005).
9. Constance E. Bagley, *What's Law Got to Do with It: Integrating Law and Strategy*, 47 Am. Bus. L.J. 587 (2010).
10. Nordic School of Proactive Law, http://www.juridicum.su.se/proactivelaw/main/planning.html.
11. ProActive ThinkTank Mission Statement, *available at* http://www.juridicum.su.se/proactivelaw/main/thinktank/missionstatement.pdf.
12. Soile Pohjonen, *Proactive Law in the Field of Law, in* A Proactive Approach, *supra* note 5, at 53, 54, *available at* http://www.scandinavianlaw.se/pdf/49-4.pdf.
13. Helena Haapio, *Introduction to Proactive Law: A Business Lawyer's View, in* A Proactive Approach, *supra* note 5, at 21, 24, *available at* http://www.scandinavianlaw.se/pdf/49-2.pdf.
14. European Economic and Social Committee [hereinafter EESC], Opinion on 'The proactive law approach: a further step towards better regulation at EU level', 2009 O.J. (C 175), *available at* http://eur-lex.europa.eu/LexUriServ/LexUriServ.do?uri=OJ:C:2009:175:0026:0033:EN:PDF. In addition to the English language version, the Opinion is also available in all other official EU languages, includ-

Insights from the parallel US and European movements were combined in 2011 with the publication of *Proactive Law for Managers: A Hidden Source of Competitive Advantage.*[15] In *Proactive Law for Managers,* Siedel and Haapio use the research developed on both sides of the Atlantic, and Siedel's Manager's Legal Plan™, to show how managers and legal professionals can, in collaboration, use law to gain competitive advantages. This Plan provides a four-step process:

- Understanding the law: Just as a legal professional must understand business practice, managers need to understand the law.
- Reactive: Managers often must react ex post to legal concerns that arise in the workplace.
- Preventive: Managers need to develop strategies and solutions to prevent future legal problems.
- Proactive: Managers should attempt to reframe legal concerns as business concerns and opportunities.

The latter three steps can be explained by a medical analogy.[16] If you develop malaria, you engage in an ex-post *reactive* action by seeking medical treatment, just as many managers think of law as an emergency room function that is utilized only after a legal problem develops. An alternative is to engage in *preventive* action by taking pills and using mosquito netting to prevent malaria. Another alternative is to use a proactive approach – such as eliminating mosquitoes through swamp drainage that addresses the root cause of the problem. Just as the drainage might provide additional economic benefits for a community, the proactive approach to the law can create competitive advantage opportunities for a business.

ing Danish (http://eur-lex.europa.eu/LexUriServ/ LexUriServ.do? uri=OJ:C:2009:175:0026:0033:DA:PDF). The Section for the Single Market, Production and Consumption, under the leadership of Mr Jorge Pegado Liz, was responsible for preparing EESC's work on the topic, and one of the authors of this chapter, Helena Haapio, acted as an expert in producing the Opinion.

15. Siedel & Haapio, *supra* note 2.
16. Haapio, *supra* note 13, at 25-26 (citing Edward A. Dauer, *Developing Preventive Law: From Lawyering to Quality*, Leadership & Management Directions Newsletter (American Bar Association ABA, Section of Law Practice Management, Law Practice Division), Summer 1998.

2.2 Manager's Legal Plan as Framework for Contract Literacy

In *Proactive Law for Managers,*[17] Siedel and Haapio apply the Manager's Legal Plan™ to contracting. This four-part application provides a framework for managers seeking to achieve contract literacy.

2.2.1 Understanding Contract Law

Contract literacy obviously requires an understanding of basic contract law principles that address questions relating to contract formation and whether the agreement is required to be in writing. But managers also must understand three areas that provide a foundation for these contract law principles: (1) two key variables that determine the source of contract law, (2) the freedom of contract philosophy and its limitations, and (3) the role of invisible (implied) terms. Because of the importance of these foundational elements and because they have received little attention in previous English language work on proactive law, they will be covered separately in 2.3.

2.2.2 The Reactive Step

In the contract arena, the reactive step usually arises when a dispute arises after a contract has been formed. When this happens, the human response often reflects the flight or fight instincts that have been documented in evolutionary biology. In legal terms, "fight" usually involves litigation while "flight" refers to the settlement of the dispute.

Contractually literate managers use legal tools in making the fight or flight decision. They use these same tools not only in the process of fighting, but also, in the process of reaching a settlement. The "decision tree" is an especially useful tool that enables managers and legal professionals to visualize linkage between various issues and to calculate an expected value of litigation that can be compared with settlement offers.[18] Visualization is discussed in greater detail in Section 3.

17. Siedel & Haapio, *supra note* 2. *See also* George J. Siedel & Helena Haapio, *Using Proactive Law for Competitive Advantage,* 47 AM. Bus. L.J. 641 (2010).
18. Siedel, *supra* note 2, at 152-57.

2.2.3 The Preventive Step

Managers wanting to move past the reactive approach to law in order to create competitive advantages proceed to the final two steps of the Manager's Legal Plan™ – preventive and proactive. The preventive step emphasizes learning from a company's flight or fight experiences (and from the experiences of other companies as well) in an attempt to minimize future legal problems.

Professor DiMatteo has noted that one form of contractual competitive advantage arises when firms engage in opportunism – that is, trying to gain advantage at the expense of the other side – as opposed to a more collaborative strategy.[19] Strategies based on gaining or preventing opportunism often arise during the negotiating process as firms attempt to develop contracts that are as legally complete as possible in protecting their rights and that also rely on past experience to allocate and manage risk.[20] The emphasis on risk management (allocation) is reflected in IACCM surveys of negotiators from around the world. The most recent survey, taken from December 2010 to April 2011, concludes that the top ten most frequently negotiated terms are: (1) Limitation of Liability, (2) Indemnification, (3) Price, Charge, and Price Changes, (4) Intellectual Property, (5) Payment, (6) Liquidated Damages, (7) Performance, Guarantees, and Undertakings, (8) Delivery and Acceptance, (9) Applicable Law and Jurisdiction, and (10) Confidential Information/ Non-disclosure.

In commenting on these results, the study concludes that: "A quick review of the 'top ten' negotiated terms reveals the extent to which negotiators are channeled into asset protection and the consequences of failure – intellectual property rights, liquidated damages, governing law and payment terms being examples."[21]

19. Larry A. DiMatteo, *Strategic Contracting: Contract Law as a Source of Competitive Advantage*, 47 Am. Bus. L.J. 727 (2010).
20. Soile Pohjonen & Kerttuli Visuri, *Proactive Approach in Project Management and Contracting, in* A Proactive Approach to Contracting and Law 75, 82 (Helena Haapio ed. 2008).
21. *2011 Top Terms in Negotiation* (International Association for Contract and Commercial Management 2011), *available at* https://www.iaccm.com/members/library/files/top_terms_2011_1.pdf. According to the introduction, the results are based on input from 1,123 organizations, representing more than 8,000 negotiators. Individual contributors came from

Closely aligned with the negotiation of protective measures is the use of alternative dispute resolution (ADR) tools in anticipation of future disputes. The negotiation of an ADR provision begins with the adoption of a company policy encouraging the use of ADR. A common corporate ADR policy statement adopted by over 4,000 operating companies states that: "In the event of a business dispute between our company and another company which has made or will then make a similar statement, we are prepared to explore with that other party resolution of the dispute through negotiation or ADR techniques before pursuing full-scale litigation."[22]

Other ADR tools include the use of suitability screens and contract clauses. Suitability screens ask managers – through a series of questions – to determine whether a binding or non-binding process should be used to resolve a business dispute.[23] Binding processes are litigation and arbitration, while non-binding processes include negotiation and mediation. ADR contract clauses typically include an agreement to use mediation or arbitration (or both, if the two are linked) in the event of a dispute.[24]

2.2.4 The Proactive Step

The proactive step is the most conceptually difficult of the four steps because the goal is to reframe legal concerns as business concerns – and, if possible, as business opportunities. This requires moving from the ground floor of the contract negotiation dance to the balcony to gain a big-picture perspective of the issues. This perspective reveals a number of potential problems of a mindset whose goal is the development of a legally perfect or complete contract:

procurement, legal and sales contracting personnel in more than 60 countries. The input comes from large international corporations and therefore may not be an accurate reflection of negotiations at a local level or between smaller organizations.

22. Siedel & Haapio, *supra* note 2, at 148, citing the Corporate Policy Statement on Alternatives to Litigation© developed by CPR, the International Institute for Conflict Prevention and Resolution.
23. *Id.*
24. *Id.* at 147.

- Length and complexity: What used to be a handshake deal can morph into a lengthy contract that the parties do not understand.[25]
- High transaction costs: These costs include the time and expense of, first, working with lawyers in drafting contracts and then returning to them later after a dispute arises to find out what the contract terms mean.[26]
- Disagreements: Problem solving between the parties tends to focus on legal remedies rather than business solutions.[27]
- Negatives: The parties begin their relationship with a negotiation that focuses on negatives.[28]
- Cross-cultural concerns: Negotiators in some cultures that emphasize relationships are uncomfortable with lengthy contracts.

Using the "from the balcony" perspective, a group of corporate lawyers in Scotland decided to move away from the "perfect contract" mentality. They realized that in contracts establishing long-term relationships with suppliers, it "is often better to leave continuing commercial relationships largely to the irresistible forces of free market economics, rather than attempt to place continuing contractual obligations on each other."[29] This philosophy led them to develop a new approach called "Pathclearer" that enabled them to shorten contracts that sometimes exceeded two-hundred pages and replace them with simple letter agreements that give each side the ability to terminate the contract at any time.[30]

The work of these attorneys parallels the 2011 IACCM survey, which revealed that negotiators recognize the need to move beyond a mindset that focuses on asset protection and the consequences of failure. When asked what terms would be more productive in supporting successful relationships, none of these top four terms are on the top ten list of terms that are negotiated with greatest frequency: change management,

25. Steven Weatherley, *Pathclearer: A More Commercial Approach to Drafting Commercial Contracts*, L. Dep't Q., Oct.-Dec. 2005, at 43.
26. *Id.* at 42.
27. *Id.* at 42-43.
28. *Id.* at 44.
29. *Id.* at 41.
30. *Id.*

scope and goals, responsibilities of the parties, and communications and reporting provisions.[31]

2.3 The Foundations of Contract Literacy

The four steps in the Manager's Legal Plan™ provide a framework for managers attempting to achieve contract literacy. The first step, understanding contract law, is especially important because it provides the foundation for the reactive, preventive, and proactive steps. This section covers three topics that, at a minimum, should be included in business school courses and company training programs on contract law: (1) key variables in determining the sources of contract law, (2) freedom of contract philosophy and its limits, and (3) importance of invisible terms.

2.3.1 Two Key Variables in Determining the Source of Contract Law

Managers should have a basic understanding of the two key variables that determine the sources of contract law. The first variable is the determination of whether the contract is governed by civil law or common law. This variable can result in differences in the form and substance of contracts. For instance, civil law contracts have traditionally been shorter than common law contracts because greater reliance in placed on implied law, which is discussed below.[32]

The other variable relates to the subject of the contract. A real estate contract, for instance, might be governed by a different set of legal rules than a contract for the sale of goods. Contracts for the sale of goods are further complicated by the fact that either a domestic law (for example, the Sale of Goods Act in the Nordic Countries or the Uniform Commercial Code in the United States) or an international law (the Convention on Contracts for the International Sale of Goods or CISG) might apply depending on whether the parties are in business, whether they are from different countries, whether and how the contract specifies the law

31. See IACCM 2011 Survey Results, *supra* note 21, at 6.
32. "Key Features of Common Law or Civil Law Systems," http://ppp.worldbank.org/public-private-partnership/node/29.

governing the contract, and whether and how countries have adopted the CISG.[33]

2.3.2 Freedom of Contract Philosophy and Its Limits

Freedom of contract is a fundamental principle of contract law. In the words of one corporate attorney: "In the world of contracts you as the writer control the script and produce the play."[34] For example, under Article 6 of the CISG, the parties to a contract can decide that the CISG does not apply or they can vary or derogate from specific provisions of the CISG.

However, managers should understand that this principle is subject to constraints (which vary from one country to another). For example, there are several legal doctrines that limit unfettered freedom of contract and provide guidelines for ethical behavior in negotiating contracts, including principles relating to fraud, fiduciary duty and unconscionability.

These legal doctrines might limit the ability of parties to use their bargaining power unfairly. For example, Hooters restaurant required its employees to sign an arbitration agreement. One employee, a bartender, claimed that she was sexually harassed by a Hooters official. When she sued Hooters, the restaurant argued that litigation was prohibited by the arbitration agreement. The trial court concluded that the agreement was unconscionable (that is, it violated principles of conscience) and the appellate court agreed, noting that the agreement: (1) Required employees, but not Hooters, to provide advance notice of their claims, (2) Provided that Hooters, but not employees, could record the hearings, (3) Gave Hooters control over the selection of the arbitrator, and (4) Allowed Hooters to change the arbitration rules at any time, "even in the middle of an arbitration proceeding."[35]

33. The CISG can be found at http://www.cisg.law.pace.edu; for the declarations and reservations applicable to the adoption of the CISG made by the Nordic and other countries *see* http://www.cisg.law.pace.edu/cisg/countries/cntries.html.
34. *How to Keep Your Company Out of Court* (Paul Allen ed. 1984).
35. Hooters of America, Inc. v. Phillips, 173 F.3d 933 (4th Cir. April 8, 1999).

2.3.3 Importance of Invisible Terms

Contract literacy requires, of course, an understanding of both the elements of a legally binding contract, such as whether an offer was made and accepted, and the express terms incorporated into the contract, such as various trade terms. However, managers must also understand the implied terms that will apply to their contract terms, which Helena Haapio calls "invisible" terms.[36] As one court noted in discussing freedom of contract under the CISG: "The CISG does not preempt a private contract between the parties; instead, it provides a statutory authority from which contract provisions are interpreted, fills gaps in contract language, and governs issues not addressed by the contract."[37] An example of a gap-filler is Article 35 of the CISG, which states that unless the parties have otherwise agreed, the seller must provide goods that were "held out to the buyer as a sample or model."

While understanding implied contract terms might be viewed as burdensome by some managers, these terms provide an opportunity to simplify business contracts. The Scottish lawyers who developed the Pathclearer approach recognized this benefit. According to them: "[The general law will] imply certain legal terms into the relationship. The general law tends to provide a fair middle-ground solution to most issues, and there are very few aspects of business dealings that are not in some way regulated by it.[38]

As a result of this realization, these lawyers conclude their letter agreements by noting that: "We have therefore agreed upon the essential elements of our contract. Rather than incur time and expense negotiating

36. Helena Haapio, *Business Success and Problem Prevention Through Proactive Contracting, in* A Proactive Approach, *supra* note 5, at 149, 170, *available at* http://www.scandinavianlaw.se/pdf/49-9.pdf. For invisible terms (and creative silence) more generally, *see* Helena Haapio, *Invisible Terms in International Contracts and What to Do about Them, Contract Management,* July 2004, 32 (National Contract Management Association NCMA), *available at* http://www.ncmahq.org/files/Articles/81EEB_cm_July04_32.pdf; Helena Haapio, *Invisible Terms & Creative Silence: What You Don't See Can Help or Hurt You, Contract Management,* September 2009, 24 (National Contract Management Association NCMA), *available at* http://www.ncmahq.org/files/Articles/CM0909%20-%2024-35.pdf.
37. Ajax Tool Works, Inc. v. Can-Eng. Mfg. Ltd., 2003 WL 223187 (N.D. Ill. Jan. 30, 2003).
38. Weatherley, *supra* note 25, at 43.

and recording in writing other non-essential terms and conditions of our contract, we have agreed to allow the general law to regulate such matters, implying such terms as it may."[39]

3. Tactical to Strategic: The Need for a Paradigm Shift

Despite all the good reasons for strategic contracting, many organizations still resist the implementation of such an approach into their corporate practices. Even where business and legal professionals are convinced that their organization needs to become more proactive there remains barriers and resistance. This section looks at these barriers and reasons for resistance and introduces ways in which they can be overcome through the incorporation of proactive methods and tools in corporate contracting practice.

3.1 Going to the Root Causes of Contract Problems

Lawyers working in the commercial world have a wealth of transactional experience. They are able to list examples of contract language and terms that were misused or misunderstood. It is likely that a large percentage of business disputes could be prevented by sharing such experience and utilizing it during proactive bid and contract reviews. However, for the purposes of this chapter, more systematic ways of enabling organizational learning and knowledge sharing of contract problems will be explored.

3.1.1 Postmortems and Legal Autopsies

Understanding organizational change has gained the attention of researchers in a variety of fields. One of the methods, considered good practice, is to conduct a *postmortem* of each business project. This is useful for organizational learning and knowledge sharing. A fundamental principle of successful contracting is learning from experience. Methods for conducting postmortems can be found in literature related to fields such as software engineering, quality engineering, risk management,

39. Template – Pathclearer Supply Agreement (Clause 6), http://ld.practicallaw.com/0-201-3576.

and project management. Yet, in the legal field, such practices are rarely discussed or performed.

An early pioneer of such a proactive learning approach was Professor Louis M. Brown who suggested practical steps to implement organizational change through a fuller appreciation of the different dimensions of using law. In the 1950s, Brown introduced the *legal autopsy* methodology as a method to learn from past mistakes in the legal field.[40] According to Brown, "the law is the only profession which records its mistakes carefully, exactly as they occurred, and yet does not identify them as mistakes."[41] In his autobiography,[42] he discussed the legal "dead body", a decided case, and how we can "open it up" by doing historical research of both sides of the dispute. This allows the researcher to recreate the whole story from the earliest beginnings of the relationship of the parties to the dispute.[43] Brown then illustrates some of the legal autopsies he and his students performed, along with their findings, and the obstacles they met on the way. He had high hopes for the methodology, yet his applications for funding for further research were unsuccessful; both the American Bar Foundation and the National Science Foundation rejected his grant applications. One explanation for the lack of interest in the academic community, he noted, paralleled the general lack of interest in the law in action as opposed to the law in books.[44]

Brown, despite his inability to complete his work, left a legacy that: "Litigation is often a symptom of legal trouble. Litigation treats symptoms rather than underlying causes. At least, if this observation is worth testing, autopsy is the method for doing so."[45] His work is reflected in those who work in the field of legal archaeology[46] and is aligned with

40. Louis M. Brown, *Legal Autopsy*, 39 J. Am. Judicature Soc'y 47 (1955).
41. *Id.* at 47.
42. Louis M. Brown, *Lawyering through Life*, 196-203 (Fred B. Rothman & Co.: Littleton, Colorado 1986).
43. *Id.* at 196.
44. "It is much easier to find the law on the printed page than the law in action." *Id.* at 202.
45. *Id.* at 203.
46. *See* Debora L. Threedy, *Dancing Around Gender: Lessons from Arthur Murray on Gender and Contracts*, 45 Wake Forest L. Rev. 749 (2010); Debora L. Threedy, *Unearthing Subversion with Legal Archeology*, 13 Tex. J. Women & L. 133, 138-39

proactive contracting's search to determine the basic causes of contractual break-downs and legal disputes.

The time has come to reinvent the autopsy methodology and develop it into a managerial-legal learning venture. This venture would look into what businesses and their lawyers did or did not do or could have done to prevent the dispute, and what they could have done to ensure performance. Additionally, successful business deals should be mined for insight. Was success achieved by mere luck or by design? What were the drivers of success and what can lawyers and business managers do to strengthen them? The increased use in the legal field of empirical cross-disciplinary methodologies provides the means to develop a more holistic, success-oriented approach to contracting.

3.1.2 Most Frequent Sources of Claims and Disputes

The Internet and the IACCM surveys provide access to information that was unavailable in Louis Brown's time. In its 10th Annual Survey *2011 Top Terms in Negotiation*[47] discussed in Section 2.2.3, the IACCM asked business managers what terms are considered the most frequent source of a claim or dispute. Table 1 on page 76 summarizes the core findings.[48]

The results show that delivery and acceptance issues constitute the most frequent source of claims and disputes. Experience tells us that this is likely due to confusion around requirements, either through ambiguity from the beginning or the implementation (or lack) of change management procedures (Number 3 on the list). While requirements management has been widely researched in other fields, it has not attracted much interest in the legal field; nor is it high on negotiators' agendas as evidenced by the list of the top ten terms that are negotiated with greatest frequency.[49] The Survey findings show a divergence between highly negotiated terms and the terms most often at the center of disputes. The good news is that most negotiators recognize that the

(2003); Richard Danzig, Hadley v. Baxendale: *A Study in the Industrialization of the Law,* 4 J. Legal Stud. 249 (1975).

47. 2011 *Top Terms in Negotiation, supra* note 21.

48. *Id.* at 8.

49. *Infra* Section 2.2.3.

Table 1: Most Frequent Sources of Claims and Disputes

Delivery / Acceptance	41 %
Price / Charge / Price Changes	38 %
Change Management	32 %
Invoices / Late Payment	30 %
Performance / Guarantees / Undertakings	27 %
Service Levels and Warranties	27 %
Payment	25 %
Responsibilities of the Parties	22 %
Liquidated Damages	22 %
Scope and Goals	21 %
Warranty	16 %
Limitation of Liability	16 %
Indemnification	14 %
Service Withdrawal or Termination	14 %
Intellectual Property	12 %
Audits / Benchmarking	10 %
Assignment / Transfer	8 %
Dispute Resolution	8 %
Data Protection / Security	7 %
Communications and Reporting	7 %

current negotiation agenda is in need of adjustment.[50] It is time to shift the focus of contracts and STCs, along with the focus of those in charge of designing them. The following sections will examine how best to change the focus of contract negotiators and designers.

50. *See id.* and *The Top Negotiated Terms: Negotiators Admit They Are On Wrong Agenda.* Contracting Excellence, July 2009 (International Association for Contract and Commercial Management IACCM), *available at* http://www.iaccm.com/news/contractingexcellence/?storyid=923.

3.1.3 Preventing Problems and Promoting Success: Not Just a Matter for Lawyers

The early pioneers of preventive law taught us that after finding the causes of legal disputes, we can prevent the breakdown of contractual relationships in the future. After this is accomplished, proactive contracting seeks to confront causes that are unavoidable and minimize any harmful effects. But the process begins with the locating of discoverable causes.[51]

In order to avoid the repetition of poorly working contracts, the current standards and framework for commercial contracting need to be shifted from their focus on terms, such as limitation of liability and indemnification clauses that deal with the *consequences* of failure to terms that can eliminate the *causes* for such failure. For example, greater clarity can be obtained by better describing the requirements related to the products, services, or solutions that are the subject of the contract. This can accomplished by incorporating contract terms that provide benchmarks to judge the progress of performance, as well as providing clear delivery times, acceptance criteria, change management procedures, and so forth. Improvement in these areas will dramatically reduce the frequency of contract disputes since many disputes are closely connected to scope of work, requirements, service descriptions, delivery terms and schedules. It is in these areas of contracts that legal issues, technical issues, and business issues become intertwined. Proactively dealing with these causes of misunderstandings should be a high priority for managers in charge of planning and specifying future sales, offerings, and procurement, as well as for contract negotiators and contract designers.

Success in business and in business contracting requires managerial-legal collaboration, which in turn requires legal astuteness in business managers and business astuteness in lawyers. Working alone, neither lawyers nor business managers can create value through strategic contracting. As noted by Professor Edward Dauer, a pioneer in preventive law, this approach takes lawyers into somewhat unfamiliar terrain. But, transactional lawyers working proactively cannot simply assume that clients design the products, the corporate culture, and environmental

51. Dauer, *supra* note 16.

integrity, while lawyers merely practice law.[52] In a highly competitive legal market, it is in the lawyers' self-interest to discover, develop, and highlight the value added nature of their services.

3.2 Changing Mindsets: Communicating Contracts Differently

One of the main reasons for existing barriers to implementing strategic contracting is the prevailing view of contracts as legal rather than managerial instruments. The potential to create value and innovate in the field of contracts is generally unknown to the business manager. The legalistic view of contracts is supported by their current "look and feel"; often these contracts consist of dense text structured according to legal logic rather than business readers' logic. They read like statutes rather than as a vehicle that provides guidance to users in the implementation of their contracts. Most contracts and contract negotiators focus on preparing for and dealing with failure rather than securing success. In order to stimulate breakthrough innovation in this area and to shift towards strategic contracting, both business executives and lawyers need to change their views and practices.

3.2.1 Contract Visualization

In order to enable executives to see the potential impact of contracts on strategy, corporate image, customer touch points, ease of doing business, and creating and maintaining good relationships, lawyers need to inform and enlighten them to bottom line outcomes. In order to accomplish this mission, lawyers need to communicate the core contents of thinking strategically about law and contracts. Visualization – adding tables, charts, and images to supplement text – can help change the way in which contracts are seen and communicated. It offers tools that can help transactional lawyers engage their business clients and change their mindsets regarding the role of law in their businesses.

Visualization is used in many areas to help reduce complexity and convey information quickly. Images can convey information in a way that makes it more accessible and understandable. In Central Europe, *visualizing legal information* has developed into a research field in its own right. In the German-speaking countries, the terms *legal visualization*

52 *Id.*

(Rechtsvisualisierung), *visual legal communication* (Visuelle Rechtskommunikation), *visual law* (Visuelles Recht) and *multisensory law* (Multisensorisches Recht) have been developed in both research and practice.[53] In the United States, the use of visualization has been studied, for instance, in the context of improving the comprehension of jury instructions[54] and facilitating the making of complex decisions related to dispute resolution.[55] Visualization has been utilized as a technique of persuasion in various settings, from the court room[56] to the board room. In today's law schools and business schools, and in executive education, graphs and other visuals are increasingly used to explain legal concepts. Visuals can enhance the classroom experience for students who have grown up in a multi-media environment and are less receptive to reading hard copy texts.[57]

A noteworthy example of using visuals to guide the use and interpretation of complex contracts comes from the United Kingdom's "New Engineering Contract" (NEC) family of contracts. This family consists

53. Colette R. Brunschwig, *Visualisierung von Rechtsnormen – Legal Design* [Visualization of Legal Norms] (Doctoral Thesis). Zürcher Studien zur Rechtsgeschichte, vol. 45. Rechtswissenschaftliche Fakultät d. Universität Zürich. Schulthess Juristische Medien: Zürich 2001); Colette R. Brunschwig, *Multisensory Law and Legal Informatics – A Comparison of How these Legal Disciplines Relate to Visual Law*, Jusletter IT, 22 February 2011, *available at* http://jusletter-it.weblaw.ch/_104?lang=en.
54. Carolyn Semmler & Neil Brewer, *Using a Flow-Chart to Improve Comprehension of Jury Instructions*, 9 Psychiatry, Psychology and Law 262 (2002); Firoz Dattu, *Illustrated Jury Instructions: A Proposal, 22 Law & Psychology Review* 67 (1998).
55. George J. Siedel, *Interdisciplinary Approaches to Alternative Dispute Resolution*, 10 The Journal of Legal Studies Education 141, 154-61 (1992); Gerlinde Berger-Walliser, Robert C. Bird & Helena Haapio, *Promoting Business Success through Contract Visualisation*, 17 The J. L. Bus. & Ethics, 55 (2011), *available as* a Working Paper at http://ssrn.com/abstract=1744096.
56. Neil Feigenson & Christina Spiesel, *Law on Display*. The Digital Transformation of Legal Persuasion and Judgment (2009); Samuel H. Solomon, *Visuals and Visualization: Penetrating the Heart and Soul of Persuasion*, DOAR Litigation Consulting, October 2006, *available at* http://tillers.net/solomon.pdf.
57. Visual legal education has been explored, for instance, by Beyond Legal Text, a research project at the University of Edinburgh, School of Law, *see* http://www.law.ed.ac.uk/beyondtext. For further examples, *see* Berger-Walliser et al., *supra* note 55; Hilgendorf, Eric, DTV-Atlas Recht, Band 2 Verwaltungsrecht Zivilrecht (2008), an extract is *available at* http://www.bilandia.de/multimedia/dtv/Hilgendorf-Eric-9783423033251-leseprobe.html.

of several contracts designed for procuring a diverse range of works, services, and supplies. The contracts come with associated guidance notes and flow charts. The latter two are not part of the contract documents but assist in their understanding and interpretation. Originally launched in 1993, the NEC has been praised for its collaborative and integrated working approach to procurement. The implementation of NEC3 contracts has resulted in major benefits for projects both nationally and internationally in terms of time, cost savings, as well as improved quality.[58]

3.2.2 Example of Contract Visualization: Making the Invisible Visible

The interests of the parties to a contract negotiation are often misaligned. One party wishes to have a long-term commitment, while the other wishes to be able to walk away from the deal with short notice. The parties' divergence in expectations relating to the intended duration of their relationship is likely to lead to a less than amicable end of the contract. Due to their different perceptions of the contractual relationship, they are likely to differ on the interpretation of contract terms, especially those that are vague and poorly written. In a Canadian case, a termination clause was interpreted differently by the two parties. The vagaries of the text lead to an eighteen month dispute over the meaning of a single comma in a clause.[59] It would have been best for the parties to have discovered their different views of the contract at the negotiation stage.

58. "What is the NEC? Achieving excellence in the procurement of Works, Services and Supply. Promoting best practice procurement, *available at* http://www.neccontract.com/documents/WhatistheNEC.pdf; and NEC Products, *available at* http://www.neccontract.com/products/index.asp. – For further examples and a sample NEC flowchart, *see* Figure 1 in Stefania Passera & Helena Haapio, *User-Centered Contract Design: New Directions in the Quest for Simpler Contracting, in* Proceedings of the 2011 IACCM Academic Symposium for Contract and Commercial Management, at 80 (R.F. Henschel ed., The International Association for Contract and Commercial Management 2011), *available at* http://www.iaccm.com/admin/docs/docs/HH_Paper.pdf.
59. Ian Austen, The Comma That Costs 1 Million Dollars, New York Times, 25 October 2006, *available at* http://www.nytimes.com/2006/10/25/business/worldbusiness/25comma.html?_r=1.

In 2002, Rogers Cable Communications Inc. (Rogers) entered into a Support Structure Agreement (SSA) with Aliant Telecom Inc. (Aliant), in which Aliant gave Rogers access to and use of certain telephone poles at a fixed rate. In order to raise its rates in 2005, Aliant gave Rogers one year's notice to terminate the contract. Rogers objected, stating that the contract had a minimum duration of five years. In addition, Aliant increased the annual rate of $9.60 per pole to $28.05 per pole.[60] The misunderstanding revolved around a single clause in the SSA:

> *8.1 This agreement shall be effective from the date it is made and shall continue in force for a period of five (5) years from the date it is made, and thereafter for successive five (5) year terms, unless and until terminated by one year prior notice in writing by either party.*

As regards the initial term of the agreement, Rogers thought that it had a five-year deal. Aliant was of the view that even within this initial term, the SSA could be terminated at any time with one year's notice. The meaning of the above duration and termination provision was reduced to the role of the last comma. In 2006, the Canadian authority CRTC (Canadian Radio-Television and Telecommunications Commission), which wrote the model SSA that the clause was taken from, sided with Aliant: "Based on the rules of punctuation," it stated, "the plain and ordinary meaning of section 8.1 of the SSA allows for the termination of the SSA at any time, without cause, upon one year's written notice."[61]

However, there was a difference between the French and English language versions of section 8.1.[62] Rogers submitted that the French version

60. Grant Robertson, *Comma quirk irks Rogers*. The Globe and Mail, 6 August 2006, *available at* http://www.theglobeandmail.com/report-on-business/article838561.ece. The full text of the Parties' SSA in English is *available at* http:/www.crtc.gc.ca/public/partvii/2005/8690/rogers/051102.pdf.
61. Telecom Decision CRTC 2006-45, Ottawa, 28 July 2006, Sections 27-30, available at http://www.crtc.gc.ca/eng/archive/2006/dt2006-45.htm.
62. In the French language version of the SSA, Clause 8.1 reads as follows: Sous réserve des dispositions relatives à la résiliation du présent contrat, ce dernier prend effet à la date de signature. Il demeure en vigueur pour une période de cinq (5) ans, à partir de la date de la signature et il est subséquemment renouvelé pour des périodes successives de cinq (5) années, à moins d'un préavis écrit de résiliation à l'autre partie *un an avant l'expiration du contrat*. (Emphasis added).

of section 8.1 provided clear evidence that the parties intended to restrict termination without cause to the end of the term. In response to Rogers' appeal, the CRTC reviewed the French-language version of the model SSA. In 2007, the CRTC sided with Rogers and held that the contract ran for a five-year initial term and could not be terminated unilaterally before the expiration of the first term.[63]

One would think that the duration of a contract would be of such strategic and operational importance that the parties and their lawyers would have made sure that what the parties intended would have been clearly stated in the contract. The answer to this quandary is that neither party had drafted the problematic clause since they had relied on the model SSA. In hindsight, the contracting parties should have carefully read the clause *before* setting the price and other terms of the agreement. Also, the SSA model form should have been more clearly drafted. Breaking the clause into two sentences would have been a way to avoid the ambiguity.[64] Had the language been clearer, the parties would probably

63. Telecom Decision CRTC 2007-75, Ottawa, 20 August 2007, *available at* http://www.crtc.gc.ca/eng/archive/2007/dt2007-75.htm. Aliant submitted that the CRTC should not use the French language version of the model SSA in interpreting section 8.1 as it was not the version that the parties executed. However, in the CRTC's view, the issue here was a regulatory one and not a contractual one, and looked to what the regulatory intent was in imposing the model SSA.
64. In a later agreement between companies within the same Groups the corresponding clause reads as follows: "The term of this Agreement shall commence on the Effective Date and, subject to the termination provisions of this Agreement, shall continue for a period of five (5) years from the Effective Date. This Agreement shall be renewed automatically for successive five (5) year periods unless terminated in accordance with Section 9 of this Agreement." *See* 2006-08-31- #8340-R31-200611039 – Basic Listing Interchange File Agreement between Rogers Cable Communications Inc. and Bell Aliant Regional Communications Limited Partnership – Agreement 1053/00, *available at* http://www.crtc.gc.ca/8340/eng/2006/R31_1053.htm. For further drafting suggestions, *see* Ken Adams, Costly Drafting Errors, Part 1 – Rogers Communications and Aliant, AdamsDrafting Blog, 7 August 2006, *available at* http://www.adamsdrafting.com/2006/08/07/costly-drafting-errors-part-1/ and other postings by Ken Adams at http://www.adamsdrafting.com. *See* also Stefania Passera & Helena Haapio, *Facilitating Collaboration through Contract Visualization and Modularization, in* Designing Collaborative Activities. ECCE 2011 European Conference on Cognitive Ergonomics 2011; The 29th Annual Conference of the European Association on Cognitive Ergonomics, August 24-26, 2011, Rostock, Germany, at 57 (A. Dittmar & P. Forbrig eds., Universität Rostock: Rostock 2011).

have noted upfront their differing understandings. Yet expectations are hard to manage or align if they are not visible. This is where contract visualization enters the picture. As illustrated in the chart below, visualizations can help make the invisible visible.

Figure 3: Example of Contract Visualization: Making Invisible Expectations Visible[65]

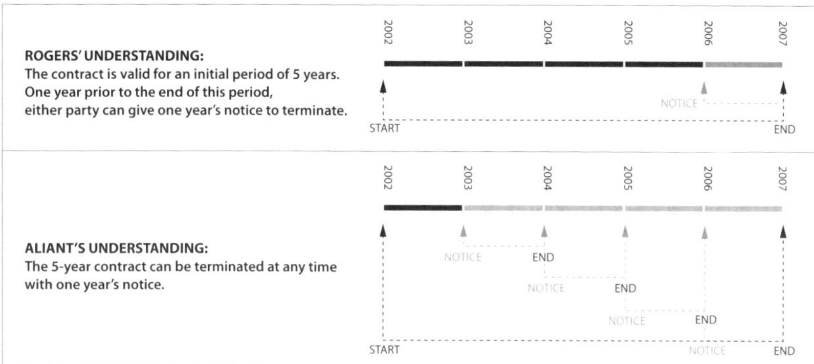

Simple timelines, as in the chart above, would have shown the parties their different understandings by making the termination clause visible and easier to understand. This would have allowed them, during the negotiations, to come to a mutual understanding and remove the ambiguity. A simple timeline could have prevented the dispute and saved the parties from spending considerable time and legal fees on resolving the dispute. In the words of Professor Brown: "It usually costs less to avoid getting into trouble than to pay for getting out of trouble."[66]

Along with invisible expectations as discussed above, *invisible terms,* too, can cause problems. The concept *invisible terms* refers to terms (such as implied terms, implied warranties, and statutory default rules) that do not appear in the contract, but become part of it unless they are expressly excluded or amended in the contract. Lawyers familiar with the contractual context should "see" these *invisible terms*. It is the lawyers' job to inform their clients of the existence of such terms.[67] Invisible terms include mandatory rules that apply to contracts in general and implied

65. This visualization is the work of Stefania Passera of Aalto University.
66. Louis M. Brown: Preventive Law 3 (1950).
67. *See infra* Section 2.3.3.

rules that are used to fill in gaps in contracts. Gaps in contracts are unavoidable, but can be minimized by legal and business astuteness at the interface of the lawyer-client interaction. Problems are often encountered not because of what the contract *says*, but because of what it *does not say*. Again, visuals can be used to make the invisible visible. They are able to show the presence and impacts of invisible terms, helping the parties obtain clarity about their rights and responsibilities, and to avoid unintended obligations, liabilities, and risks.

3.2.3 Enhancing Managerial-Legal Decision Making through Visualization

The use of visualization to increase the clarity of knowledge-laden communications is being researched on numerous fronts. Knowledge visualization in the context of risk management, for instance, has been researched at the University of St. Gallen's Institute for Media Communications and Management.[68] Its research findings relating to risk communication, especially the communication of knowledge between experts and decision makers, are highly relevant to the enhancement of communications between managers and their legal advisors. In a recent case study conducted at the University of Oslo, a group of lawyers, managers, and engineers were asked to analyze the risks related to a contract proposal using a method based on graphical language and diagrams. The case study showed that graphical language was helpful in communicating risk among the case study participants. However, the need for simplicity and usability also led to some limitations and the need for a combination of graphical and natural language for improved decision making.[69]

At Aalto University, a multi-disciplinary research project seeks to develop and apply new methods for cooperation, co-creation, and inter-

68. *See, for instance,* Martin J. Eppler & Markus Aeschimann, *A systematic framework for risk visualization in risk management and communication.* 11 Risk Management 67 (2009) and the resources mentioned at USI HSG Knowledge Communication – Publications, http://www.knowledge-communication.org/publications.html.
69. Tobias Mahler, *Legal Risk Management – Developing and Evaluating Elements of a Method for Proactive Legal Analyses, With a Particular Focus on Contracts* 237-262 (Doctoral Thesis, Faculty of Law, University of Oslo: Oslo 2010).

action.[70] Drawing upon research on proactive contracting-proactive law, information design, user-centeredness, and other fields, the goal is to develop, prototype, and test new approaches to commercial contracts. This project aims to develop contracts that will increase understandability and usability across cultures and disciplines. The project is researching visualization techniques, modularization, user-centered contract design, and other possible methods for simpler contracting.

Early experiments indicate that many business and legal problems could be prevented if visualizations were more widely used. They also suggest that visualizations have the potential to enhance managerial-legal decision making, as well as higher quality communications and knowledge sharing, through greater clarity and shared understanding. Visualization is a means to enhance the use of strategic contracting to produce greater returns and increase the ease of doing business.[71] Through visualization, and more importantly, through proactive lawyering and enhanced managerial-legal communication, the view of contracts as merely tactical, transactional and legal risk shifting instruments can be transformed to reflect the possibilities of their use as strategic, relational, and value-creative assets. The final section explores the expanded role that strategic contracting requires of transactional lawyers.

70. The project looks into contracting in the Finnish Metals and Engineering Competence Cluster (FIMECC) as part of UXUS (User Experience & Usability in Complex Systems), a five-year research program funded by Tekes, the Finnish Funding Agency for Technology and Innovation.
71. For early experiments with and examples of contract visualizations, *see* Passera & Haapio, *supra* note 58; Passera & Haapio, supra note 65; Thomas D. Barton, Gerlinde Berger-Walliser & Helena Haapio, *Visualization: Seeing Contracts for What They Are, and What They Could Become, in* Proceedings of the 2011 IACCM Academic Symposium for Contract and Commercial Management, at 3 (R.F. Henschel ed., The International Association for Contract and Commercial Management 2011); Helena Haapio, *Contract Clarity through Visualization – Preliminary Observations and Experiments, in* Proceedings of the 15th International Conference on Information Visualisation IV2011 / 7th International Symposium on Knowledge Visualization and Visual Thinking KV2011, 13-15 July 2011, London, UK, at 337 (E. Banissi et al. eds., IEEE Computer Society 2011).

4. Proactive Contracting as Learning to Think Strategically

This section will explore a number of topics related to the negotiation and drafting of contracts, and the role of lawyers in this process. In previous research, Siedel and Haapio took the perspective of the manager in the strategic use of the law.[72] This perspective rejects the narrow, but common, view that law acts, at best, as a mere a facilitator to deal-making and, at worst, as an obstacle to deal-making. Transactional lawyering and contract law as facilitators of deal-making are generally confined to providing legal templates for the various types of transactions found in the business world. This view, which sees the transactional lawyer as a mere scrivener brought in at the conclusion of a deal in order to consummate the deal through a legal memorialization, poses numerous problems and a variety of lost opportunities.

The hypothesis of this chapter is relatively simple: Proactive contracting requires the manager to view contracts as a means to create value and to create competitive advantages. Proactive contracting also requires lawyers to innovate to better use contracts to obtain strategic advantages for their clients. In short, before the parties and their lawyers can plan, design, and draft a strategic contract they must first think strategically about the use of contracts and contract law. It is important to note that the "original position" is that contracts are inherently value creative. The contract creates value, for instance, by binding parties to exchanges that create value based upon the different values the parties place on the items being exchanged. Proactive contracting is a move from the original position to the use of contracts to maximize values and to provide mechanisms for future unknown or unanticipated value creation.

A generic management textbook states that "the job of a business manager is to continuously search for and exploit new opportunities."[73] If a manager is responding to an external change, then the manager should think and act strategically to develop an internal response to capture value and competitive advantages. A change in the law is an external force that can be internalized and used strategically to create value. The manager needs to be enlightened to the value creation pos-

72. Siedel & Haapio, *supra* note 2.
73. Michael A. Hitt, J. Stewart Black & Lyman W. Porter, *Management* 22 (2005).

sibilities of law. Transactional lawyers often need to do the enlightening. In order to best accomplish this task, the lawyer must obtain business astuteness in the same way that a manager needs to gain legal astuteness as discussed in Section 2.

Another popular management textbook equates conceptual skills to being able to think strategically. First, it notes that such skills include the "cognitive ability to see the organization as a whole and the relationships among its parts."[74] Second, it "means the ability to think strategically – to take a broad, long-term view."[75] This broadening of context and breaking out of the perspective of short-termism is captured in the Manager's Legal Plan™, as explained in Section 2, by the concept of "climbing to the balcony." In this respect, the essence of proactive contracting is opening the viewfinder of the manager and lawyer alike to capture value in the present and far into the future. Strategic contracting at its best captures not only anticipated opportunities, but also provides mechanisms to capture unanticipated opportunities.

4.1 Managers and Lawyers as Business Partners

A review of generic management and human resource management (HRM) textbooks provides insight into the business person's perspective of the role of law in their business operations. One HRM book refers to the law as just "another significant external force."[76] Interestingly, the HRM literature speaks of the need to use human resources as a strategic partner: "HR executives must work with top management in achieving concrete plans. They must understand the operational side of the business and comprehend the complex organizational design. This means participating in and being responsive to the rapid changes that are occurring in business today."[77] This same template holds true for the company's in-house and external lawyers – they should take the perspective of a business partner with a deep understanding of the business, and not just act as transactional, independent task servers.

74. Richard L. Daft, *Management* 12 (7th ed. 2005).
75. *Id.*
76. R. Wayne Mondy, *Human Resource Management* 8 (5th ed. 2008).
77. *Id.* at 14.

Another management textbook describes the internal-external environments of business, and places legal considerations within the "mega-external" environment.[78] The laws referred to include intellectual property, workplace, environmental, and products liability laws. Proactive lawyering and proactive contracting require the internalization of legal and strategic considerations within the business decision-making structures of a company. In business planning, one study of Business Week 1000 companies showed that many business plans included the following components: customers, products or services, geographical market, technology use, survival concerns, philosophical priorities, recognition of weaknesses and competitive advantages, public image, and concern for employees. However, these plans gave no consideration to the value-creating role of law.[79]

The notion of "lawyer as business partner" is not meant to be literal in that the lawyer does not ordinarily have a proprietary interest in the business enterprise or the business transaction. Instead, it represents the idea that good transactional lawyers are able to place themselves in the position of business partners. One commentator explains: "For a deal lawyer not knowing about business is akin to a litigator not knowing the evidence rules. To do deals, lawyers must understand business, their clients' business, and the business deal."[80] An important role of strategic transactional lawyers is the design and management of contracts and STCs protective of client interests which often requires an understanding of the contracting parties' mutual interests. The next sections explore the areas of contract design and theories of contract writing. Both of these areas are analyzed through the prism of proactive lawyering.

4.2 Contract Design

Often the best contract, especially for relational, long-term, and repeat transactors, focuses on providing mechanisms and governance structures that are likely to preserve the business relationship by deterring op-

78. Kathryn M. Bartol & David C. Martin, *Management* 71 & 73 (2d ed. 1994).
79. Nash, Laura, *Mission Statements – Mirrors and Windows*, Harv. Bus. Rev., March-April 1988, pp. 155-56.
80. Tina L. Stark, *My Fantasy Curriculum and Other Almost Random Thoughts*, 2009 The Tenn. J. Bus. L. 3, 4 (2009).

portunism and litigation. Such contracts provide flexibility that allows the parties to make adjustments in response to future developments. The normative position in drafting such contracts is that of the contract writer as a reasonable person. The client with superior bargaining power provides leverage to its attorney to write a one-sided contract. Lawyers should at times counsel their clients that overly one-sided contracts may work to a strategic disadvantage. Reasonable person contract drafting provides a framework for the design of contracts and will be discussed in more detail in a later section.

Negotiating parties may possess relatively equal bargaining power. This is often the case when competitors seek to create a collaborative alliance or a joint venture project. Here, the reciprocal and fairness norms that underlie a reasonable person theory of contract design may not be necessary or possible. Instead, in order to design a contract that will provide incentives to maintain the alignment of interests between the competitor-partners and provide penalties to deter opportunistic takings, a "bad person" theory of drafting may be the more appropriate drafting posture.

In 1897, Oliver Wendell Holmes, Jr. postulated the bad man theory of law. This theory asserts that the law is not what a good, law abiding person sees it as, but what a bad person determines is needed to avoid the sanctions that the law authorizes: "You can see very plainly that a bad man has as much reason as a good one for wishing to avoid an encounter with the public force ... A man who cares nothing for an ethical rule which is believed and practiced by his neighbors is likely nevertheless to care a good deal to avoid being made to pay money, ... if he can."[81] However, proactive contracting sees such penalty-induced performance as a last resort. Instead, proactive contracting deters opportunistic behavior by building a blueprint that views the contract as a collaborative enterprise. It trades the stick – known in law and economics (LAE) as "penalty defaults" – with a carrot that ensures performance through positive incentives that appeal to the parties' mutual interests.

81. Oliver Wendell Holmes Jr., *The Path of the Law*, 10 Harv. L. Rev. 457, 459 (1897).

4.2.1 Transaction-Type

There are numerous contextual factors that impact contract design. Two important generic factors are: (1) contractual subject-matter and (2) transactional-relational focus. The first factor refers to the type of transaction, such as, exporting, licensing, technology transfer, long-term supply contracts, agency and distribution agreements, construction of a turnkey operation, and mergers and acquisitions. The second factor refers to whether the parties are single transaction partners or repeat transactors. Matthew Jennejohn notes a general international trend away from vertical integration and towards horizontal collaboration. Contract design in a long-term alliance or collaboration is profoundly different than in a vertical integration (merger or acquisition). Jennejohn states that "firms enmesh themselves in webs of collaboration – joint ventures, strategic alliances, just-in-time production arrangements usually in hope of cost-cutting but also with an eye to securing competitive advantage through innovation."[82]

In the area of contracting for innovation, proactive contracts that incentivize "information exchange" and provide for "internal" dispute resolution mechanisms become essential.[83] In such contracts, the goal of the formal contract is to incentivize what is normally an informal exchange of information and to provide for internal consensus building to prevent resort to external dispute resolution between the collaborators: "So instead of specifying objectives, the contract establishes transparency through information exchange, open inspection, and mutual learning."[84] In this way, the parties are able to police each other's performance, exchange mutually informational benefits during the performance stage, and to build trust.

4.2.2 Business and Deal-Relationship Preserving Norms

Lawyers will surely misunderstand business clients if they think that business people are interested in detailed, unambiguous planning or in

82. Matthew C. Jennejohn, *Collaboration, Innovation, and Contract Design*, 14 Stan. J.L. Bus. & Fin. 83, 84 (2008).
83. Ronald J. Gilson, Charles F. Sabel & Robert E. Scott, *Braiding: The Interaction of Formal and Informal Contracting in Theory, Practice, and Doctrine*, 110 Colum. L. Rev. 1377, 1382 (2010).
84. *Id.* at 1408.

holding each other to expectations as legally defined; to be an effective transactional lawyer means becoming knowledgeable about "business norms."[85] In real-world deal-making, "legal doctrine is typically, at most, a faint shadow over a small corner of the stage."[86] Often lawyers "do not delve into the mechanics of how businesses and individuals, sometimes aided by lawyers but often not, adjust their deals to preserve relationships and reputations to the greater glory of making money, keeping customers and suppliers happy, and spending as little as possible on law."[87]

The importance of an inter-disciplinary view of contracting is that it allows the manager and the lawyer to bridge the different perspectives they possess on the role of contracts. Instead of a bright line separation at the frontiers of the business-legal interface, proactive contracting sees this interface more like a field or a continuum. Managers with a working knowledge of the law relevant to their particular type of business will be better able to discover the value-added potential of contracts. Lawyers possessing a reasonable level of business astuteness, especially relating to their clients and the clients' businesses, are best able to remove the shackles of legal formalism and use client-specific, business-specific, and deal-specific information to write a contract that serves as a clear and practical blueprint for success.

Furthermore, benefiting from business acumen allows the lawyer to write contracts and STCs that can be more easily implemented by those involved in the actual performance of the contract. Knowing the business facts and the context of the contract relationship allows the lawyer to be more proactive and creative in designing the contract to serve the above objectives. It is through "proactive creativity"[88] that lawyers can best serve clients and produce contracts that frame deals as collaborative

85. Jean Braucher, "The Sacred and the Profane Contracts Machine: The Complex Morality of Contract Law in Action," Arizona Legal Studies, Discussion Paper No. 11-18 (April 2011) (Contact Machine), 2.

86. *Id.* at 4.

87. *Id.*, citing Stewart Macaulay, *Non-Contractual Relations in Business – A Preliminary Study*, 28 AM. SOC. REV. 1 (1963).

88. Sandra Ohly & Carmen Binnewies, *The Ambiguity of Creativity and Innovation*, 2 Industrial & Organizational Psych. 360, 361 (2009), citing, K.L. *Unsworth, Unpacking Creativity*, 26 Acad. Mgt. Rev. 289 (2001).

enterprises. This is especially important in certain industries, such as contracting for innovation, R & D joint venture, and construction, where parties often face both internal and external changes in circumstances.[89]

Contracts are often viewed as blueprints for performance. This idea relates to the longstanding premise that contracts are primarily plans for future action. But, since contracts are inherently incomplete, especially in the era of complex contracting,[90] the blueprint is at best a starting point that will need to be revised along the way. It is in the open recognition of this incompleteness and the relational or corroborative nature of contracting where proactive contracting seeks to change the blueprint.[91] Instead of writing a contract in the *Shadow of the Lawsuit*,[92] proactive contracting seeks to prevent the lawsuit and to maximize value by placing mechanisms into the contract that encourage information exchange, trust-building, change management, renegotiation, and internal dispute resolution. The proactive contract primarily aims at business success and deal preservation, rather than simple risk allocation.

Berger-Walliser, Bird, and Haapio succinctly surmise the current problem of the business-legal interface in the writing of contracts when they state that "most contracts seem to be written by lawyers for lawyers."[93] As such, contracts and, in particular, STCs are primarily a form of legal posturing in which lawyers attempt through legalese to position their clients to take advantage of an unexpected contract-generated surplus, to create technical loopholes that avoid contractual liability in the event the deal turns bad, to lay the foundation for a future legal claim or defense, and to allocate as much of the risk as possible to the other party.[94] Proactive contracting begins with the premise that the contract should

89. See William A Klein & Mitu Gulati, *Economic Organization in the Construction Industry: A Case Study of Collaborative Production under High Uncertainty*, 1 Berkeley Bus. L.J. 137 (2004).
90. See Claire Hill, *Bargaining in the Shadow of the Lawsuit: A Social Norms Theory of Incomplete Contracts*, Del. J. Corp. L. 191 (2009).
91. For an analysis of the relational element in complex contracting, see Claire A Hill, *A Comment on Language and Norms in Complex Business Contracting*, 77 U. Chi.-Kent L. Rev. 29 (2001).
92. Hill, *supra* note 90.
93. Berger-Walliser et al., *supra* note 55, at 56.
94. *See* Claire A. Hill, *Why Contracts are Written in 'Legalese,'* 77 U. Chi.-Kent L. Rev. 59 (2001).

reflect the understandings of the parties and incorporate deal-preserving provisions that encourage and guide cooperation and renegotiation.[95] Instead of providing fodder in anticipation of litigation, the contract should reflect the collaborative nature of successful businesses. This entails the use of contract provisions to encourage dispute resolution to prevent a breach from occurring or becoming adversarial, as well as post-breach means of ADR that are more likely to result in the settlement of disputes and preservation of the relationship.[96]

4.3 Reasonable Person Theory of Contract Writing

A theory of reasonable person contract writing serves a number of purposes including the drafting of enforceable contract terms and the incorporation of fair or deal-preserving clauses. Under this theory of drafting, the post-hoc reasonable person standard used in the interpretation of contracts is brought forward to the time of the writing of the contract. This temporal shift provides the perspective needed to write a contract that will likely be honored by the parties, diminish the back-end costs of litigation or ADR, and ensure the enforceability of clauses important to the party inserting the clauses. This type of contract writing aligns well with the proactive contracting view of contracts as collaborative enterprises: "Instead of providing the most advantageous solution to one of the parties ... the proactive contracting process and documents seek to align and express the interest of both sides of the contract in order to create value for both."[97] The rest of this section will discuss the adversarial model of contract writing and argue for the superiority of the theory of reasonable person contract drafting.

In many instances, even between large entities, one party may possess superior bargaining power. The issue becomes whether that party, as a matter of strategy, should use the full extent of that power in negotiating as one-sided a contract as possible. Unfortunately, many transactional lawyers feel it is their duty to draft contracts that are one-sided in favor of

95. See Jeswald W. Salacuse, *Renegotiations in International Business*, 4 Negotiation J. 347 (1988).
96. For a case for the cost-effectiveness of ADR and the wastefulness of litigation, see Stewart Macaulay, *Renegotiations and Settlements: Dr. Pangloss's Notes on the Margins of David Campbell's Papers*, 29 Cardozo L. Rev. 261 (2007).
97. Berger-Walliser et al., *supra* note 55, at 61.

their clients. This mandate is understandable given the advocacy model of lawyering prominent under lawyers' codes of ethics and imbued in legal education. This model, as stated in the American Bar Associations' Code of Professional Responsibility provides that the role of the lawyer is that of "zealous advocate." This view of lawyering sees contract writing as a zero-sum game.

The principle of zealous advocacy is easy to justify in the context of defending a client in a criminal proceeding, but loses its strength in transactional lawyering. One commentator notes that the principle was "never designed to guide lawyers' transactional work, including the drafting of contracts, which is often non-adversarial and cooperative."[98] This view does not mean that transactional lawyers should not advance the interests of their clients to the utmost degree. But the key focus should be on what truly advances the clients' interests. In many cases, overly extensive one-sidedness may work against a client's best interests.

Astute observers have noted that "[c]ontract theory does not address the question of how parties design contracts under the existing adversarial system."[99] The best we can do is to adopt the view of the contractual enterprise as a cooperative venture and the importance of deal-preserving norms that allow lawyers to forsake maximizing the leverage of superior bargaining power in the interest of deterring future breach. In an overly one-sided contract, the weaker party may feel justified in not performing if the one-sidedness is strictly enforced by the other party and when all contractual surplus, expected or unexpected, is captured inequitably by the other party. In the role of enterprise builder,[100] transactional lawyers must be careful to write contracts that protect the interests of their clients as seen by their clients. Once again, clients, in consultation with their lawyers, are the final arbiters of the level of the one-sidedness, as opposed to the level of collaborative, deal-preserving characteristics of the contract. The best a proactive lawyer can do is to provide these two alternatives.

98. Gregory M. Duhl, *The Ethics of Contract Drafting,* 14 Lewis & Clark L. Rev. 989, 995 (2010).

99. Robert E. Scott & George G. Triantis, *Anticipating Litigation in Contract Design,* 115 Yale L.J. 814, 814 (2006).

100. See George W. Dent, Jr., *Business Lawyers as Enterprise Architects,* 64 Bus. Law. 279 (2009).

It should be noted that the position here is not that lawyers should avoid taking advantage of superior bargaining power, but that lawyers need to strategically decide to what extent they use that power in the negotiation or drafting of contracts. A reasonable person theory of contract writing advances the idea that the degree of the one-sidedness should be tempered by the need to write a contract that will likely be honored by the weaker party. Transactional lawyers are required to advance the interests of their clients, but that advancement will usually require a broadened focus that looks to the integrity of the transactional relationship in building trust between the contracting parties and enhancing the probability and quality of performance.

The dual focus upon client interest and transactional integrity is really one and the same. Unfortunately, transactional lawyers often suffer from a degree of short-termism – drafting a contract most favorable to their clients – at the expense of the long-term health of the deal and the parties' relationship. The focus on the preservation of the deal is an example of "climbing the balcony," as discussed in Section 2, in which the lawyer sees the interests of the parties as not being mutually exclusive. The balcony perspective enables a lawyer "to build trust among commercial parties that is critical to the success of business relationships."[101] In the end, a contract "can be both pro-client and pro-contract relationship."[102]

Model contracts produced by a neutral third-party association often, but not always, are products of reasonable person drafting. The International Chamber of Commerce describes its model contracts as giving contracting "parties a neutral framework for their contractual relationships" by providing "an even-handed agreement acceptable to both sides."[103] Another advantage, other than deal preservation, of using the reasonable person theory of writing is the back-end concern of enforceability. A clause or contract that is extremely one-sided may encourage a court to not enforce certain provisions or to "misinterpret" a term to make it fairer in effect. Clauses written under reasonable person

101. Duhl, *supra* note 98, at 1033.

102. Larry A. DiMatteo, *Contracts and Precedents*, 2009 The Tenn. J. Bus. L. 262, 269 (2009).

103. International Chamber of Commerce, "Model Contracts and Clauses," *available at* http://www.iccwbo.org/policy/law/id272/index.html.

drafting theory, if properly done, will be enforced under the reasonable person theory of contract interpretation.

4.3.1 Transactional Lawyers as Strategic Engineers

The earlier sections of this chapter highlighted the different elements of strategic contracting including preventive and promotive use of the law, as well as the need to strategically plan for future disputes. The three key roles of transactional lawyers are: providing as clear and complete a contract as transaction costs will bear, providing contractual incentives to encourage performance, and providing a cost-effective means of alternative dispute resolution. The third role can be supported by the strategic use of a "force majeure clause that excuses performance under various conditions, a clause that requires prompt notification of dissatisfaction, a clause that mandates informal procedures to be followed in the event that dissatisfaction cannot be resolved immediately, and a valid liquidated damages clause."[104] In the event of a dispute, the most important strategic term in many cases is the arbitration or ADR clause, which was discussed earlier.

Professor Schwarcz describes the same aspects of strategic contracting, but uses terminology found in Law and Economics (LAE) and other areas of research, such as the negotiation literature. He notes that transactional lawyers acting strategically add value by reducing transaction costs and by acting as reputational surrogates and as identifiers of risk.[105] These categories of value-added tasks support the expanded role of the lawyer and law in the negotiation and formation of contracts. This expanded role is the essence of proactive lawyering and strategic contracting.

The role of transactional lawyers and strategic contracting in lowering transaction costs will be extensively discussed in a subsequent section. This section will briefly explore Schwarz's other concepts. First, transactional lawyers provide value by acting as "reputational

104. Donald C. Langevoort & Robert K. Rasmussen, *Skewing the Results: The Role of Lawyers in Transmitting Legal Rules*, 5 S. Cal. Interdisciplinary L. J. 375, 414 (1997).

105. Steven L. Schwarcz, *Explaining the Value of Transactional Lawyering*, 12 Stan. J.L. Bus. & Fin. 486, 487 (2007).

intermediaries."[106] This hypothesis asserts that transactional lawyers are generally "repeat players" who add value by renting their good reputation to clients.[107] Renting, a major LAE concept, in the current context views the good reputation of specific lawyers as fair bargainers as being attributed to their clients, which signals to the other party that the prospective contracting party is a reputable transactor.

Second, transactional lawyers use experience to act as identifiers of risk. The lawyer's ability to serve this function is attributable to two elements: objective detachment and being a contextual purveyor. Both of these elements are interrelated and are captured by the "climbing the balcony"[108] step previously discussed in the Manager's Legal Plan™. Experienced transactional lawyers have been exposed to deals and cases where anticipated and unanticipated occurrences resulted in problems, disputes, and sometimes the premature termination of contracts or business relationships. This experience provides a vantage point of objective detachment for future dealings.

The lawyer is able to assess the risks in a deal involving similarly-situated parties. However, this general knowledge has limited use unless it is clearly applicable to the deal at hand. The fit of ex-post risk assessment to a current risk assessment requires the lawyer to be a contextual purveyor. As noted previously, transactional lawyers must possess general business acumen, understand their clients and the clients' business, and familiarize themselves with the transactional details of the current negotiation. In this way, lawyers can best provide both business and legal perspectives. In the end, any good contract writer must answer the following questions: Have I determined each imaginable risk? Have I assessed the probability of such risk occurring? Have I allocated the risk in a way that reasonably protects my client from such risk? Have I provided protections to deal with unanticipated risks?[109]

106. *Id.* at 493.

107. *Id.*

108. Wisdom has been defined as having "total perspective – seeing an object, event, or idea in all its pertinent relationships." Will Durant, *What is Wisdom?*, WISDOM, II, NO. 8 (1957), at 25-26.

109. *See* Sam Jacobson, *A Checklist for Drafting Good Contracts*, 5 J. Ass'n Legal Writing Directors, 79 (2008).

A closing thought before leaving the lawyer's role as risk identifier. Transactional lawyers are excellent risk identifiers – perhaps to the extreme! This is the point of the question above regarding the assessment of the probability of a risk occurring. The reputation of lawyers as obstacles to deal-making is likely due to their ability to identify risks. These risks are often illusory – that is, they have very low probabilities of occurring. In addition, lawyers may be more risk averse than their clients. Dealing with risk and the probability of its occurrence should be a client-centered enterprise. This requires the lawyer to act as an information enabler – providing information relating to legal risks and probabilities, and receiving information from the client as to the most important elements of the transaction and the level of risk the client is willing to assume. This engagement should be guided by the principle that the client is the ultimate decision maker.

4.4 Economic Theory of Strategic Contracting

Despite the importance of the lawyer gaining business and client-targeted acumen, the lawyer's primary value is knowledge of the law and its application to solving real-world problems.[110] This role can be assessed by analyzing the efficiency of contract law and its application to contract writing. This section will examine contracting through the lens of the economic analysis of law. A simple description of LAE as it applies to contract law can be summarized by the goal of developing efficient legal rules and the ancillary idea that such efficiency results in the reduction of transaction costs.[111] This section begins with a rather pessimistic assessment of the benefits of LAE scholarship to contract law.[112] However, this pessimism is complicated by the distinction between mainstream LAE and the more specific area of the "economics of contracts."[113] The first relates specifically to the law, whether its rules

110. *See* Ronald J. Gilson & Robert H. Mnookin, *Foreword: Business Lawyers and Value Creation for Clients*, 74 Or. L. Rev. 1 (1995).

111. See Jeffrey L. Harrison, *Trends and Traces: A Preliminary Evaluation of Economic Analysis of Contract Law*, 1988 Ann. Surv. Am. L. 73 (1988).

112. *See generally*, Jeffrey L. Harrison, *Egoism, Altruism, and Market Illusions: The Limits of Law and Economics*, 33 UCLA L. Rev. 1309 (1986).

113. Karen Eggleston, Eric A. Posner & Richard Zeckhauser, *The Design and Interpretation of Contracts: Why Complexity Matters*, 95 Nw. U.L. Rev. 91, 93 (2000).

are or are not efficient, how they can be made more efficient. Economics of contracts relates to the private nature and the "optimal design of contracts."[114] It is the second use of economic analysis that is relevant here.

One LAE scholar notes the internal contradiction relating to the value of the economic analysis of contract law.[115] On one hand, the economic perspective provides a broader view for placing a given transaction into the context of an efficiency assessment. Akin to the notion of climbing the balcony, contract law and contract design can benefit by the "use of the broad lens of economic analysis to develop a holistic picture of contractual relationships."[116] On the other hand, due to the complexity of contracts, "any economic theory of contract law may ultimately suffer from a lack of granularity."[117]

This section concludes, counter-intuitively, that despite LAE's failure to explain the law of contracts (descriptively and normatively), the concepts of LAE, such as transaction costs, signaling, and the efficient insurer, provide explanatory power in the writing of contracts. Eric Posner made a similar claim in his determination that three decades of LAE have failed to explain contract law or to provide a means to reform contract law.[118] However, he notes that the use of economic analysis has made contract law research more rigorous: "The literature now speaks in an economic idiom, with concepts like transaction costs, risk aversion, default rule, and efficiency substituting for similar but vaguer notions in the earlier writings."[119] The assertion made here, and elsewhere, is that economic concepts are useful in designing contracts.

4.4.1 Risk and Uncertainty

Given the complexity and the incompleteness inherent in contracts, no contract can anticipate all future events. Thus, a strategically written

114. *Id.*
115. George S. Geis, *Economics as Context for Contract Law*, 75 U. Chi. L. Rev. 569, 570 (2008).
116. *Id.*
117. *Id.*
118. Eric A. Posner, *Economic Analysis of Contract Law After Three Decades: Success or Failure?*, 112 Yale L.J. 829, 830 (2003).
119. *Id.* at 880.

contract needs to address risk and uncertainty.[120] Different approaches to dealing with risk and uncertainty are partly a product of the characteristics of the contracting parties. Experienced and sophisticated parties tend to focus on risk identification and allocation in the negotiation of their contracts and to a lesser extent deal with the issue of uncertainty. Risk is foreseeable; however, the probability of certain risks varies greatly. The parties are in the best position to negotiate the sharing of various risks or obtain appropriate insurance. Uncertainty relates to unforeseeable events. Unforeseeable events are those that reasonably expert parties in a given business or industry would not be able to foresee given their business experience.[121] Mahler and Bing explain the connection between risk, uncertainty, and proactive lawyering:

> [R]isk management is motivated by the need for a proactive legal analysis, which identifies probable or possible future problems, and which seeks to mitigate these ... A proactive legal analysis also includes elements which determine the relevant law, but in addition it needs to deal with an unknown future in which the client wants to protect his assets (of a certain nature) from crumbling.[122]

However, unlike risk that can be addressed explicitly and precisely by a contractual risk allocation, a contracting party who is uncertainty averse will want to negotiate more complex, expansive clauses to capture future uncertainty. This does not mean that the uncertainty-averse party will be satisfied by expansive but vague and ambiguous contract clauses. This is due to the fact that uncertainty's surrogate in contract writing is ambiguity. Contractual ambiguity means greater uncertainty. The party wanting to strategically manage uncertainty will be ambiguity averse.

120. For a brief summary of the concepts of incompleteness and complexity, and their interrelationship, see Jeffrey M. Lipshaw, *Contingency and Contracts: A Philosophy of Complex Business Transactions*, 54 DePaul L. Rev. 1073, 1084-91 (2005).

121. Eric L. Talley, *On Uncertainty, Ambiguity, and Contractual Conditions*, 34 Del. J. Corp. L. 755, 759 (2009).

122. Tobias Mahler & Jon Bing, *Contractual Risk Management in an ICT Context – Searching for a Possible Interface between Legal Methods and Risk Analysis, in* A Proactive Approach, supra note 5, at 339, 341, *available at* http://www.scandinavianlaw.se/pdf/49-20.pdf.

An ambiguous term creates uncertainty relating to its actual meaning and scope.

In the end, contracting strategically requires the management of both risk and uncertainty. Dealing with uncertainty is more problematic due to its unfamiliarity and unforeseeable nature. The most precise way of dealing with uncertainty is to provide clear terms relating to the parties' rights in the event of an occurrence of a "material adverse event." Professor Talley asserts that a highly ambiguity-averse party may "make the contract's very enforceability contingent on the 'ambient' amount of uncertainty they face."[123] This could be reflected in the inclusion of a right to recession.

Talley also notes that the tremendous amount of uncertainty produced by financial and economic crises is likely to impact contract design: "One can reasonably expect that the challenge of allocating uncertainty will increasingly come to confront courts, practitioners, and legal scholars. Developing an appreciation for such challenges, as well as the analytical tools for addressing them, is an investment whose return is significant."[124] The uncertainty of the times has resulted in litigation over the meaning of commonly used clauses in complex contracts, such as material adverse event (MAE) or material adverse change (MAC) clauses.

Professors Choi and Triantis have already anticipated that current litigation and renegotiation of MAE and MAC clauses will provide transactional lawyers and contract scholars much to analyze in future contract designs.[125] For example, as a result of unprecedented and unanticipated economic and financial shocks, as well as volatile stock and commodity prices, it is important that contracts include well-reasoned "excuse, or walk-away, provisions such as closing conditions, force majeure clauses, and termination or cancellation rights."[126]

The economic argument for risk allocation is that a strategically drawn contract would allocate a risk to the party most capable of bearing the risk. Alternatively stated, the more risk averse and capable party

123. Talley, *supra* note 121, at 760.
124. *Id.* at 806.
125. Albert Choi & George Triantis, *Strategic Vagueness in Contract Design: The Case of Corporate Acquisitions*, 119 Yale L.J. 848, 851 (2010).
126. *Id.*

should be willing to pay for such an efficient risk allocation. However, risk allocations can serve numerous strategic purposes, including signaling by the party accepting the risk to the risk averse party that the likelihood of the risk event happening is small. Other strategic purposes served by the proper contractual allocation of risk include providing "incentives for a party to take measures to minimize the risk (efficient investment)." More importantly, the inability to agree on a risk allocation due to asymmetrical information deters efficient contracting.[127] In the end, proactive, strategic contracting involves more than just the express allocation of risk. The recognition of risks in the negotiation stage is a beginning. But how the risks are allocated, hopefully to the most efficient insurer, is just as important – all geared toward enabling sound risk taking and effective risk management. Furthermore, the strategically drawn contract provides governance structures, strategies, and internal dispute resolution mechanisms that will enable the parties to process uncertainty in order to preserve the contractual relationship.

4.4.2 Proactive Contracting and Transaction Cost Theory

Transactional lawyers have been dubbed "transaction cost engineers."[128] If this is true, it supports a more proactive role for lawyers prior to and at the time of contract formation. In reducing transaction costs, the lawyer assesses the level of transaction costs among the different stages of the contract: formation, performance, and termination. The existence of contractual incompleteness and ambiguity can been associated with transaction costs – the higher the level of completeness and clarity, especially in complex contracts, the higher the costs of due diligence, negotiation, and drafting. The avoidance of transaction costs is the reason why contracts may incorporate inefficient risk allocations and improperly manage uncertainty.

Transaction costs are incurred not only in the execution of a contract, but also during the performance and enforcement stages of contracting. At the contract formation stage, the more complete and clear a contract

127. *Id.*

128. Ronald J. Gilson, *Value Creation by Business Lawyers: Legal Skills and Asset Pricing*, 94 Yale L.J. 239, 293 (1984). In Siedel & Haapio, supra note 2, lawyers are also called "Opportunity Engineers."

the higher the transaction costs expended, but the greater the likelihood of transaction cost savings at the time of performance (due to the clarity of obligations provided by the contract) and the lower the likelihood of end of contract transaction costs (dispute resolution). From an efficiency perspective, the lawyer plays the strategic role of balancing higher transaction costs at one stage against lower transaction costs at another stage of the contract relationship. [129]

Some legal theorists have argued that sophisticated commercial parties are willing to incur additional front end costs in order to design a contract that will have more predictable interpretive outcomes. Kraus and Scott argue that such parties prefer the strict enforcement of their contracts rather than the courts' use of rules of interpretation that allow for the use of extrinsic evidence and contract doctrines, such as mistake, to "save" the parties from their contracts.[130] Such a formalistic contract law regime would lower back-end costs – the uncertainty of judicial contract interpretation – and justify the upfront costs of drafting a more complete contract.

However, if a contract is relational in nature, making a more complete contract will result in prohibitive transaction costs and is likely to be cost-ineffective. The nature of relational contracts requires greater flexibility at the performance stage. Greater flexibility means a certain level of vagueness in contract terms and more standard (greater discretion) obligations than highly-specified, rule-like obligations. Thus, in certain types of contracts, lower transaction costs at formation and higher transaction costs at performance (cooperation, good faith obligations, and renegotiation) may be a prudent allocation. This is a very careful balancing act that only transactional lawyers with business acumen and client-specific knowledge can hope to manage. For example, in some relational contracts – such as, alliances and joint ventures between competitors – additional transaction costs upfront are justified in order consummate the deal and provide governance terms to ensure its success.

129. Robert E. Scott & George G. Triantis, *Anticipating Litigation in Contract Design*, 115 Yale L.J. 814 (2006) (discusses the relationship between front-end and back-end costs in contract design).

130. Jody S. Kraus & Robert E. Scott, *Contract Design and the Structure of Contractual Intent*, 84 N.Y.U. L. Rev. 1023 (2009).

Contracts that are a product of extreme asymmetrical information are likely to result in a contract ripe with moral hazard and alignment of interest problems. Transactional lawyers can proactively attempt to reduce the degree of asymmetrical information through due diligence and the procurement of information from the other side during the negotiation process. More importantly, the lawyer should strategically negotiate terms that will preserve the relationship and ensure cooperative performances. This could include clauses that provide incentives for the parties to share information and penalties to deter opportunism.

Complex contracts that create a governance structure to manage the contract relationship and insure alignment of interests come with high transaction costs, but the downstream savings in minimizing the risk of non-performance and termination costs outweigh the upfront costs. An example should clarify such transaction costs analyses. Two competitors want to enter into an alliance to create and market a new product. A key concern is that one party or both may usurp assets of the alliance (new technology, know-how) to gain a competitive advantage over its alliance partner in areas where they are competitors. The contract will need to provide mechanisms to prevent such opportunism and subsequent destruction of the alliance. There are numerous strategic tools that the contract writer can use in dealing with these issues. The following is a less than exhaustive list of such contract terms gleaned from the literature:

- Rewarding a party for sharing information through an additional allocation of profits.
- Providing penalties for a party that withholds alliance-related information.
- Requiring both parties to provide key personnel to manage the alliance in order to build trust.

Strategic investment requiring each party to expend sunk costs at similar rates in order to incentivize collaborative behavior.

These types of contract provisions create a "mutual hostage" situation.[131] Such a situation deters opportunism and reduces transaction

131. Stephen R. Salbu & Richard Brahm, *Strategic Considerations in Designing Joint Venture Contracts*, 1992 Colum Bus. L. Rev. 253, 303 (1992).

costs in ensuring performance. As noted by the above list, the mutual hostage scenario can be created through "reciprocal penalties, reciprocal benefits, or the strategic investment of mutual sunk costs."[132]

Choi and Triantis state the above proposition – the efficiency of expending high transaction costs at the negotiation-drafting stage to reduce performance and termination costs – in the alternative: "Contract theorists focus on the cost of verifying facts and typically posit that parties avoid terms that are costly to verify. Vague contract provisions fall in this category because of the cost and uncertainty of judicial interpretation."[133] Just as risk allocation is highly dependent on probability estimates, the amount of transaction costs allocated in the negotiation of a contract is determined by the probability of a contract's term-focused event happening or the probability of future litigation over the contract term in question. Lower probabilities justify expending lesser costs to produce a more complete and clearer term. In sum, vagueness and incompleteness can be cost effective – but only if they do not prevent the parties from reaching their business goals. For strategic, proactive contracting, the predictability of business goals deserves more attention than the predictability of the outcomes in possible future litigation.

It is also important to note that factors other than transaction costs determine whether a contract is simple or complex and the level of its completeness: "[T]here are many other reasons why parties may avoid complexity when drafting contracts, including: asymmetric information, monitoring dynamics, evolutionary pressures, conventions, reliance on trust and reputation, enforcement costs, bounded rationality, and renegotiation."[134] Transaction cost theory demonstrates the complexity of economic analysis and its ability to justify almost any conclusion using economic jargon. Nonetheless, if used in modest proportions economic nomenclature can be used strategically to clarify and support transactional lawyers' arguments in favor of specific contract language or provisions.

132. DiMatteo, *supra* note 19, at 756.
133. Choi & Triantis, *supra* note 125, at 852.
134. Eggleston et al., *supra* note 113, at 92-93.

5. Conclusion

Business managers and their lawyers need to shift towards a proactive, strategic method of contracting. This entails preventing contract drafters and users of contracts from continuing to do what they have always done – that is, assuming that business persons do deals, negotiate the deal terms, and secure business success, and their lawyers write one-sided contracts with legal terms that attempt to allocate risk to the other party and protect their clients in case of a failure or dispute. Instead, we need to change current mindsets and educate business persons on the strategic use of contracting to create value and competitive advantages. Using visualization to communicate contract and other legal information offers one way to initiate this change. Also, transactional lawyers, many of whom already possess business savvy, need to use their business and legal acumen to be proactive in the development of contracting processes and documents. Proactive contracting is strategic in nature – requiring lawyers to view contracts, especially complex ones, as collaborative enterprises. This may also require them to forsake one-sided contracts based on the utilization of superior bargaining power for the sake of contracts that serve the mutual interests of both parties. The current inertia and path dependence of the adversarial, short-term view of contracting needs to be replaced with an enterprise model of contracting and a reasonable person model of contract writing, with successful implementation and deal-relationship preservation as the ultimate goals, rather than risk allocation that is focused on winning in court.

Collaborative Contracting as Preventive/Proactive Law

By

Thomas D. Barton[1]
Louis and Hermione Brown Professor of Law
California Western School of Law,
San Diego, California

1. Introduction

Preventive/Proactive Law ("PPL") offers a different, and arguably deeper, way of understanding law, legal problems, and how lawyers can help clients achieve their goals. As a method of practice, PPL urges early and frequent communication between lawyer and client – and between clients and those with whom the client is connected in an economic, organizational, or personal relationship. Such communications should not be limited to instrumental goals or positions, but should also explore more expansive interests, purposes, and contexts. PPL seeks to understand both problems and goals systemically, uncovering the connections that may cause risks to grow into costs and injuries, or that may offer opportunities. PPL has the potential to substitute understanding, trust, and consent for power and coercion in a broad range of undertakings. Doing so can save money as well as relationships.

PPL could have especially valuable application in commercial contracting, because of the conscious, voluntary nature of the human relationship that is formed by a contract. The professional process of contracting – which involves counseling each party to an agreement, negotiating the terms, drafting documents, implementing and enforcing the undertakings, and troubleshooting difficulties – may strongly benefit from the communications that are inherent to PPL methods. To

1. Louis and Hermione Brown Professor of Law, California Western School of Law, San Diego, California.

date, however, relatively few contractual relationships have taken full advantage of the approach.

Several obstacles can slow the adoption of PPL in commercial contracting: the inertia of traditional attitudes and stereotypes; the difficulty of effective communication within organizations; limited grants of authority to depart from accepted practices; short-term balance sheet imperatives; and asymmetries in parties' motivations toward forming stronger relationships.[2] This Essay, however, focuses primarily on one recurring barrier: an exaggerated and largely unnecessary separation between the business goals that clients seek to achieve, and the legal methods by which contractual relationships are created and managed. Business people want to create exchange relationships, and at least sometimes welcome the personal relationships that may accompany that exchange. Both such relationships, however, can become too strongly detached from legal relationships. In practice, business combinations and legal rules seem to migrate to distinct realms, employing different languages and ways of thinking. When that happens, the strong communication and interactions that are foundational for PPL never materialize.

Understanding this "separate worlds" barrier is not difficult. Business clients – from management to engineers to production personnel – cannot easily access the legal language in which their formal contractual relationships is typically expressed.[3] And yet they cannot dispense with

2. These obstacles and more are thoughtfully discussed in a 2010 webinar conversation about Collaborative Contracting between Tim Cummins and Jacqui Crawford conducted under the auspices of the International Association of Contract and Commercial Managers (IACCM). Although their specific topic was Collaborative Contracting, their analysis can be analogized to apply to PPL. As this Essay hopes to clarify, Collaborative Contracting could be one important vehicle toward accepting PPL more generally. Their webinar is archived in the membership library of IACCM at https://www.iaccm.com/members/library/files/Ask_The_Expert_Recording-Jacqui_Crawford-April10.mp3https://www.iaccm.com/members/library/files/Ask_The_Expert_Recording-Jacqui_Crawford-April10.mp3https://www.iaccm.com/members/library/files/Ask_The_Expert_Recording-Jacqui_Crawford-April10.mp3https://www.iaccm.com/members/library/files/Ask_The_Expert_Recording-Jacqui_Crawford-April10.mp3 (hereafter "*Webinar*").

3. Stewart Macaulay, *The Real and the Paper Deal: Empirical Pictures of Relationships, Complexity, and the Urge for Transparent Simple Rules*, 66 Mod. L. Rev. 44, 46-47 (2003) (hereafter *"The Real and the Paper Deal").*

the legal relationship, or even readily change the language in which it is so often expressed. If business people want to make a binding agreement, they seem locked in to satisfying legal requirements. The legal requirements, in turn, also seem locked in: to difficult vocabularies and narrow assumptions.

The parties to commercial contracts thus depend, rather helplessly, on legal recognition of their relationship. Neither party can fully understand nor control how the legal system will interpret their intentions or rule if there is trouble. But rather than opening out the dialogue with their lawyers, business clients sometimes do the opposite: they limit the dialogue, often severely. They may foreclose stronger conversations by re-using again and again a standard form contract that parties feel they can safely sign without even reading. Or they may delay consulting with the lawyers until the deal is fully negotiated. Clients may wait until all that remains – in their minds – is for lawyers to supply the indecipherable and potentially deal-upsetting technicalities that add nothing to the value of the relationship.

For their part, the lawyers who create and often are called upon to manage the rights and duties of contractual relationships too seldom educate themselves fully on the business context or goals that prompt the formation of a particular contractual relationship. Lawyers too often limit their counsel and practice as though they were system technicians the experts who operate a relatively arcane but indispensable machine that produces legal legitimacy.

As with the business people who become reluctant to consult them, the lawyers are not operating in bad faith. Instead, they are playing out a role that is too narrowly defined under a traditional adversarial model. That role regards the primary task of each lawyer as creating a set of legally strong – hopefully unassailable – rights for one party to the agreement. Accomplishing that requires expert understanding of legal rules, and managing those rules through highly precise, specialized language – concepts and devices that do not necessarily depend on the particulars of what is exchanged within the agreement.

But this detachment from substantive context or contract purposes reinforces the very client attitudes that postpone summoning legal advice until the content of the agreement is agreed upon. The traditional strongly adversarial role also perpetuates an instinct of secrecy toward communications with the other parties to a contract. The spiral of separation thus continues, and perhaps deepens, between exchange relationships, personal relationships, and legal relationships.

It bears repeating that neither business clients nor their lawyers intend to act irresponsibly. Yet both can become gripped by attitudes and practices that block the stronger value that could be captured by the PPL approach.[4] Lawyers want contracts to create a strong, but confined, relationship that formally ties the parties together and yet keeps them at arm's length. Business people want relationships that are more flexible[55] and (at least sometimes) more trusting and personal.[6]

The exchange relationship is distinct from the legal relationship, and both are crucial.[7] Yet they need not be linguistically or conceptually walled off from one another. This Essay, beginning from the assumption that the PPL approach really could supply stronger mutual benefits to contracting counterparts, explores one promising vehicle for lowering the barriers among exchange, personal, and legal relationships: Collaborative Contracting.

2. Organization of the Essay

Still in its infancy, Collaborative Contracting attempts to build identify links between collaborative methods and the goals of PPL: better relationships, better communication, and contextual understandings that will prevent problems and facilitate success. Along the way, analyzing

4. As developed in the webinar conversation between Tim Cummins and Jacqui Crawford, the blockages extend into the organizations and their contracting partners. Overcoming the barriers beyond those of lawyer and client is difficult, especially in challenging economic times, but sensible advice is offered by Cummins and Crawford. *See generally, Webinar, supra* note 2.
5. In a poll taken among the members of the International Association of Contracts and Commercial Managers (IACCM), nearly 90% said that "flexibility and greater agility" is important for their contracts. http://contract-matters.com/2011/09/21/stuck-in-a-negotiation-rut/, last visited September 24, 2011.
6. Stewart Macaulay, *Freedom from Contract: Solutions in Search of a Problem?* 2004 Wis. L. Rev. 777, 790-795 (hereafter *"Freedom from Contract").*
7. David Campbell and Donald Harris, *Flexibility in Long-Term Contractual Relationships: The Role of Co-operation,* 20 L. & Soc. Rev. 166, 178 (1993).

these links may pay additional benefits. The analysis may shed new light on an old conundrum about commercial contracts, and may prompt new research about systems or networks of communication.

The section immediately below begins by examining that old conundrum, what I here call the "disjuncture puzzle." This is the historical, but ongoing, pattern of heavy investment in strong legal rights during the formation of contracts, but the later abandonment of those rights just when they might be most useful: when trouble arises. The Essay examines this puzzle economically, but concludes that economic analysis alone is not likely to explain the phenomenon fully.

That leads to the next section, one which may prompt further research into understanding contracting as a network for human communications. This section first describes Harvard Law professor Larry Lessig's framework of "smart" versus "simple" communications networks, and then applies that framework to the disjuncture puzzle.[8]

To preview that discussion, "smart" communications networks or systems are typically expert constructed, internally complex, and require input or operation to follow templates or fit within particular structures. The creative focus of smart networks is internal, and usually confined to highly skilled designers. Smart networks are optimized to work efficiently, and effectively, for a relative narrow set of applications. Old-fashioned dial-up telephone technology is one illustration of smart networking.[9] Users can do only one thing on the network: make phone calls to speak with one other person (or in later refinements of the system, to more than one person). The user input is confined to dialing a number. Behind the phone dial live highly engineered, complex switching and transmission systems.

"Simple" networks, by contrast, are far more flexible and open to diverse inputs. They do not operate by elaborate internal rules or channel usage narrowly. The creative focus of a simple system is external, in the users rather than the designers. The Internet illustrates a simple

8. This part applies by analogy the framework developed by Harvard Law professor Larry Lessig, who writes insightfully about Internet design. *See* Lawrence Lessig, The future of Ideas (2001).
9. The example is taken from Lessig, *supra* note 8, who introduces and explains the example at pp. 26-34.

network. It is designed as simply as possible, to move packets of information – textual, graphical, or audio – through a virtually limitless variety of software applications, from all comers and without restriction on destination.

The Essay concludes that traditional contracting constitutes a smart communications network. It is governed by legal rules that are created by legal experts and largely useable only by lawyers or other trained personnel. The creative focus of the contract system is basically internal, within the legal rules and their interpretation in courts; not, in other words, on the users. And as with other smart networks, the contracting rules are optimized for particular operations. But the sort of transaction for which it is optimized is becoming less important in the Information Age.

The analogy between contracting and communications networks thus offers a new way to articulate the tension of the disjuncture puzzle. Lawyers are comfortable and creative within the (smart) contracts system. But the operation of the system is largely inaccessible to their clients. The client role is reduced to supplying input information that is more elaborate but structurally akin to dialing a phone number. The Essay asserts that clients would prefer that contracting become simpler – i.e., more accessible to lay persons and more open to their creative contributions. And by so doing, the communications prerequisites to using the PPL approach would be furthered.

The final section discusses Collaborative Contracts, a promising device by which the system might be pried open to let in more of that participation and creativity. After briefly explaining its values and methods, the Essay suggests that collaboration could be a way to make the contracting system more "simple," *and therefore to facilitate relationships among lawyers, clients, and contracting partners in ways that accord with PPL.* Collaborative Contracts could thus become an important vehicle toward making commercial contracting practice more preventive and proactive.

3. The "Disjuncture Puzzle" of Strong Contractual Rights

Close to fifty years ago, Stewart Macaulay published his now-famous empirical study of how American business people respond to contract breaches.[10] Macaulay found that users of contracts (*i.e.*, business clients) related to their contracts differently than the drafters of the contracts (*i.e.*, lawyers) probably expected. The lawyers worked scrupulously to create legal rights for their clients that were tightly enforceable in a courtroom, in the event that the other side breached the agreement. The clients, however, often chose not to exercise these rights. Even in the face of a clear breach, the clients would seek a mutual adjustment to enable the contract – or at least the business relationship – to continue.

Half a century later, Macaulay could still find the same phenomenon.[11] Lawyers tend to use comprehensive, precise language to establish legal protection for their clients in the event of trouble, but their clients then work with their contractual counterparts – especially in the event of a disruption or dispute – to avoid the legal consequences both counterparts had probably paid significantly to insure.

Lawyers and their clients thus seem, at least at first blush, to be working at cross purposes. Why would businesses invest significant time, attention, and money in assets (namely strong contractual legal rights) that then are frequently given away? And if this "disjuncture between formal contract law and actual relationships among businessmen"[12] is actually as inefficient as it seems, why has it not been better addressed?[13]

10. Stewart Macaulay, *Non-contractual Relations in Business, 28 Amer. Sociological Rev. 55* (1963), *cited and described* in Lawrence Rosen, LAW AS CULTURE: AN INVITATION 14-23 (2006) (hereafter "LAW AS CULTURE").
11. *See, e.g., Freedom from Contract, supra* note 6, at 778-783; Ross E. Cheit and Jacob E. Gersen, *When Businesses Sue Each Other: An Empirical Study of State Court Litigation, 25* L. & SOC. INQ. 789, 790 (2000).
12. LAW AS CULTURE, *supra* note 10, at 22.
13. A valuable update by Stewart Macaulay characterizes the disjuncture as the "real deal" versus the "paper deal" and helpfully analyzes many of the structural issues addressed in this Essay. *See generally, The Real and the Paper Deal, supra* note 2. For a fine introduction to transaction cost analysis in this context, *see* David Campbell, *The Incompleteness of Our Understanding of the Law and Economics of Relational Contract,* 2004 WIS. L. REV. 645.

Two issues are embedded in these questions: First, is the "disjuncture" really inefficient, or is it instead a sensible way of insuring against exploitative, rent-seeking behavior by one's counterparts in a contract? Second, if the disjuncture is inefficient, what may explain its persistence? This second question is important because if plausible hypotheses can be generated, perhaps recommendations can be made that would reduce the transaction costs embedded in the disjuncture of commercial contracting.

The first issue is empirical, but we may at least speculate on the framework for its assessment. Investing in careful legal language at the formation stage of contracting may be reasonable as a deterrent against exploitation by one's contractual counterparts. But if the legal rights are widely known to be acted upon only rarely, their deterrent value is obviously undermined. We do know, however, that some commercial contract disputes are indeed fully litigated.[14] So perhaps accumulating strong legal rights is efficient even though the rights are not *always* used. Furthermore, the legal rights may be relinquished only at a price – not simply charitably donated to the other side. Their adjustment is typically the result of negotiations that may lead to mutual adjustments between the disputing parties.

Perhaps, ironically, the existence of strict legal rights in a contract actually introduces a healthy flexibility and resilience into the everyday functioning of contracts. In other words, perhaps the formal language in the contract enables business people to adopt a non-legal, cooperative, and relational voice when trouble arises, *a potential that could not as easily be realized absent the power of the legal right.*[15] That speculation has some theoretical as well as empirical support. Legal economists identify that negotiations flounder when neither party holds a reasonably clear legal entitlement, i.e., when neither party knows who should be buying out

14. And asking the question why any disputes should escalate toward litigation rather than settle is Jacob E. Gersen, *Markets and Corporate Conflict: A Substitution-Cost Approach to Business Litigation,* 24 L. & SOC. INQ. 789, 790 (1999).
15. *Freedom from Contract, supra* note 6, at 782-784 for examples. On the relationship generally between coercive mechanisms and self-enforcing provisions, see generally Robert E. Scott and Paul B. Stephan, *Self-enforcing International Agreements and the Limits of Coercion,* 2004 WIS. L. REV. 551; William C. Whitford, *Relational Contracts and the New Formalism,* 2004 WIS. L. REV. 631.

whom.[16] Perhaps, therefore, clients demand (or at least tolerate) being equipped with the unshakeable legal rights their lawyers recommend, *even while* the clients expects that these legal entitlements will not be employed in the event of an actual breach. In other words, the clients may demand, and the lawyers may supply, the strategic stockpiling of rights.

This threshold issue is important not simply because the formal language inserted into contracts represents significant transaction costs, costs that no doubt could be reduced by drafting contracts using language that is less precise and more relationship-building.[17] If the stronger legalistic language actually *facilitates* mutually accommodative behaviors by business people in the event of trouble, then the disjunctive phenomenon should be tolerated or even encouraged. But if inserting strong rights-asserting contractual language *inhibits* flexible, value-creating adjustments by business people when trouble arises – inhibitions that business people often manage to overcome – then lawyers should seek to serve their clients better by altering the voice with which they express contractual arrangements. Seeking legal empowerment from the outset may, for example, inhibit a power-based mentality in the event of trouble that discourages a dialogue of mutual accommodation.

The truth may lie somewhere in between. It may be that defining a relationship through strong legal rights at the outset may also *confine* that relationship, limiting its potential growth. But within those confines, negotiation and accommodation is enabled through clarifying initial entitlements. Empirical investigation is not likely to put such questions to rest.

But this much can scarcely be disputed: If business people struggle against the strong "rights language" of their own contracts, managing nevertheless to find mutually acceptable, relationship-preserving out-

16. Guido Calabresi and A. Douglas Melamed, *Property Rules, Liability Rules, and Inalienability: One View of the Cathedral* 85 HARV. L. REV. 1089, 1093-1096 (1972).
17. Ichiro Kobayashi, in his insightful Essay *The Interaction between Japanese Corporate Governance and Relational Contract Practice,* NYU JOURNAL OF LAW & BUSINESS (2005) explains that many Japanese contracts drafted in the aftermath of World War II were strongly relational because of the shortage of lawyers: the drafting costs of achieving more precise, "discrete" contract language were too high. Businesses economized by reducing contract precision, even though enforcement costs were likely to be higher because of such imprecision.

comes, then *even if negotiations are facilitated by the economists' concerns for clarity of entitlements,* we should ask additional questions. We should determine how much *better* the relationship between those parties could be, and how much *more* value the parties to the contract could realize, were the contract language designed from the outset to provide good communication and flexibility by the parties throughout the life of the contract. How much better would the contract be, in other words, where it is consciously structured preventively – to avert problems or disputes from arising – and proactively, to facilitate ongoing adjustments through which the value of the commercial relationships may be enhanced? Put even more broadly, if business people were to have a stronger role in defining and managing their relationship, how much more like a partnership or friendship would it be than the relationship that is defined by legal rights and duties?[18] And does traditional legal treatment of that relationship constrain its development?

Finding out would require bringing closer together the worlds of the business content of contracts with the legal and human relationships of the parties. Stronger connections could be built in at least three possible ways: (1) reform the world of legal contract rules so that the rules are more simple;[19] (2) make the expression of those legal rules more accessible or intuitive for the users of contract documents; or (3) expand the legal recognition of the non-legal aspects of the exchange relationship that may be desirable to the contract users.

These three options are not mutually exclusive. The first option, to reform legal rules so as to better mimic business behaviors, is the approach of the Uniform Commercial Code in the U.S., and the CISG that in some respects is modeled on the UCC. Although this aim of moving legal rules more organically toward business practices is admirable, it has not been achieved to the extent foreseen by the designers of the

18. *See* Linda Alvarez, *Discovering Agreement,* http://www.discoveringagreement.com, last visited Sept. 21, 2011; Ethan J. Leib, *Contracts and Friendships,* 59 EMORY L. J. 649 (2010); *cf.* Daniel Markovits, *Contract and Collaboration,* 113 YALE L. J. 1417 (2004); George Dent, *Lawyers and Trust in Business Alliances,* 58 BUS. LAW. 45 (2002).

19. *See The Real and the Paper Deal, supra* note 3, at 44-45 in which Macaulay cautions about the limited capabilities of a contract law based more on standards than rules.

UCC,[20] nor is that process of conforming legal recognition to business behaviors free of potential undesirable side-effects.[21]

The second option, that of making contract documents more accessible – thus inviting more participation in every phase of the contractual process – is the aim of "plain language" efforts in contracts and more recently to incorporate graphic images or "visualization" to contract documents.[22]

The third option is the one explored in this paper: building better recognition and connections among the exchange, personal, and legal relationships. This option may possibly be furthered by adopting the PPL approach, a process that perhaps can be better understood by imagining contracting as a communication system that could have "smart" or "simple" attributes.

4. Contracting as a "Smart" versus "Simple" Communication System

As introduced above, Lawrence Lessig's masterful work, The Future of Ideas[23] describes the Internet and World Wide Web and the conditions under which innovation thrive within them. The analytical framework he builds for understanding telecommunications systems can be valuably applied to contracts, imagining contracts as a process of human communication. After drawing points of comparison and contrast be-

20. Robert E. Scott, *The Rise and Fall of Article 2,* 62 LA. L. REV. 1009 (2002). *See generally Juliet Kostritsky, Taxonomy for Justifying Legal Intervention in an Imperfect World: What to Do When Parties Have Not Achieved or Drafted Incomplete Contracts,* 2004 WIS. L. REV. 323.
21. Omri Ben-Shahar, *The Tentative Case Against Flexibility in Commercial Law,* 66 U. CHI. L. REV. 781 (1999).
22. Gerlinde Berger-Walliser, Robert C. Bird, and Helena Haapio, *Promoting Business Suc-cess through Contract Visualization,* 17 J. LAW, BUS. & ETHICS 55 (2011); Thomas D. Barton, Gerlinde Berger-Walliser and Helena Haapio, *Visualization: Seeing Contracts for What They Are, and What They Could Become,* submitted for publication, 2011.
23. Lessig, *supra* note 8. Lessig's historic, analytical, and policy treatment of the Internet and its relationship to innovation is outstanding. Use of the Internet metaphor in this paper to help understand contract relationships is thus heavily indebted to Lessig's work.

tween Lessig's Internet analysis and the contracting system, we may better understand the divergent mentalities or values between legally-trained contract drafters and the business persons who use contracts to achieve a broad variety of commercial and research ends.

Combining the work of others as well as his original contribution, Lessig describes the Internet as a network for human communication. And so also could we imagine the enterprise of making, performing, and enforcing contracts. Although formal contract law does not stress the point, ideally a commercial contract should be considered as a communications system, a device for facilitating connections between parties and to effectuate the agreed intentions of the parties.

The analogy between the Internet and contracting may be fruitful for its points of agreement, but also for its contrasts. One such contrast can open our understanding of the disjuncture of contracting and point the way for possible reform. This contrast reflects a fundamental difference between the Internet and contracts as a means of communication. In Lessig's terminology, the Internet is basically a "simple" (or "stupid") network,[24] whereas contracts – especially contract law – is a "smart" network. Almost immediately most people would compliment contracts for having achieved "smartness." In general, of course, intelligence offers huge advantages over stupidity; smart phones are more functional than phones with simply telephony capabilities. But as Lessig uses the terms, the matter is far more subtle.

A smart versus simple communications system is best understood by thinking about those who use it at each end: as examples, the people who pick up telephones to dial, and on the other end when they ring; or those who create any sort of website and those who visit it; or, finally, those who want to sell a good or service via a contract, and those who wish to purchase it. A simple network works like a highway, electricity system, or bridge over a river.[25] Its function is simply to enable transport from one end to another, be it an automobile, truck, bicycle, or pedestrian. The bridge asks no questions about what it is – vehicle, human, or animal – that wants to travel the highway or cross the bridge. Similarly, the purposes of the crossing are no business of the highway or bridge.

24. Id., at 34-48.
25. Id., at 38-39.

These structures of a bridge or highway are neutral among a huge variety of possible users, with only occasional control or restrictions like speed limits, weight limits, or exclusions of pedestrians from high speed highways. For the most part, anyone can use the highway or bridge as and for whatever purpose they choose.

That is how the Internet also works, certainly in its inception and continuing today with some emerging challenges.[26] It is an "end to end" (or "E2E") simple network.[27] The Internet is consciously designed to be extremely simple, functioning merely to facilitate the communications between one end-user with another. It does not restrict or control the purposes of the communications. As a network, it has no idea what the content of the communication between end-users may be. The Internet simply transports on a first-come, first-served basis any bits of information that properly employ its technical protocols.[28]

The originators of the Internet designed it that way, because of what Lessig rightly calls the laudable humility of those first-rate engineers: they simply could not foresee the forms that the communication made possible by this new technology might take, and they wanted a system that was completely open to the innovations of the end users.[29] The complexity of Internet computing is not, therefore, in the Internet itself. The Internet itself is profoundly simple, a neutral "information superhighway." The complexity comes from the end users themselves – the E2E – who devise all manner of software to enable new ways for humans to share information.

So maybe the simple Internet is not so stupid after all. By eschewing controls, rules, and conscious allocations, its simplicity empowers the imagination of those who use it. Millions of minds are thus freed to explore and develop the Internet, rather than a few gifted computer scientists who could have crafted an elaborate, "smart" system of Internet rules and controls. Had they done so, they would not have been evil scientists bent on totalitarian control. Instead, they would have been devising a set of rules that optimized certain sorts of communications on

26. Id., at 34.
27. Id.
28. Id., at 34-37.
29. Id., at 35.

the Internet. That is, they would have devised rules that seemed to them at the time to make most efficient those transactions on the Internet that seemed most likely to prevail. But had they created such a system of rules and control *within* the Internet itself – not spread out to the edges for the end users to determine for themselves – the remarkable innovation that has characterized the Internet evolution may not have happened.[30]

That is the trade-off of a simple versus a smart network. A simple network is transparent and open, making itself available for the creativity of its users on a completely non-discriminatory basis. A smart network, in contrast, is internally complex, comprised of rules and controls that are optimized to work best for the functions that those in charge of the network perceive to be most important or useful. But by the expert system engineers creating a rule-structured network that favors particular applications, innovation by *users* becomes far more difficult. They must overcome the rules that are not designed for their uses.

Contrast the simple Internet communications system with contracting, especially taking into account the legal regulation of contracts. Contracting is far more smart, being full of classical contract law rules that frame many aspects of contract formation, conditions on performance, modification, breach and repudiation, plus remedies. Contract rules are in play in every agreement, even where not explicitly invoked. The "invisible" default rules that Helena Haapio identifies are buried in statutes, case law, even trade customs – but still control contracts unless specifically overwritten.[31]

Through seeing contracting as a smart network, we could now re-articulate the disjuncture between how business people and lawyers regard contracts. We can speculate that business people yearn for contracting to be a far simpler network, whereas by training and mentality lawyers support the existing smart network.

30. Id., at 34-46.
31. Helena Haapio, *Invisible Terms in International Contracts and What to Do About Them,* CONTRACT MGMT., July, 32 (2004), *available at* http://www.ncmahq.org/files/Essays/81EEB_cm_July04_32.pdf, last visited Sept. 22, 2011.

Business people may experience the contracting system as frustrating, full of controlling but often irrelevant rules that seem to require more precision and structure than the business proposal can or should tolerate, and that they cannot usually fully access, must less control. Lawyers, by contrast, are steeped in the elaborate smart framework of contract law. After their years of study, lawyers work as familiars within the smart system, able to harness the power represented by the controlling rules. The logic of the rule system can be appealing to lawyers, and their work may feel like an appropriate realm for creativity, because that is precisely the way in which a smart network is set up. It is optimized for a particular set of applications, and lawyers are trained to operate within that set. But for business people who are legally untrained, the flexibility and creativity that is internally available within the network of contract rules is not readily available. The contracting system may be experienced by clients as inaccessible, and resistant to the creativity – creativity likely of a different sort than would come from lawyers – than clients would like to exercise from the "edges" of the system.

Perhaps we can advance the dialogue between lawyers and clients, bringing somewhat closer together the exchange and legal relationships, by re-phrasing our initial inquiry about the disjuncture puzzle. We first posed the issue in terms of language and rights: under what conditions does strong, precise language facilitate mutually accommodative behaviors by business people, and when might such words instead inhibit flexible, value-creating agreements? We can now frame the issue differently: in what ways can, or should, the contracting system be smart, and in what ways can or should it be more simple?

Put that way, we will assume that legal rules (together with their authoritative interpretation in the courts) are what make classical contracting a smart network. Being smart, the network is optimized for certain kinds of economic exchange. Viewed historically, contracting can be seen as a system that co-evolved with the Industrial Revolution, furthering its transactions and distributional patterns.[32] The Information Age, however, creates structural demands on economic exchange that

32. Thomas D. Barton, Preventive Law and Problem Solving: Lawyering for the Future 256-264 (2009).

may well not be optimized by the smart network of classical contracts.[33] At least for *some* contracts – perhaps the more strategic, more densely relational contracts – a "simpler" rather than "smarter" system would be more efficient and better suited toward emerging business conditions in the Information Age.

Economic conditions may be ripe, then, for making the contracting system more simple. In the remainder of this Essay I will elaborate the idea of using Collaborative Contracting to do just that. It could perhaps become a vehicle for ***both*** (1) steering disjuncture behaviors toward its positive role of promoting mutual accommodating post-dispute behavior; and (2) opening up the contracting system – making it simpler – and thus promoting the sorts of communication between lawyer and client, and between client and contractual counterpart, that may help to prevent those disputes from arising even while proactively advancing the purposes of the exchange.

5. Collaborative Contracts and Practice

"Collaborative" practice among lawyers and other professionals began in the context of family law and divorce.[34] But the collaborative move-

33. As I have written elsewhere,

> "What once may have been efficient forms of organization – forms with centralized authority that projected standardized goods, services, or ideas outwards – may not be able to harness Information Age efficiency potential. What may work better are inter-firm networks: webs of relationships among distinct contributors that can couple and decouple to suit particular projects. To accomplish this, businesses will need a collaborative mentality and inter-firm communication.
>
> ***[B]uilding trust and strong relationships are crucial in these web relationships,*** ... because of the need for speed, flexibility, and the ability to deal with high complexity."

Id., at 260-261.

34. *See* Forrest S. Mosten, Collaborative Divorce Handbook: Helping Families Without Going to Court (2009) (hereafter "Mosten"); Sherri Goren Slovin, *The Basics of Collaborative Family Law: A Divorce Paradigm Shift,* 18 AMER. J. Of Family Law 74 (2004). Mosten's book offers a comprehensive description of the values and methods of collaborative lawyering. For a review of Mosten's fine work, see

ment may be useful in many areas of law since, like PPL, it reflects emerging structural changes in how lawyers think; how they relate to their clients and other professionals; and the methods with which they address problems. The breadth of those changes may have valuable application to the formation and performance of commercial contracts.[35] In the section below I explore and assess some possible ways in which collaboration might improve communication, lower transaction costs, and advance the goals of everyone involved with making and implementing contracts.

In a useful Ethical Opinion, the American Bar Association describes and approves Collaborative Law practice (assuming that appropriate counseling is given to the client, and informed consent obtained).[36] In Collaborative Law, "The parties and their lawyers commit to work cooperatively to reach a settlement. ... Participants focus on the interests of both clients, gather sufficient information to insure that decisions are

Thomas D. Barton, *Collaborative Divorce: A Model for Effective Problem Solving and Prevention,* in the online journal of Harvard Negotiation Law Review (www.hnlr.org), December 28, 2009 http://www.hnlr.org/?p=505, last visited Sept. 13, 2011.

35. Mosten, *supra* note 34, at 1-20.

36. ABA Formal Op. 07-447 (2007). For example, the Opinion describes a "four way" agreement that is typical in a collaborative divorce setting:

> "Although there are several models of collaborative practice, all of them share the same core elements that are set out in a contract between the clients and their lawyers (often referred to as a "four-way" agreement). In that agreement, the parties commit to negotiating a mutually acceptable settlement without court intervention, to engaging in open communication and information sharing, and to creating shared solutions that meet the needs of both clients. To ensure the commitment of the lawyers to the collaborative process, the four-way agreement also includes a requirement that, if the process breaks down, the lawyers will withdraw from representing their respective clients and will not handle any subsequent court proceedings."

That latter provision–requiring a withdrawal by both lawyers in the event of lack of settlement--is known as the "Disqualification Clause." A related practice called "cooperative" rather than "collaborative" lawyering is distinguished by omitting the Disqualification Clause from the four-way agreement. *See* John Lande, *An Empirical Analysis of Collaborative Practice*, 49 Fam. CT. Rev. 257, 257-58 (2011).

made with full knowledge, develop a full range of options, and then choose options that best meet the needs of the parties."[37]

Just as collaborative lawyering is typically used to structure healthy ongoing interactions of a family – even following a divorce – so also could collaborative practices organize a healthy, ongoing contractual commercial relationship. "The parties structure a mutually acceptable written resolution of all issues without court involvement. ... The structure creates a problem-solving atmosphere with a focus on interest-based negotiation and client empowerment."[38]

Forrest S. Mosten, a prominent analyst and advocate of collaborative lawyering, elaborates the values that underpin a collaborative agreement:

- Respect and dignity for the other party and other professionals
- Direct and open communication with the other party and professionals
- Voluntary and full disclosure of relevant information and documents necessary to make agreements
- Commitment to the healing of the family
- Use of interest-based negotiation to try to meet the needs of both parties.[39]

Mosten views the collaborative movement as a paradigm shift in legal relationships. Citing Julie Macfarland,[40] he draws out the contrasts. Traditional lawyering is characterized through its orientation toward individual rights; its confidence in court-based adjudication; and its assertion that lawyers should be in charge of those procedures.[41] As so structured, the traditional relationship between lawyer and client, tends to be channeled narrowly by legal rules and the securing of rights for the client under those rules. That rule/rights orientation may confine the

37. Id.
38. Id.
39. Mosten, *supra* note 34, at 21.
40. Julie Macfarlane, The New Lawyer: How Settlement is Transforming the Practice of Law (2008).
41. Mosten, *supra* note 34, at 2, *quoting* Macfarlane, *supra* note 5, at 61-62.

relationships among contracting parties, especially if a dispute arises. Inter-party communication may then wither into silence as broader discussion is gradually displaced by their respective lawyers' analysis of legal rights and duties. Collaborative practice, by contrast, attempts to move away from that adversarial engagement. It attempts instead to find a relationship more akin to a partnership among lawyers, clients, related professionals, and all those who share involvement in a common problem or enterprise.[42] But how might it work in contracts, and, as importantly, how could it find legal legitimacy?

One idea is to be explicit in the actual contract about both the collaborative intentions and responsibilities of the parties. Doing so has the strong advantage emphasized by Jacqui Crawford of Rolls-Royce: the parties disclose from the outset their respective interests, their baseline expectations, and a process for addressing and managing the changes that will inevitably occur over the life of a longterm contract.[43] Collaborating contractors could pledge, in the preamble to a contract or separate document:

- to improve the quality of information they share, focusing from the beginning on their underlying interests and the risks they perceive;
- to work toward clauses that share risks in a balanced way, striving for maximal realization of *both* parties' interests;[44]
- to communicate in regularly scheduled meetings about the progress and quality of performances;
- when needed, to cooperate and perhaps even provide affirmative assistance toward another party's performance of its contractual duties;
- to work toward understanding and accommodating the needs of one another in response to changes, and to be open to modifying terms where conditions suggest the need for adjustment; and

42. Mosten, *supra* note 34, at 2.
43. *Webinar, supra* note 2.
44. If one party consistently forces the other to accept unbalanced risks, the subordinated party may eventually be forced into breach–at which point both parties very likely lose value. Accepting a balanced sharing of the risks throughout the contract, even where opportunistic rent-seeking is possible, may well produce the best results over the life of a contract (or relationship). Id.

- in the event of a dispute, to negotiate in good faith and to seek mediation and other alternative dispute resolution methods where initial efforts at negotiation fail.[45]
- in the event of litigation, interpretation of the agreement should not be limited to its explicit language. Instead, all interpretations of the commitments and understandings of the parties should be augmented by the collaborative spirit in which the agreement was entered.

Inserting such clauses into a contract, or into a separate document that could be incorporated by reference, would be relatively easy. But several questions would nonetheless remain.

First, would such collaborative terms be warranted in *every* exchange? Probably not, although the collaboration need not be all-or-nothing. Some of the provisions above are more demanding of time, money, and organizational coordination than others. The duties of ongoing consultation, for example, would clearly require an organizational commitment that may not be justified by the levels of complexity, duration, and economic value of a given contract.[46] But on the other hand, seeking a bright line between adopting a collaborative communication style for "strategic" contracts but reverting to traditional adversarial qualities for "commodity" contracts may be unrealistic as well as ultimately unproductive.[47] Authorizing and enabling a collaborative style within an organization involves significant investment in thoughtful structures and personnel.[48] But having done that, certainly *some* elements of collaborative contracting become affordable even for shorter-range transactions[49] or for those transactions in which one party may be more desirous than the other of a stronger relationship.[50]

Second, would courts enforce collaborative clauses such as proposed above? The PPL and collaborative approaches are designed to avoid litigation, not to spawn it. If collaboration must rely on judicial enforce-

45. *See Freedom From Contract, supra* note 6, 784-788 reporting successes and limitations of such a clause in the form of the CPR Pledge.
46. Tim Cummins, *Webinar, supra* note 2.
47. Id.
48. Id.
49. Crawford, *Webinar, supra* note 2.
50. Cummins, *Webinar, supra* note 2.

ment, it probably will not work from the beginning. Even if its clauses are imperfectly observed and not legally pursued, they may create normative expectations among the parties that can be helpful to the personal relationship and thus to smoothing out trouble in the exchange relationship. But if one party's reliance on a clause really were to cause significant, measurable injury when the clause is breached by the other party, could a court enforce the collaborative clause? Or is the language too vague? We cannot be sure, but may note that the idea of a commitment to collaboration is probably no less difficult to apply than concepts like "reasonableness," "good faith," and "unconscionability."

Finally, we should face the possibility that collaborative clauses could themselves give rise to new opportunistic behaviors: to provide new tools, in other words, by which one party can threaten another with expensive litigation. One can only hope that no one with such cynical motives would agree to collaboration in the first place. But if they were to do so, courts could see instrumental rent-seeking uses of such clauses as themselves violations of the general duty of good faith.

6. Conclusion

If collaboration were successful, contracting partners could improve their economic prospects along with their interpersonal relationship. Collaborative contracts hold out the possibility of lower formation and performance costs, as parties share from the outset their key interests in making the agreement. That knowledge, plus ongoing communication between the parties suggests that fewer disputes will occur, or escalate significantly. But where disputes must be addressed, easier resolution may occur through mandatory mediation sessions. Finally, collaboration can facilitate conversations that may discover additional opportunities for mutual benefit.

All three relationships of a contract – the exchange, the personal, and the legal – can be made stronger if the legal system can become simpler, opening itself to broader, more creative participation by users as well as legal experts. Collaborative contracts, by bringing contract personnel into more meaningful contact with one another, may be one worthy experiment toward that goal.

Great Expectations (Part 1): Towards *Relational* Contract Modelling as a Strategic Competence in B2B Agreements

By

John Jørgensen
Commercial Manager

"The ***behaviour*** that does occur in relations must occur if relations are to continue, and hence ought to occur so long as their continuance is ***valued***"
(MacNeil, emphasis added)

1. Introduction – why relational contracts matter to the proactive law movement

The second European Proactive Law Conference call for papers seeks approaches to merging best practice from legal, contract, project and risk practice management, towards the provision of a framework for integrating legal astuteness into the tangible practice of everyday business. In response to that call this paper seeks to provide an approach that is grounded in relational contract theory, as espoused by MacNeil[1] and advanced more lately by commentators such as Diathesopoulos[2] and Austen-Baker[3].

Taking a broad-brush approach at this stage, I attempt to merge the norms-based school of thought with economic analysis of the relation (or organisational economists), notably Klein's "self-enforcing range"[4]. Then, by having regard to the "contracting journey", I emphasise certain aspects such as:

- the importance assigned to the "social contract" as advocated by Lax and Sebenius[5] amongst others; and
- one of MacNeil's key norms the "implementation of planning" which in a negotiating context ex ante is supported by Ertel and Gordon[6] and previous contributors to the proactive law movement;[7] and
- the overall contractual structure that is "best-fit" to the requirements, including ex-post matters such as dispute management.[8]

Drawing all of these strands of commentary together starts to create a paradigm within which lawyers, contract managers, project managers and sales professionals can consider the best-fit approach to meeting the objectives of a B2B relationship to ensure its success.

The proposed framework neither seeks to attain full presentiation in agreements, nor to leave agreements awash with uncertainty as neither pole's are satisfactory, and remains cognisant of the tensions and interplay between rights based and interest based approaches ex ante and ex post. It is hoped each area may be fleshed out in more detail as and when time permits. It should be made clear at the outset that the focus on 'relational' contracting should not be confused with a solely paternalistic or highly co-operative behaviour, indeed a relational contract may be to the contrary.

Why should "legal astuteness" have a concern with the relational aspects surrounding any given agreement, and why should it be addressed within the proactive law movement? The quick answer here is of course any deal that is not based on a genuine agreement is simply not sustainable. However there are more dimensions for consideration, as information and power asymmetry and a "multiplicity of unforeseen contingencies"[9] may well arise, especially so in longer-term complex agreements. On the 20th September the IMF announced that the global economy was entering "a dangerous new phase", the very next day Vince Cable, the UK Coalition Governments Business Secretary, at the Liberal Democrat Party conference likened the current economic climate to being at war, and Mervyn King, the Governor of the Bank of England, has stated that the current global economic collapse "may end up worse than the Great Depression of the 1930's". To compound the depressing rhetoric, recent articles investigate the economies' concern with highly relational contract structures such as outsourcing for businesses to achieve their outsourcing goals[10], and indeed part of that reaction can be seen in an increasing appetite for shorter contracting terms and selection of more suppliers across multiple deliverables.

In such depressed economic conditions the age-old adage "when poverty knocks on the door, love jumps out of the window" springs to mind, and this can be supported by the growing number of litigation cases, for example the 2009/10 Annual Report of the Technology and Construction Court in England and Wales summarised that, *despite the heavy mitigation of new claims through the LJ Woolf reforms* (e.g. mandating companies to at least attempt ADR), that since the onset of the current global financial crisis in 2008, new claims have increased almost 30%[11].

It is therefore understandable that, in what is already a very complex globalised environment, the myopia impacting the business world today makes it extremely difficult for parties to plan ahead, and **therefore relational aspects ex post will be of ever increasing importance,** as Hart expounded:

> "First, in a complex and highly unpredictable world, it is hard for people to think very far ahead and to plan for all the various contingencies that may arise. Second, even if individual plans can be made, it is hard for the parties to negotiate about the future, it may be very difficult for them to write their plans down in such a way that, in the event of a dispute an outside authority…can figure out what these plans mean and enforce them."[12]

This presents particular challenges, and opportunities, for the proactive law movement to address, to the benefit of "real-world" B2B relations by providing a framework that takes a balanced approach between presentiation and legal formalism on the one hand, to effectively addressing ex-post matters in an ongoing B2B relationship, particularly in a volatile world. This is supported for example by the EESC Opinion Paper published on the proactive law approach:

> "…the EESC would argue that rules and regulations are not the only way, nor always the best way to achieve desired objectives; at times the regulator may best support valuable goals be refraining from regulating and, where appropriate, **encouraging self-regulation and**

> **co-regulation.** This being the case, the fundamental principles of subsidiarity, proportionality, precaution and **sustainability** take on new importance and a new dimension."[13]

As such, a contract does not just consist of a set of written obligations, but of attitudes, power, planning and a wider social context which, if left to self-regulation and subsidiarity, means that we must focus on these aspects within the contractual domain.

2. Relational Contract Theory – a refresh, and latest developments

This paper does not attempt to regurgitate the early works of Macauley or MacNeil and the mass of commentary that has since followed over the last half-century, however I will surmise the key norms defined by MacNeil, and most recent work by Diathesopoulos and Austen-Baker in a practical analysis of these norms against contract provisions, because it is this norms system that is core to the consideration here.

Firstly MacNeil's view was that contracting is a phenomenon and was not an isolated exchange separate from the social context that informs upon it, and that because contracts are "generators of future exchange" **no unique law (i.e. contract law) can govern every contract for its term, because such exchange(s) cannot simply be consented, planned and isolated from the present and future social and relational context. Hence understanding any transaction necessitates understanding all essential elements of its enveloping relations.** Therefore, gaining clarity about the party's expectations on entering an agreement are fundamental for the establishment, development and continuation of every relation, but especially so in longer-term complex arrangements.

2.1. The relational spectrum

The first consideration we should make is the extent to which relational aspects require consideration by the contracting parties. Whilst MacNeil's work contended that all contracts were relational, the polar opposites range from discrete one-off or "spot-market" transactions, where buyers and sellers may trade remotely for supply-only of commodity items, through to highly relational, complex, long-term, possibly multi-party contractual structures, such as outsourcing, joint-ventures, partnership agreements etc.

Indeed MacNeil proposed 12 variables or axes upon which one may determine the extent of a relational exchange or a discrete exchange: duration, extent of planning, number of participants, extent of measurability, the degree of future co-operation that would be required, the extent of obligations and so forth[14].

In summary, relational contract theory proposes that every contract may be related to a social background, and therefore whilst the stated economic provisions play a legitimate role, their significance depends upon their compatibility with the current relational circumstance, hence the relational aspect cannot be ignored if the given transaction benefits are to optimised.

Moving on then to MacNeil's norms system (these are summarised under Appendix A of this paper), we now ask how this system may actually be applied proactively to optimise contract design and determining obligations?

Diathesopoulos in his paper 'paradigm for the application of the Theory of the Norms' seeks to use management contracts which offered a good environment as a paradigm for the **implementation** of relational contracts theory, as by their nature being highly relational such that its "specific content is determined by relational variables…their content can only be examined in the framework of the various and changing aspects of the specific total relation"[15].

Diathesopoulos presents three questions:

- **What is the content of the relation between the parties and which are the factors that govern this relation?**
- Why do management contracts have a highly relational element?
- **How effectively do the norms succeed in conveying each obligation's content?**

Diathesopoulos summarises his analysis as being distinguished into two categories of obligations, on the one hand certain specific predefined actions, and on the other specific but more general overall behaviour, "where the core refers to specific actions and the overall relative behaviour has a complimentary role." This is interesting as it alludes to the distinction between the "economic" and the "social" elements of the contract, which other commentators such as Lax and Sebenius have focused on (see later). In the final analysis Diathesopoulos' findings are summarised as follows:

Diathesopoulos – Incidence of Norms by Obligation in a Management Contract

Austen-Baker 4-Norm System:	SATISFYING PERFORMANCE EXPECTATION				PRESERVATION OF THE RELATION			HARMONI-SATION WITH THE SOCIAL MATRIX		SUBSTANTIAL FAIRNESS		
MacNeils' Norms:	Implementation of Planning	Role Integrity	Effectuation of Consent	Creation and Restraint of Power	Contractual Solidarity	Preservation of the Relation	Harmonisation of the Relational Conflict	Harmonisation with the Social Matrix	Supra contract Norms	Reciprocity	Creation and Restraint of Power	Proprietary of Means
TOTALS (MacNeil):	4	9	4	5	12	12	5	5	4	8	5	3
TOTALS (Austen-Baker):	22				29			9		16		

As we can see, the most evident norms in the set of obligations were preservation of the relation, contractual solidarity, role integrity, reciprocity, and creation and restraint of power (being duplicated in Austen-Bakers approach). Whilst the number of incidences of a particular norm should not be taken as the only factor in determining highly relational contracts, clearly most of the more relational norms identified by MacNeil are reflected as most prominent here. Whilst this analysis may reconfirm what we would naturally expect to see from such an agreement type, of course what we don't know is whether the contract under analysis was itself a sound one and that met the parties' expectations and whether it **optimised** that relation.

One of the key MacNeil norms not addressed above is that of 'flexibility'. However the writer concurs with the views of Austen-Baker and Diathesopoulos on this specific norm; "In relational exchanges the flexibility is achieved inside the relation, and is determined by the parties actions, planning and behaviour within the relation...Flexibility is a pre-requisite for the relations solidarity...a means for parties to resolve their relational conflicts that may be caused by unpredictable events... to change their priorities within the relation, thus asking for a change of the content of their, or their counterparty's commitments because of an alteration of parameters of the ongoing relation...**(flexibility) is not actually a norm (in relational theory) but a pre-requisite for the effectuation of all other norms."**[14]

The key consideration is what determines the extent of that flexibility, which the writer contends as being the (healthy) tension between the norms and the 'self-enforcing range' (see below).

Graphical Representation of the Incidence of Obligations in Diathesopoulos' Paper:

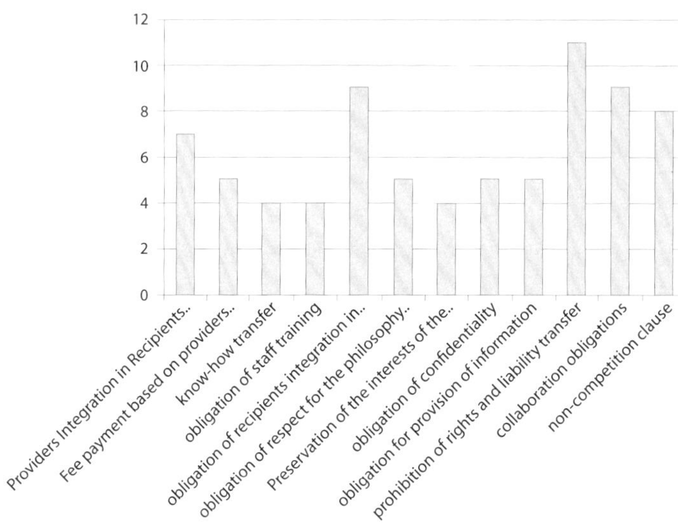

It is interesting to note that of the top 5 referenced clauses to which the norms were applied, the top one was liability transfer – essentially risk allocation, this directly influences cost and therefore to some extent plays into the self-enforcing range of the deal (see below). However the others are; collaboration obligations, the obligation of provider and recipients integration into the others organisation and non-competition clause – all of which are highly relational obligations. Compare this to IACCM's study "2011 – Top Terms in Negotiation", it's 10th annual survey, where the top 5 terms included limitation of liability, indemnification, charges, IPR and payment terms, whereas other more relational provisions such as scope and goals, responsibilities of the parties, change management, dispute resolution, service withdrawal, governance aspects and most favoured client languish in the bottom half. Despite this inversion it is acknowledged by the same negotiators that the latter set are the more productive in supporting successful relations, and such myopia hence forces IACCM to conclude that this "results in key areas of the contract content being overlooked or paid inadequate attention – specifically, clarity over scope and goals and over the on-going governance and management procedures for the relationship."

I have just referred above to the "self-enforcing range", what is this and how does it apply to the norms-based approach? In most cases people cooperate not due to altruism, but in order to increase their own utility...**the tension lies in the parties' self-interest, between short term and long term prioritisation.** The cooperative context to this imposes on us certain obligations that limit our behaviour (and one can refer to the norm of creation and restraint of power in that regard). The limits of that behaviour can largely be defined by the amount of reputational capital a party may gain or lose from any agreement, both with the other party and in the marketplace at large, which draws us onto the "self-enforcing range" as a complimentary consideration to the norms framework.

3. Economic boundaries – the "self-enforcing range"

Aside from MacNeil's model of relational contracts, another school of thought comes from an organisational economists approach. On this general approach I concur with the writings of Mouzas and Blois who state that the two approaches are converging ones, but "they are assessing the subject matter through completely different ontological views", expanding on the organisational economists view, Mouzas and Blois further, "The underlying assumption is that transaction costs are important and (such approach) investigates the efficiency of different forms of governance"[17]... however, they go on to critique that, whilst discrete contracts may be certain and an economic analysis may take place, in many cases the level of assumptions in the analysis of highly relational contracts becomes fraught, as "complete, fully contingent, costlessly enforceable contracts are not possible"[18], this is because in the real world, as Mouzas and Blois explain, "First a large number of possible contingencies may exist and it may be costly or impracticable to specify in advance responses to them. Second, transaction costs such as unforeseen contingencies, the costs of writing and enforcing contracts and renegotiating make it expensive or unfeasible to measure contractual performance, and thirdly information asymmetries will exist"[19].

Klein however contends that a party's **reputational capital** is a key variable that must be determined by the parties in what is termed as an 'efficient breach' situation triggered by opportunism, and hence the more explicit and transparent the terms the clearer a self-enforcing range, the more reputational capital that can be gained or lost in any agreement the more a **flexible** adjustment process will play into consideration, or rather the more elastic the "self-enforcing range" becomes, essentially the contracting parties seek incentive NOT to renege as **"reneging would bias future trade terms against the deviator or even end the relationship... the fundamental economic motivation for the use of contract terms is to supplement self-enforcement. Court enforced explicit terms are a necessary evil that is used by transactors solely because the transactions possess limited reputational capital."**[20]

Hence Klein's "self enforcing range" can be summarised as being where the party's relational payoff (being the relational payoff within the immediate relation and the risk to reputational capital in the wider market place) exceeds the spot market payoff AND the delta is equal to or greater than the party's maximum reneging temptation.

I concur with Klein's view here, that essentially the parties' interests may be aligned by reputational considerations, and that reputational capital is a key consideration, however, it is not the sole consideration, at the core of the relationship is the behaviour of the parties, and the expectations set – at the outset. For example, contracts may well be delivering the expected economic value to both parties, but may still be terminated earlier than expected because the relational expectations are not aligned.[21]

4. Relational Contract Theory through the agreement lifecycle ex ante and ex post

Having summarised the relational norms theory of MacNeil, and how that has been analysed and aggregated by others against certain contract scenarios, I now wish to consider aspects of those norms in the contracting lifecycle, and how they are reflected in the negotiating phase therein. In a typical outsource scenario for example, this could be the scope: – transition, transformation, service commencement/ongoing delivery, dispute management and exit provisions and the overlaying governance to it, and the focal point will be upon MacNeil's implementation of planning norm.

4.1. The Implementation of Planning

Previous submissions to the Proactive Law movement have already focused on this aspect of the contracting cycle[22] and, despite the observations from Diathesopoulos where this particular norm did not score highly (until aggregated under Austen-Bakers 4-norm system), the writer considers this to be one of the key norms in a relational contract when ***setting expectations.*** By reference to IAACM's study, this norm reflects on those terms considered most productive in supporting successful relationships (scope, goals, responsibilities).

By seeking to maximise discreteness/presentiation, Rekola advocates that defining the service product clearly, accurately, concisely and exhaustively through the "Service Design" that this approach provides a preventive contracting approach, effectively this can be seen as **"shifting left"** using the implementation of planning norm. Sitting beside this is the "Service Guideline", which is based on the mission and strategy of the company. Combining the Service Design with the "Service Guideline" provides a "positive and mutually reinforcing cycle", which to some extent provides a practical application of, and reflects the distinction between, the economic and social contracts espoused by Lax and Sebenius (see below). However, Rekola's "Service Guideline" is internal facing, it refers to the company brand and how that company "does things", hence for the writer it does not adequately address the relational aspects, for example, where there may be an obligation on the client to undertake an induction/training session with service provider staff in their culture and strategic goals, and hence how the suppliers operation dovetails with that so there is a clear cultural fit. Indeed, where Rekola refers to the Customer experience and emotional attachment, she underlines the point, ***"…It is often those elements that are deemed unimportant by the developers of industrial services…that actually are the most visible and concrete to the customer. There are no best practice guidelines on how to develop these elements…"*** – Rekola's approach nevertheless offers a good starting point for then generating the "social contract" aspects with the contracting party.

In my opinion, Ertel and Gordon's[23] work reinforces MacNeil's norms based approach generally, notably with regards to that of enhancing discreteness and presentiation through the implementation of planning and effectuation of consent. Their approach is to examine how one transitions from a "deal-maker mentality" to having an ***implementation mind-set, from the outset***, and having the resulting agreement articulate not just the deal shape but how the parties get to the final destination, with the clear view that there is no point to negotiation "victories" if they cannot be subsequently implemented. Identifying some common pitfalls and how to address them, they are all behavioural in approach.[24]

Ertel and Gordon also refer to work done by Lax and Sebenius[25] who suggest that the parties seek to build a "social contract" to supplement the economic contract, going beyond just a good working relationship, they advocate for a social contract that governs the parties expectations about the nature of the venture and the way unforeseen events will be handled.

4.2. The "Social Contract"

Lax and Sebenius, as part of their "3D" approach to negotiating, focus on the social contract as an important aspect that requires serious attention in the negotiating phase of any agreement, such that the design of a deal must ensure that the contracting parties minds have truly met on what is the underlying social contract. Lax and Sebenius start with the "1D" view that many negotiators get trapped in, which is a negotiation based on what they term as the "Zone of Possible Agreement", and this "Battle line" becomes a single dimension of Price. To some extent this has connotations with Klein's self-enforcing range, however Lax and Sebenius expound that their model is focused on unlocking more value out of the deal, hence as the writer sees it, the more elasticity that can be played into the deal design phase, the more the relationship norms can survive and thrive. **Their key message is that a negotiation that leaves both parties feeling they have something they can live with that is one step better than 'no-deal', is not a win-win situation. Current negotiating practice as evidenced by the IACCM suggests parties are in danger of exactly that accusation.**

Lax and Sebenius' view of the social contract focuses on three key aspects:

a. The real nature of the relationship;
b. How the relationship will proceed, i.e. how will decisions be made, unforeseen events managed, communications and dispute management (what might be seen as traditional governance models);
c. That the social contract is complimentary to the economic one and vice versa (or as the writer analogises, biscuits and cheese – different but complimentary, rather than peaches and nectarines – similar, but different).

Their concerns are that in many negotiations on what are highly relational agreements, the underlying social contract is left implicit, and that rather than have serious discussions about the expectations on a business goal and relational level, the parties project their own assumptions, which can lead to dispute and termination downstream, even where the economic facets of the agreement are being successfully delivered.

Under point (a) above, Lax and Sebenius seek to encourage the contracting parties to ask themselves, do they both see the contract as a starting point for a problem-solving relationship (interest based), or do they see it as an end-point (rights based)[26], as entrepreneurial or bureaucratic, as centralised or de centralised, as focused on finance or focused on operations etc.

In seeking to construct deals that last, Lax and Sebenius recommend some points for treatment:

- Watch for discrepancies in the contracting parties views on the social aspects, especially if the deal is being driven by third parties (i.e. it gets done to them);
- Ensure that there are explicit and periodic audits of all sides perceptions;
- Do not see it (the social contract) as being subjective to the economic objective;
- *Acknowledge that a social contract, as with relational contract theory, does not have to be co-operative, democratic and anticipatory. Indeed it may be necessary to be the exact opposite, the point is that the parties understand that and there is a meeting of the minds;*
- Provide incentivisation to stay in the relationship, provided that is the intent of the parties, i.e. do I want a 100% one-off return, or a 30% return recurring over several years, from my investment (the writer has acknowledged that the surrounding economic environment will greatly influence the strategies undertaken by parties, as such the more myopic the environment the less one can plan, and hence taking shorter term returns may be a business goal);
- Anticipate external shocks and their effects on attitudes;
- Consider the overall structure of the agreement, move away from single party single issue domains by purposefully negotiating an expanding web of involvement and dependencies (this may of course also present further risks and contingencies).

4.3. The Contract Structure

Having taken a check on where in the relational spectrum the contracting parties sit, and understanding the best-fit approach should be considered, this may sound obvious but it is important that the parties do not put together for example a structure that reflects a Managed Services agreement, when in fact it is an Outsource or a Systems / Service Integration Agreement, we should now consider the contents of the agreement, and the distinction between the economic contract and the social contract then. Let us first look at the typical ingredients in a "deal-shape":

Traditional View of a Client-Focused Contract Structure

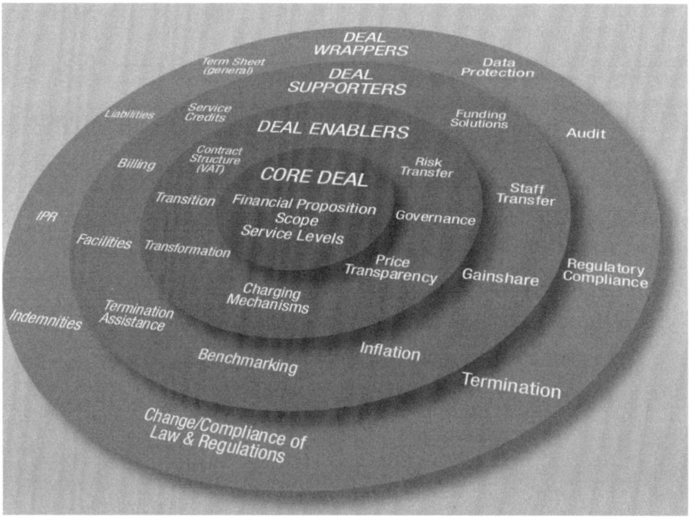

(Reproduced by kind permission of Fujitsu Services Limited. © Copyright Fujitsu Services Limited 2011)

This view at least has scope at the centre of the deal, and all of its constituent elements will cover the deal aspects, however, how might the above be reconstructed when taking a relational contract modelling approach?

Assuming a highly relational contract had been determined, and having regard to the analysis of such a type of agreement by Diathesopoulos observed above, the writer contends that the parties should then utilise the relational norms **across the lifecycle of the contract,** having specific regard to:

- Shifting left through the implementation of planning (getting to the point of the deal); and
- Adopting the approach advocated by Lax and Sebenius in treating two mutually reinforced work-streams of social and economic facets to the Agreement; and
- Considering how parties should address the self-enforcing range of the Agreement

and question how any specific obligation maps through the norms system (as identified above, any specific obligation will be repeated several times).

Austen-Baker's aggregation of MacNeil's norms into a 4-norms system, and tiered based on Diathesopoulos' analysis of management contracts.

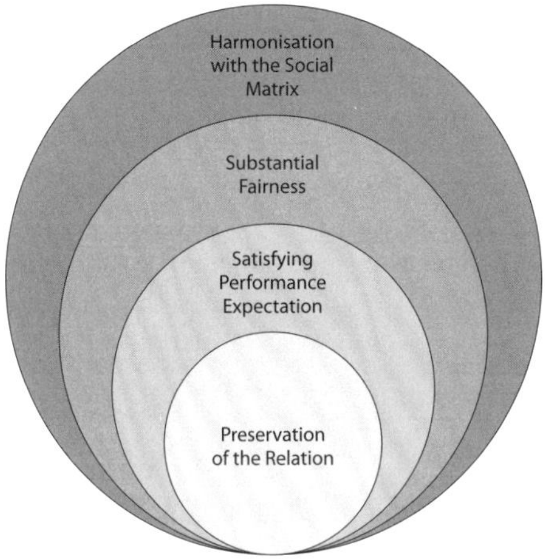

Having regard to each one's contents the parties should analyse each requirement through this spectrum. Take for example Transition, a usual initial component in a highly relational Agreement such as an Outsource.

Typical Outsource Lifecycle

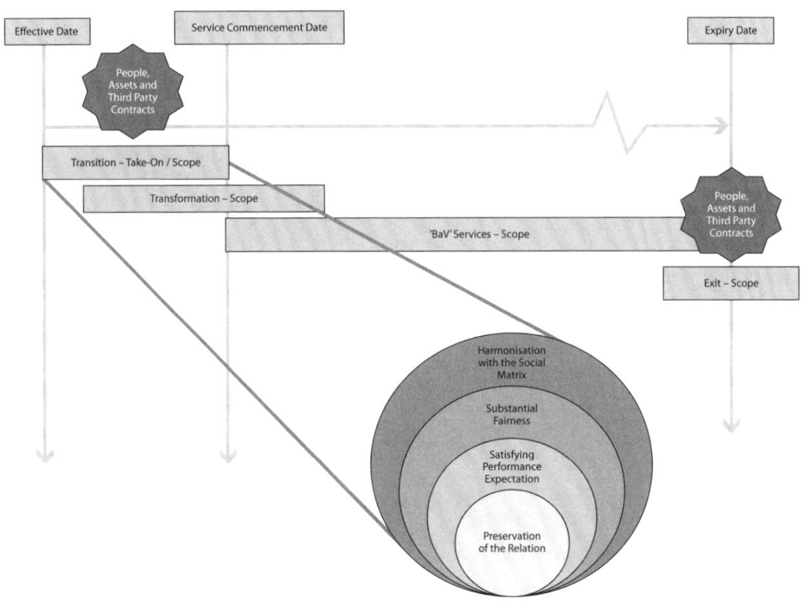

Now we can drill down to analyse the typical component elements of the Transition phase across the relational norms, for example (not exhaustive):

Austen-Baker 4-Norm System:	**SATISFYING PERFORMANCE EXPECTATION**				**PRESERVATION OF THE RELATION**			**HARMONISATION WITH THE SOCIAL MATRIX**		**SUBSTANTIAL FAIRNESS**		
MacNeils' Norms:	Implementation of Planning	Role Integrity	Effectuation of Consent	Creation and Restraint of Power	Contractual Solidarity	Preservation of the Relation	Harmonisation of the Relational Conflict	Harmonisation with the Social Matrix	Supra contract Norms	Reciprocity	Creation and Restraint of Power	Proprietary of Means
Contractors Deliverables	✓											
Customers Deliverables	✓											
Milestone Scope and Dates												
Milestone Criteria Acceptance			✓									
Charges and Payment Terms	✓		✓							✓		
Governance – specific Transition Governance Board						✓	✓					
Assets – Transfer												
Staff – Transfer								✓	✓			
3rd Party Contracts – Novation												

Whilst the above may represent simply a box ticking exercise, the purpose is to illustrate how each stage of the agreement lifecycle is broken down into segments, and to consider each in turn against the norms. Then, in each element, one would consider the "who/what/where/why/

when/ how" to articulate the respective obligations. Take for example an obviously highly relational aspect such as staff transfer as part of an outsource agreement. Whilst under the traditional model illustrated above where one can see "staff-transfer" as a deal supporter, in reality one would expect this subject to be treated:

a. within the core deal of the financial proposition, that staff cost assumptions would be transparent, that the risk allocation at any one point was clear, whether post contract verification against such assumed costs applied, this would be supported by the indemnities given by one party to another; and
b. as part of the on-boarding of in-scope staff in the Transition phase, from knowledge transfer to other staff members to on-boarding in terms of the company culture to which they were transferring to, to contract education; and
c. that both parties would adhere to their regulatory obligations under TUPE law and other regulations such as data protection; and
d. in terms of governance this would engage all disciplines in a typical outsource team – Transition Programme leads, HR advisers, commercial managers, subject matter experts for the relevant roles in scope, hence all of the above would in fact be managed through the governance structure between the parties.

Hence such aspects under norms of behaviour can be seen under all four of Austen Baker's norms system and arguably all of the norms espoused by MacNeil, whether determining obligations for the timing and content of staff transfer under implementation of planning and role integrity that supports that, to adherence to the legal duties to consult under TUPE legislation (supra contract norms and harmonisation with the social matrix).

4.4. Dispute Management – rights-based and interest-based approaches

To refer to Lax and Sebenius, where a deal is seen in a single dimension approach, or is focused on 'just doing the deal' then more sensitive aspects of the management of the ongoing relationship can be if not totally ignored then "boiler plated" and also one dimensional by referring to static hierarchical structures of each parties organisations. Macauley has asked the question "Perhaps the law could impose a duty to renegotiate as part of the duty of performing in good faith?"[27], and within England and Wales the Lord Justice Woolf reforms have gained traction in this direction[28]. Expounding on that paper, the authors Gould, King and Britton comment on standard form contracting in the construction industry and refer to the NEC3 set as including a partnering option and PPC2000 providing a contractual "team" framework to encourage collaboration, between employer, designers, main and key sub-contractors, from early conceptual design stages of a project onward. The authors summarise that the literature repetitively suggests two specific aims:

1. Make carefully considered dispute avoidance mechanisms part of the contractual matrix (between the parties);
2. Choose formal dispute resolution and the personnel to operate them that have a "best fit" to the circumstances.

Supporting this view, work carried out by Lumineau and Malhotra[29] against 102 business disputes in analysing when and how contracts (referring to the rights based and interest based approaches – and acknowledging that these are not mutually exclusive) will be effective in reducing costs associated with inter-firm conflicts and whether they prevent conflicts. Their analysis suggests that the effect of contract choice on dispute resolution approach is moderated by the degree of co-ordination required by the relationship, that the effect of dispute approach is moderated by power asymmetry and the choice of contract structure has important strategic implications.

Clearly then as part of the proactive law agenda within the context of this paper for relational contract modelling, following through on all aspects of the chronology of the agreement means ensuring that the more sensitive areas of the ongoing relation are appropriately addressed by both parties, such that the principles advocated by the EESC Opinion Paper continue to flow down within the agreement (subsidiarity, proportionality, precaution and sustainability).

5. Conclusions - drawing up the Relational Framework

This paper has considered a number of existing fields of study, which the writer contends are complimentary to each other, and attempted to draw their salient elements pertaining to relational contracts together into a framework, which might serve to guide contracting professionals in architecting agreements that will best meet the strategic objectives of the parties, sustain the intended purpose, and deliver more value.

- Consider where in the relational spectrum the contracting parties sit when determining the overall contract structure;
- Analyse the relational norms, and consider which ones require treatment across the chronology of the Agreement (the Service Journey), and treat accordingly, having regard to best practice in deal behaviour (the point of the deal);
- Seek to "shift left" relational contracts. That is to say, all parties need to ensure presentiation and discreteness of agreements as far as is possible, without constraining the horizon;
- Seek to create two mutually reinforcing streams between the economic and the social contract, again having regard to the chronology of the Agreement (e.g. governance aspects changing to reflect different staff, skills at different junctures of the journey);
- Seek to ensure that the (healthy) tension on the level of flexibility in any Agreement is fully understood by all parties having regard to the behavioural expectations and the "self-enforcing range" – This will challenge laggards in the marketplace. The extent of flexibility in a contract will depend upon two key aspects – the amount of reputational capital, and the clarity between on the parties on expectation of behaviour, seek to externalise these aspects into the contract.

In its Opinion Paper on the proactive law approach, the EESC "*...calls for a paradigm shift...a focus on how the law is used and operates in everyday life...involving stakeholders...aligning objectives...a shared vision....and successful implementation*". I believe that the framework analysis in this paper provokes further thoughts to answer to this call, upon which the writer shall further develop proposed solution, and I close by referring to Macauley;

> "If one reads Ian Macneil's work on relational contract…one finds *a list of factors to consider in making a judgment rather than neat answers.* This leaves us uncertain about the judgment in a particular case. Uncertainty has its costs, but so do certain and precise rules that defeat actual expectations and reasonable reliance."[30]

Next Steps…This paper is titled "Great Expectations Part 1", to underline the relational aspects of contracting but also as an initial shaping paper that suggests a framework for further analysis. Indeed each element could in its own right become a detailed study. Further work is therefore required in analysing in more depth how relational contract theory can be progressed into a pragmatic and proactive management tool for developing relational contracts. Such analysis will attempt to draw upon case-law, current thinking in the industry and further research into the norms based approach.

References

1. MacNeil's major works on relational contract theory are cited in the bibliography, see also Wikipedia, also Campbell, D. "Ian MacNeil and the Relational Theory of Contract" CDAMS Discussion Paper 04/1E March 2004 and "The Relational Theory of Contract: Selected Works of Ian MacNeil" Sweet & Maxwell, 200.'
2. See bib. Below, for example Diathesopoulos 'First Approaches Towards Relational Contracts'
3. See bib. below, for example Austen-Baker
4. See bib. below for Klein's article on the self-enforcing range of contracts
5. See Lax and Sebenius' '3D Negotiating' in bib. below.
6. See Ertel and Gordon, 'The Point of the Deal' in bib. below.
7. Mouzas and Blois
8. The Trouble with Outsourcing, The Economist http://www.economist.com/node/21524822 Schumpeter July 30th 2011, which refers to a 60% decrease in the last year in 'mega deals'.
9. An increase of 30% in new claims since 2008 is a general view, albeit within a specific Court such as Technology and Construction, in fact the vast majority of cases are related to the Construction industry, whereas IT related claims have been static. This indicates that how separate industries approach contracting, including relational matters and dispute resolution, is an important factor for consideration, and could also be compared to industries relative resistance to economic peaks and troughs. See also SCL article at http://www.scl.org/site.aspx?i=ne22911, where at a meeting for the Society for Computers and Law Vivian Ramsey Head of the TCC calls for a 'clear framework, and flexible horizon'.
10. See Hart, O in Bib.
11. See EESC Opinion Paper in Bib.
12. MacNeil, Restatement of Contracts, 595.
13. Diathesopoulos – it should be noted that each analysis of contracts using the norms system will be subjective, however the writer is contending that the approach should be used by both parties as a means for better grounding of the parties expectations in any agreement, hence such subjectivity is externalised.
14. Diathesopoulos – see Bib.
15. Mouzas and Blois – see Bib.
16. Klein, "Transaction cost determinants of 'unfair' contractual arrangements' The American Economic Review Vol.70 No.2 May 1980, p356.
17. See Mouzas and Blois article in bib.
18. Klein see above.
19. Further work will be undertaken beyond the scope of this paper by the writer in assessing the extent to which disputes are not essentially being driven by a

breach of the 'self-enforcing range'. See for example Lax and Sebenius' reference to the failed merger between Deutschebank & Dresdner (see 3D Negotiating p165)

20. See for example in Katri Rekola's paper for service design as a basis for successful commercial contracting
21. Ertel and Gordon's work on effective negotiating 'The Point of the Deal' and correcting the 'deal maker' mentality when based on 'doing the deal'
22. Ertel and Gordon in identifying common pitfalls, call out:
    - Creating a 'deal department'
    - Relying on third parties to do your deals usually means you end up with their deal, not yours
    - Using deal-making metrics for measuring success
    - Allow negotiators to 'protect the deal' and 'close early and often'
    - Many negotiators believe that they must deploy tactics to push the counterpart to agreement as efficiently as possible (close fast) which may actually limit the value the deal could ultimately deliver, also that disclosing information can make the negotiator weaker, and that therefore it is up to the other side to do their due diligence and discover whatever information they need in order to proceed (or not).
    - And therefore they suggest...
    - The real purpose of a negotiation is not to sign a deal, but to accomplish something! So treat it as integral to the implementation of the deal
    - Make sure all stakeholders are aligned, consulted, early and often.
    - Recognise the way you deal with each other in a negotiation will impact how you work together in implementation.
    - Confront the hard issues, not repressing them to 'sign the deal' – table concerns openly and honestly, having regard to the costs and benefits of putting the 'nightmares' on the table
    - Ensure joint understanding
    - Disclose information as early as possible (minimise information asymmetry)
23. See Lax and Sebenius' work on "3D Negotiation" (see bib.)
24. Understanding this nature of the relationship feeds into other works, such as Jennejohn's work on 'collaboration, innovation and contract design', whereby he presents contract design as a learning process through its lifecycle.
25. See Macauley 2007 Wisconsin law school paper (see bib.).
26. See "Mediating Construction Disputes" (2010) by Kings College London (see bib.).
27. See Lumineau and Malhotra article in bib.
28. See Macauley 2007 Wisonsin law school paper (see bib.)
29. See Lumineau and Malhotra article in bib.
30. See Macauley 2007 Wisonsin law school paper (see bib.)

Bibliography

MacNeil:

"Restatement of Contracts and Presentiation" (1974) 60 Virginia Law Review 589

"The Many Futures of Contract" (1974) 47 S. California Law Review, 691

"Contracts: Adjustment of Long Term Economic Relations..." (1978) 72 Northwestern University Law Review" 854

"The New Social Contract"

Opinion of the European Economic and Social Committee on "The proactive law approach: a further step towards better regulation at EU level" (2009/C 175/05)

Austen-Baker, R. "Comprehensive Contract Theory: A Four Norm Model of Contract Relations" (2009) 25 Journal of Contract Law 216-243

Austen-Baker, R. "A Relational Law of Contract?" (2004) 20 Journal of Contract Law 125-144

Rekola, K. Service Design as a Basis for Successful Contracting, Proactive Law Conference paper.

Diathesopoulos, First Approaches towards Relational Contracts,

Diathesopoulos, M. Cambridge University, June 2010. "Relational Contract Theory and Management Contracts – A Paradigm for the Application of the Theory of the Norms" http://mpra.ub.uni-munchen.de/24028/ MPRA Paper #24028

Jennejohn, Matthew C, June 2007, "Collaboration, innovation and Contract design" Working Paper 379 Centre for Law and Economic Studies Columbia University NY http://papers.ssrn.com/paper.taf?abstract_id=1014420

Hart, O. (1995) Firms, Contracts and Financial Structure 23

Adar and Gelbard, 2009, "The role of remedies in the relational theory of contract – a preliminary enquiry" http://ssrn.com/abstract=1416750

Klein, "Why Hold-Ups Occur: The Self Enforcing Range of Contractual Relationships" (1996) 34 Economic Inquiry, 444-463

Sebenius and Lax "3D Negotiation", Harvard Business School Press, 2006

Ertel and Gordon "The Point of the Deal" Harvard Business School Press, 2007

Kings College London, Centre of Construction Law and Dispute Resolution, Gould, King and Britton, 2010 "Mediating Construction Disputes" (2010)

Mouzas and Blois, University of Lancaster, Relational Contract Theory: Confirmations and Contradictions (2007)

Blois and Ivens, "Measuring Relational Norms – some methodological issues" (2006) Emerald Group Publishing

Mitchell, C. 2009, Oxford Journal of Legal Studies 675, "Contracts and Contract Law: Challenging the

Distinction Between the 'Real' and 'Paper' Deal"

Glasspiegel M, "Pricing the outsourcing deal: financial drivers for outsourcing contracts" The Outsourcing Revolution 2005 p 431

Lumineau and Malhotra, "Shadow of the Contract – How Contract structure Shapes Inter-Firm Dispute Resolution", Strategic Management Journal, 32(5) 532-555

Macauley, "Renegotiations and Settlements: Dr. Pangloss' Notes on the Margins of David Campbell's Papers", Legal Studies Research Paper Series Paper #1045, May 2007, University of Wisonsin Law School.

International Association of Commercial Contract Management "2011 Top Terms in Negotiation" study paper.

Appendix A

Summary of MacNeil's Relational Norms, extracted and summarised from Diathesopoulos paper "First Approaches towards Relational Contracts":

Norm	Summary Explanation
Role Integrity	Anticipation standards, about what each party are going to do, and **HOW** they are going to fulfil their obligations. This is more than the Implementation of Planning norm, because it is focused on the other Parties **behaviour** being a platform for developing and continuing every relation.
Reciprocity	More than mere consideration in a legal sense and as a measurable provision, but having regard to the adequacy of one's overall behaviour in providing and earning benefits back.
Implementation of Planning	A 'shift-left' continuum on the relational axis, it is critical to maximise the extent to which obligations within the full lifecycle of both the economic and social contract can be pre-defined, without then strangling the ability to flex.
Effectuation of consent	MacNeil refers to this norm as the consent to future actions which are determined by the rules of the ongoing relation, it is essentially that all parties have clarity on the ethos and approaches and the strategic objectives of the parties, not just on the delivery of the economic benefits expected.
Flexibility	Flexibility is ultimately determined by the parties actions, their planning and behaviour, within the relation. A pre-requisite for all other norms
Contractual solidarity	Being a norm of contractual law, i.e. as an enforcement and hence providing a pre-emptive legal mechanism which serves to shape our behaviour
Creation and restraint of power	Ex ante and ex post creation of obligations and the subsequent restraint of exercising that power by one party in favour of the other, having regard to the relational aspects, seen in the overall co-operative context which may impose non-contractual limits on our behaviour.
Proprietary of means	Certain behavioural patterns will be adopted depending upon the specifics of each relation and the wider social context, such as e.g. specific industry norms. This can be observed in the relational contracting approach in the construction industry.
Harmonisation in the social matrix	Effectively MacNeil refers to the relational aspects of the exchange being integrated with everything else that is required in order that the exchange may occur.

MacNeil's 'linking norms' of Restitution, Reliance and Expectation are not covered here, although they are important for MacNeil's theory as being necessary for adjusting the relationship ex post.

Pre-Contractual Mediation in Negotiation – Transplanting Techniques from Mediation and Introducing a Neutral Contract Facilitator

By

Camilla Baasch Andersen
Senior Lecturer (University of Leicester)
Cand.jur., Ph.D.

1. Introduction

As a new recruit into the ranks of the believers in pro-active law, I am perhaps more prone to commit some of the rookie-mistake of the fresh convert, which – it must be noted – are borne of enthusiasm. Two such potential rookie-mistakes especially spring to mind concerning the present paper.

The first may well be an over-enthusiastic re-invention of the wheel, as I discover aspects of this new psychology of contract management that others may have known for aeons, but which are new and exciting to me. Getting carried away is a given for the fresh convert.

The second error will undoubtedly be the fact that in this re-invention I may not be utilising the right schematics. As I familiarise myself with this (for me) new way of considering the role of law, I may not be employing the right taxonomy, the right and recognized perspectives or the acknowledged sources. Hopefully, in time, this problem will evaporate – for now I fear it must be tolerated.

The present paper attempts to make two points which I believe to be innovative:

a. that there are techniques from the established theories of mediation which can be transplanted into pro-active pre-contractual negotiation, and
b. that mediation and mediators do not just belong in resolution of disputes, but have a potential place in pro-active contract negotiation by introducing neutral contract facilitation.

In doing so, this paper first examines the role of mediation as a more amicable and pro-active dispute resolution mechanism today, and then explores the utility of these techniques in other areas of law in the name of "pro-activity". In doing so, the paper analyses three case studies where a mediating entity was in the right place at the right time to facilitate negotiations or re-negotiations.

Ultimately, it is posited that the use of such a neutral contract facilitator should not be hinged on the chance of someone being in the right place at the right time, but can be organised through the deliberate use of such contract facilitators in negotiation. The paper will conclude with some thoughts on how this may be achieved.

2. Mediation Today

> ***"...it is no longer possible to regard curial methods of resolving disputes, notably mediation, as insignificant appendages..."***[1]

Mediation is sometimes referred to as the "handmaiden of settlement",[2] and settlement is an unavoidable part of all dispute resolution now. The time of conflict-driven law is waning – and the time of compromises and understanding (should be!) dawning. For instance, pre-litigation protocols in the UK now require some form of evidence of attempts to secure agreement through bargaining and settlement. Even after litigation has commenced, a Court will not only stay its proceedings, it will bend over

1. extraMediation in England-- an overview by Neil Andrews available at http://www.dike.fr/IMG/pdf/Mediation_in_England_by_N_1_._H._Andrews_Cambridge_.pdf.
2. Neil Andrews' *"Modern Civil Process"* p. 216, (Mohr Siebeck 2008).

backwards to encourage it, to the extent that Courts in most Common Law jurisdictions (like England, Australia and most US state courts) can incur costs on a party unreasonably rejecting attempts at mediation. In Civil Law countries, a more diverse picture is painted – but in Italy, mediation has recently become a compulsory avenue to pursue before traditional litigation. In his "Access to Justice, Interim Report (1995)" in Chapter 7, para 7(a) Lord Woolf refers to the fact that "the philosophy of litigation should be primarily to encourage early settlement of disputes…" and supports all settlement through mediation as a necessary recourse to be pursued. This is a great victory for a more amicable role of law in settling disputes post-conflict.

Mediation has also become less stigmatized; where before it was perceived as a weakness, its (cheap and amicable) advantages have won most commercial practitioners over,[3] and it is now safe to say that mediation clauses are common in commercial agreements.

Due to this phenomenal rise in the popularity of mediation, and the awareness of its potential to solve issues once they arise, a multitude of theories, books and disciplines have arisen around it. One of the most comprehensive sources of these is Hans Boserup and his "Six Ways in Seven Days",[4] which compares and outlines the variety of styles in mediation in a novel way. Boserup lists an astounding array of schools of mediation, and says there are many more. He refers to Generic Mediation; Peer Mediation; Systemic Mediation & Cognitive-Systemic Mediation; Narrative Mediation; Humanistic Mediation; Transformative Mediation; Settlement-Driven Mediation; Mediation through Understanding … the list goes on with tools that help parties to see eye to eye in reaching agreement once a dispute has arisen.

But – sadly for proactive law as a whole – mediation and its impressive arrays of negotiation techniques remains fairly firmly entrenched on the dispute resolution side. Mediation retains the wisdom and psychology it has developed for gluing the egg back together once a dispute has arisen, rather than contributing to preventing the egg from breaking in the first place. Especially in the light of the extent to which pro-active

3. *IDIBEM,* p. 217.
4. Hans Boserup *"Mediation: Six ways in seven days : special part of the mediation pro-cess"*, DJOEF Publishing 2007.

law relies on Louis Brown's ideals of preventive law, it is folly to disagree with the basic notion that it is cheaper to stop something from breaking that to try to fix it – however amicably. So it would be a shame if the wealth of mediation techniques could not be used to improve contract negotiation to prevent the proverbial egg from breaking in the first place.

It is my submission that many of the techniques developed for mediation in dispute resolution can be used at the negotiation stage in planning and achieving contracts. In other words – to use the taxonomy of the "bible" of proactive law – mediation too, can play an even greater role in supporting proactive law in the 4th step of the Managers Legal Plan™.[5] We can move it from step 2; borrow techniques from mediation and transplant them into negotiation stage of contracts, where we plan contracts "from the balcony".

3. Centrality of Neutrality

Georg Simmel, the pre-eminent sociologist, identified the need for neutrality in mediation thus as early as 1908:

> *"The non-partisanship that is required for mediation has one of two presuppositions. The third element [the mediator] is non-partisan either if he stands above the contrasting interests and opinions and is actually not concerned with them, or if he is equally concerned with both."*[6]

In a modern commercial context, the latter is a rarity. Case study C below will explore an example, but usually we assume the former. A mediator's role is thus to ensure a calmer (swifter & cheaper) settlement of a dispute from a neutral perspective. At the negotiation stage, a mediator could use this neutrality to help formation, by aid in giving insight into special circumstances, mediating between cultural differences, easing communication where it has broken down, and also by proposing innovative

5. The Managers Legal Plan is designed by Helena Haapio and George Seidel, explained in *"Proactive Law for Managers"* esp. Chapter one.
6. G Simmel, *The Sociology of Georg Simmel,* edited by K. Wolf (1950, originally 1908) Free Press Glencoe Illinois, p. 149.

alternative solutions which more entrenched partisan representatives may not have considered. Neutrality is key for many of these functions, as it is often a question of trust and perceived non-partiality.

The centrality of neutrality in the mediation process stands out if we attempt to compare some of the key traits of traditional negotiation, with those of mediation. The schedule below outlines some of the main differences between classic negotiation techniques.

3.1. Negotiation v Mediation

Typical traits of Negotiation:

- Interest based, goal-driven on partisan interests
- Biggest lie maintained in Commercial Law: Equality of bargaining power…
- Partisan ideology of: "Getting to YES" and "Getting past NO"
- "Deal-breaker" immobility causes entrenchment
- Compromises not perceived as a strength, but as giving in to the other side

Typical traits of Mediation:

- Neutral Mediator
- Equality guaranteed
- Goal is to reach <u>an</u> agreement, by rethinking the possibilities
- Ideology of "seeing eye to eye" and promoting mutual understanding (helps eliminate deal-breakers)
- Compromises are strengths because they evidence recognition and understanding of the other party and a step towards agreement

One glance at the above demonstrates the most significant difference, namely the neutral approach, the essence of the success of mediation, as explained above. The central role that neutrality plays is seen in the strength of establishing trust, being non-partisan, and thinking outside the box to reach a mutually amicable agreement. This essential neutrality can be transplanted into the negotiation stage of contracts in different ways, and there are numerous potential benefits to be had in transplanting or transferring this neutral philosophy of mediation into earlier stages of the contract – notably the negotiation phase.

As mentioned in the introduction, this can happen in two basic ways: First and foremost, by transplanting the idea of a neutral entity – a mediator of contract formation and negotiation, labelled a "neutral contract facilitator" in the following. This is dealt with in section 5 and a number of case studies are offered as examples of where such a mediator has been in the right place at the right time.

However, even without a decidedly neutral facilitator, some of the techniques of mediation can benefit more "partisan" negotiators if they put aside their partisan stance. This is not news – the secret of "getting to YES" and "getting past NO" for a successful contract negotiator has long been a more flexible approach. But by removing the focus from the Agreement Itself and placing it on the enabling and empowerment of the parties, a greater flexibility may be had. This is one example of how mediation techniques may be helpful in facilitating negotiation; namely by employing tricks from transformative mediation. This is outlined below.

4. Transferring Neutral Techniques

As early as 1987, Lord Donaldson referred to mediation as "...in the public interest" since it enabled parties to "appreciate the true strengths and weaknesses of their positions at the earliest possible moment."[7]

Appreciating each other's strengths and weaknesses is at the heart of good negotiation as well. And in following this logic, the "earliest possible moment" is before a conflict arises. But is it feasible to transplant mediation techniques from dispute resolution to a negotiation stage? The answer is some, but not all, and it is purely a question of rethinking the way we negotiate, plan and manage contracts.

While section 5 below will argue that the introduction of a "Neutral Contract Facilitator" can benefit negotiation in some cases, it is still possible to bring some of the neutrality of the mediation techniques to the negotiating table, even without such a neutral entity.

7. Court of Appeals (1987) *Naylor v Preston Area Health Authority*, 1 WLR 958, 967-8.

Some techniques, which can be successfully employed, include the following:

- Cognitive Systemic
- Microdynamics & psychology
- Generic mediation in accessing cultural understanding
- Improvised mediation, intuitive mediation: What ever else works!

However, the mediation technique I have chosen to isolate in proving the point about transplantation from mediation to negotiation is transformative mediation, for the simple reason that it conveys many points about neutrality and transforming basic negotiation attitudes well.

4.1. Transformative Mediation – One Example of a Technique Transposed

A good way to illustrate the transposition of techniques is to examine "transformative mediation". Although the term "transformative mediation" has roots that go back to the 1970s, the prevalent understanding of the term today is defined by Bush and Folger.[8] Essentially, transformative mediation is a contrast to problem-solving mediation, because it does not primarily focus on arriving to a solution to the problem or conflict at hand, but rather focuses on "recognition" and "empowerment" of the parties. This may sound counter-intuitive, but the main idea is that through this empowerment and recognition of the parties, a solution – which might not otherwise be visible – will present itself. "Empowerment", according to Bush and Folger, means enabling the parties to define their own issues and to seek solutions on their own problems and issues, avoiding mediator directiveness where possible. "Recognition" represents the ability of parties to see and understand the other parties' perspective; understand how they define the problem and why they seek the solution that they do (without necessarily agreeing with those views). Transformative mediation will thus foster the parties' ability to approach their current problem, as well as any later issues, with confidence and a better understanding of their respective needs

8. R. Baruch Bush, J.P. Folger *The promise of mediation: the transformative approach to conflict*, John Wiley & Sons, 2005.

and perspectives, thus keeping their options for alternative approaches and solutions open.

Some of this is immediately attractive in a negotiation situation. If the parties are negotiating a contract by respective representatives, then empowerment may seem a given. But considering the age-old LIE of equality of bargaining power, this is not always so. Imagine a small computer hardware company in negotiations with Microsoft… Is there a true equality of bargaining power?

In dispute resolution, Folger and Busch argue that there are ten "Hallmarks" of achieving transformative mediation.[9] These can be adapted to suit the relevant situation in achieving recognition and enforcement in settling disputes, and some of these may also be employed – either by a neutral contract facilitator or by the parties themselves – in trying to achieve recognition.

Transformative Mediation:

1. In the opening statement, the transformative mediator will explain the mediator's role and the objectives of mediation as being focused on empowerment and recognition.
2. The transformative mediator will leave responsibility for the outcomes with the parties.
3. A transformative mediator will not be judgmental about the parties' views and decisions.
4. Transformative mediators take an optimistic view of the parties' competence and motives.
5. Transformative mediators allow and are responsive to parties' expression of emotions.
6. Transformative mediators allow for and explores parties' uncertainty.
7. Transformative mediators remain focused on what is currently happening in the mediation setting.
8. Transformative mediators are responsive to parties' statements about past events.

9. R. Baruch Bush, J. P. Folger *"Transformative Mediation and Third-Party Intervention: Ten Hallmarks of a Transformative Approach to Practice"* Mediation Quarterly Volume 13, Number 4 (1996).

9. Transformative mediators realize that conflict can be a long-term process and that mediation is one intervention in a longer sequence of conflict interactions.
10. Transformative mediators feel (and express) a sense of success when empowerment and recognition occur, even in small degrees. They do not see a lack of settlement as a "failure."

Some (while not all) of these techniques can be successfully superimposed on difficult negotiations. I imagine these Hallmarks transposed thus:

Transformative Negotiation:

1. At the opening of the negotiations, the respective negotiators will explain how they perceive their own roles, and the role of the other representative, and recognize the goal of achieving mutual empowerment and recognition.
2. Negotiators will endeavour not to judge decisions and ideas which may be perceived as obstructive to a mutual agreement, but instead to inquire into the motivation behind it.
3. Negotiators promise to take an optimistic view of all parties' competence and motives.
4. Negotiators endeavour to remain attuned to expressions of emotions relevant to the negotiations: frustration, anger, optimism – these are important indicators.
5. Negotiators explore any uncertainties and allow for alternative approaches.
6. Negotiators focus on what is currently happening in the mediation setting.
7. Negotiators are responsive to parties' statements about past events and respect the experiences of both parties.
8. Negotiators feel (and express) a sense of success when empowerment and recognition occur, even in small degrees. They do not see a lack of agreement as a "failure" as long as an important step has been taken in understanding what currently hinders agreement.
9. Negotiators realize that difficult negotiations can take a long time to settle, but that the key to a mutually successful contract is a mutual understanding.

10. Negotiators try not to make assumptions about any meanings or goals, but explore and clarify all aspects of a contract.

This may seem like a lot of trouble to go to for negotiation of a contract. But sometimes, a difficult negotiation is worth the effort to ensure an egg that will not break. It is worth remembering that the vast majority of disputes between commercial parties occur where there are misunderstandings or mistaken assumptions about the actual intention of a specific aspect of a contract. Working hard to ensure actual understanding – and avoiding false assumptions of understanding – is thus often worth the effort.

It may be challenging to impose this sort of empathetic negotiation on a negotiator who is given a range of values within which to seek a successfully formed contract. Thinking "outside the box" to reach an alternative agreement can be particularly difficult when acting on a specific mandate. Empowering the negotiator is therefore the first important step. But it can also be helpful to introduce a neutral contract facilitator to ensure minimal partisan attitudes, ease trust, and introduce a fresh perspective on the possibilities available to the parties.

5. Transferring a Neutral Entity – The Neutral Contract Facilitator

In negotiation, a neutral facilitator can help in cases where negotiations are particularly difficult. While this may represent an additional expense, which will need justification in the eyes of a commercially viable party, the additional expense may be worth entertaining in cases where:

- Negotiations have broken down due to a "deal breaker" clause, but there is a general willingness to pursue this further.
- Negotiation is difficult due to cultural differences.
- One or both sides is perceived as "difficult".

Each of these three situations will be explored further in this section, illustrated by three case studies. Each of these case studies has occurred in situations where an individual with mediation experience happens to be present ("right place right time") entirely by coincidence. To the best of my knowledge, no mediation or arbitration institutions offer such a service. Inquiries have been made with selected larger ADR institutions, who do not offer this service, but would consider it if there were an interest. This will be revisited in the conclusion.

Case Study A – The Deal Breaker

Case study A demonstrates the problem of assuming equality in bargaining power in contract negotiations, and the usefulness of a more careful understanding and empowerment of each party.

A large US corporation is refusing to continue negotiations with a small German company: they insists on their boilerplate US dispute resolution clause. The smaller German company is unwilling to potentially litigate in the US as they fear potential court costs. Negotiations are brought to a halt by the US corporation as they label this a "deal breaker". The German negotiator takes offence at this immobility and intimating breach of pre-contractual liability, as negotiations are taking place on German soil, threatens suit. A mediator is initially introduced by the US Corporation to salvage and settle the issue of pre-contractual liability (which has taken the US corporation somewhat by surprise, being unfamiliar with such a notion). However, after meeting both parties, and understanding what prompted the breakdown in negotiation, the mediator senses that both parties are still inherently interested in pursuing the contract. The mediator then interferes directly in the negotiations, acting as a neutral contract facilitator, calculating the risk-assessment for the German firm, and manages to convince them that risk of actual litigation is very small. Additionally, the mediator gets the US Corporation to agree to cover the (minimal) cost of US legal claim insurance, as a sign of goodwill if the German firm agrees to the US dispute resolution clause. The German firm is thus convinced that US litigation is a small and surmountable liability, and that it is not a "trick" from the giant US Corporation. The contract is thus concluded – a surprising solution to the pre-contractual negotiation mediation, but one which would bear years of mutually beneficial commercial enterprise.

Not only does this case study emphasize the importance of risk calculation and compromise – but it underlines a neutral contract facilitators potential for rethinking parties positions, even in a situation where parties were ready for settlement and had abandoned the pursuit of a contract.

Case study B – Culture Shock

Where Case Study A was a triumph for careful diplomacy and pursuit of alternative methods for removing fear of uncertainty, case study B is a triumph for comparative law and cross-cultural understanding. Both demonstrate the value of knowing the motivation of the other party better than what is apparent on the surface or what can be assumed.

Again, the case hinges on a mediator being in the right place at the right time, this time brought in specifically to salvage negotiations but consulted by one party solely for multi-cultural understanding.

A large Japanese exporter of goods enters into negotiations with a small and newly established UK importer of goods. Both would benefit greatly financially from the deal, but the Japanese exporter is very hesitant and clearly stalls negotiations constantly. The UK company has no idea why, and turns to an expert in comparative law (who also happens to be a mediator) for help with these difficult negotiations.

The problem is clear to the mediator, who has some experience with the Japanese market. The small UK firm is entirely unknown in Asia and the honour-bound system of (1990's) Japanese contracting, where litigation is rare and honour and trust is a bankable commodity, cannot easily accommodate such an unknown foreign company. Despite the lure of profits, the Japanese exporter is thus very unwilling to negotiate, but unhappy to disclose this as real reason. It would not be polite to require references. The mediator takes steps to provide references from other firms outside Asia, with which the Japanese exporter has done business, and provides them unsolicited. Negotiations may then proceed. A lucrative contract is concluded, and the UK company is subsequently used to provide "references" for other importers to other Japanese firms.

The author is given to understand that this practice of establishing trust by references from trusted business-partners is diminishing in Japan. But it was, at the time, easy to see why a European firm in the 1990's could not conceive of this necessity references, and was frustrated by the inability of the Japanese exporter to voice this need.

This demonstrates the need for expert insight into the *real reason* behind negotiation issues. In mediation, this might be categorised as "Mediation through Understanding",[10] which is also transformative. But it primarily highlights some of the difficulties faced by those negotiationg cross-culturally. Assumptions about approaches and requisites can be dangerous. It may well be true that business is slowly merging its approaches across the globe, but we are not yet the "Global Village" that keen comparative uniformists would have us think, and there are still pit-falls for the unwary negotiator. Cross-cultural understanding is a difficult pre-requisite for in-house counsel, and a neutral expert will have insight into issues that may not even be anticipated otherwise.

Case Study C: Entrenchment

This final example of a neutral contract facilitator is yet another case where a mediator happened to be in the right time at the right place to salvage a contract.

In this example, a large UK heath club was running childcare facilities on ground owned by a large University. On negotiation of renewal of the lease, the University notes that proper planning has not been changed to run the facility legally. An (admittedly unpleasantly curt) letter is sent. As a reaction to this letter, there is a knee-jerk reaction from the Central UK Office of the health club: they elect to close the facility to avoid bad publicity and a fine, and to be able to maintain the health club on the grounds as a whole. In other words: they entrench defensively against the University's strong position by taking drastic measures. A letter is sent to parents informing them that the university will not permit the child care facility to continue. The university hears of this letter, as some parents are (angry) university employees. The University takes great offence at the allegation that they sought the closure of the child care facility, and are angered by potential press-reaction, and they entrench themselves in a defensive position of discrediting the reason for the closure. Neither party takes any step to negotiating a compromise which will allow the facility to continue.

10. Most notably known from Gary J. Friedman, Jack Himmelstein, & Robert Mnookin: " *Saving the Last Dance: Mediation through Understanding*" DVD from Harvard Programme of Negotiation (2001) available at: http://www.pon.harvard.edu/shop/saving-the-last-dance. In book form see Friedman & Himmelstein "*Challenging Conflict: Mediation Through Understanding*" ABA Publishing (2009).

A parent takes action, mediating between the University and the Health Club, to suggest various means by which the child care facility can continue. After a few days of diplomacy, and a hefty dose of recognition and empowerment to enable both sides to understand the reactions of the other, new terms are renegotiated, allowing retroactive planning to be permitted, and a renegotiated contract can be formed. Childcare facility continues (many parents relieved!) and the lease is renegotiated.

Case Study C illustrates the importance of communication and a non-partisan mediator to ease communication once parties become entrenched. It provides an unusual situation where the mediator has a vested interest. But the interest is NOT partisan – it is merely an interest in seeing the contract succeed. So, returning to the quote from Louis Brown on neutrality in Section 3 above, it is a party whose neutrality is expressed by having an equal interest in each side of the negotiations.

Case study C was particularly difficult to negotiate, as the psychology of the involved parties had caused them to entrench themselves defensively, even though such defensiveness was not actually called for. Micro-dynamics and recognition was essential. In Case Study A, where parties were in nearing actual dispute, there was still a mutual interest in pursuing the contract. But in this case, entrenchment and defensiveness made constructive pursuits very difficult. It can be categorised as an example of "settlement driven mediation", in the context of ensuring a contract is formed, but using "narrative mediation" styles to achieve understanding and empowerment of both parties,[11] by offering an opportunity to map the problem and the reasons for the mutual reactions, and then encouraging parties to understand their respective reactions sufficiently to see the bigger picture and appreciate that a mutual understanding (and thus a successfully renegotiated contract) is still possible. This can perhaps be described as a sort of cognitive behavioural therapy for contract negotiation... but perhaps that is stretching the psychological metaphors a tad.

11. Winslade and Monk, *"Narrative Mediation – A New Approach to Conflict Resolution"* Jossey-Bass Publishing, (February 2000).

6. Conclusion: Future of Mediation in Negotiation?

As explained in the introduction, these methods and techniques may well seem excessive for some negotiations, and will solely be useful for the more problematic where specific issues arise. But it is clear that any form of neutrality can be relied upon to present trustworthy alternatives, and that it can help ease communication and mutual understanding.

The "neutral contract facilitator" may seem an unnecessary and far-fetched idea in some negotiation contexts. However, in the above examples it is an undeniable fact that these contracts would not have been completed without the incidental involvement of a mediator who was in the right place at the right time. And in other difficult negotiations, it may be worth pursuing that that mediator can assist in negotiations other than merely by coincidence.

The shared additional expense can be worthwhile if the contract is worth pursuing. Alternatively, one neutral facilitator may also be shared between two negotiating parties instead of two partisan negotiators, reducing costs. So the neutral facilitator needs to be:

1. EITHER an additional investment from large companies to engage with expert contract mediators to identify potential contracts, and aid difficult negotiations.
2. OR cost-efficient shared negotiator: small/medium size businesses share the cost of a neutral contract mediator, rather than hire negotiator each.

Of course, regardless of which of the above is pursued, one of the first things which the negotiating parties will have to agree is to both respect the negotiator and empower him/her as a neutral entity. So the mediating negotiator – or "neutral contract facilitator" – needs to understand the parties businesses and their predicament, and not just the law of the issue. As illustrated by Case Study B above, comparative understanding of different national legal cultures will sometimes also be necessary. The real challenge will lie in finding the RIGHT person for the job.

The expense of a neutral contract negotiator can perhaps even be justified if it comes with a guarantee of sorts. Changing the mentality of negotiation: from "if there is an issue my client will win" to "no issues will arise" will be more pro-active and cost-efficient in the long term. Thus, a professional mediator could add a Best Efforts guarantee to mediate any dispute arising out of a contract he/she has negotiated, confident that there will be very few disputes as their clients really DO see eye-to-eye. This may further strengthen client confidence in the efficacy of a neutral facilitator.

For now, this remains a novel idea which it is hoped that mediation centres will consider examining. With a large network of mediation experts in various areas of business, law and culture at their disposal, they seem best placed to start initiatives in introducing this sort of service at the stage of negotiation. Efforts to see this begun in practice in a more institutionalised manner will continue.

Exclusive Choice of Court Agreements and the Brussels I Regulation

By

Peter Arnt Nielsen
Head of Department and Professor,
the Law Department,
Copenhagen Business School

1. Choice of Court Agreements

For businesses, choice of court agreements is of manifest importance in international cases. A choice of court agreement stipulates for the purpose of deciding disputes, which have arisen or may arise in connection with a particular legal relationship, the courts of a State or one or more specific courts of a State to the exclusion of the jurisdiction of any other courts. However, a choice of court agreement may also stipulate that courts of two or more than two States are to have jurisdiction, but such agreements are rare.

The purpose of choice of court agreements are to give predictability and certainty as to in which State litigation can and will be instituted. At the same time, such agreements usually also protect the parties against forum shopping, because proceedings instituted in another State than the chosen one will be dismissed due to lack of jurisdiction. Most States have national provisions in their civil and procedural legislation to those effects.

On a global scale, the Convention on Choice of Court Agreement signed in the Hague in 2005 (cited as the Hague Convention) is of paramount interest to businesses in respect of exclusive choice of court agreements. The Convention applies to exclusive choice of court agreements in civil and commercial matters. The purpose of the Convention is to promote international trade and investment through enhanced judicial cooperation by enhancing uniform rules on jurisdiction and on recognition and enforcement of foreign judgments. In particular, the Hague Convention shall provide certainty and ensures the effectiveness of exclusive choice of court agreements between parties to commercial transactions.

The Hague Convention has not yet entered into force, but it has been signed by the US and the EU and ratified by Mexico.

According to Art. 3 of the Hague Convention, an "exclusive choice of court agreement" is defined as an international agreement concluded by two or more parties that designates, for the purpose of deciding disputes which have arisen or may arise in connection with a particular legal relationship, the courts of one Contracting State or one or more specific courts of one Contracting State to the exclusion of the jurisdiction of any other courts. Such an agreement is deemed exclusive unless the parties have expressly provided otherwise.

The Convention also sets up formal conditions for a choice of court agreement in Art. 3. Such an agreement must be concluded or documented in writing or by any other means of communication, which renders information accessible so as to be usable for subsequent reference. Finally, the Convention establishes the doctrine of separability; an exclusive choice of court agreement that forms part of a contract shall be treated as an agreement independent of the other terms of the contract. The validity of the exclusive choice of court agreement cannot be contested solely on the ground that the contract is not valid.

As far as the operative provisions of the Convention are concerned, Art. 5 determines the obligations of the chosen court or courts, and Art. 6 determines the obligations of other courts, that is to say any court or courts not designated in the choice of court agreement.

According to Art. 5, the court or courts of a Contracting State designated in an exclusive choice of court agreement shall have jurisdiction to decide a dispute to which the agreement applies, unless the agreement is null and void under the law of that State. The reference to "the law of that State" includes the choice of law rules of the Forum State.[1]

A court of a Contracting State other than that of the chosen court shall suspend or dismiss proceedings to which an exclusive choice of court agreement applies; see the Hague Convention, Art. 6. However,

1. *Trevor Hartley and Masato Dogauchi*, Explanatory Report on the 2005 Hague Choice of Court Agreements Convention (2007) 43.

that court may nevertheless take the case, if: a) the agreement is null and void under the law of the State of the chosen court; b) a party lacked the capacity to conclude the agreement under the law of the State of the court seised; c) giving effect to the agreement would lead to a manifest injustice or would be manifestly contrary to the public policy of the State of the court seised; d) for exceptional reasons beyond the control of the parties, the agreement cannot reasonably be performed; or e) the chosen court has decided not to hear the case.

The Hague Convention does not provide for a lis pendens provision, because there are no alternative grounds of jurisdiction under the Convention.

In the European Union, the *Brussels I* Regulation (cited as *Brussels I*) governs international jurisdiction and the recognition and enforcement of judgments in civil and commercial matters.[2] It is the successor to the Brussels Convention from 1968, and it rests upon the revision of the Convention that took place in 1998/99.[3] It also contains provisions ensuring the efficiency of choice of court agreements.

2. Brussels I

Brussels I is a cornerstone within the area of EU Law on Justice and Home Affairs. It has created free movement of judgments within the EU and harmonised the rules of international jurisdiction in cases where the defendant is domiciled in a Member State. On the other hand, the Member States apply their national rules of international jurisdiction where the defendant is domiciled in a non-Member State, and they ap-

2. Regulation 44/2001 of 22 December 2000 on jurisdiction and the recognition and enforcement of judgments in civil and commercial matters (as later amended). It entered into force on 1 March 2002. For a general treatment of the Regulation, see, for instance, *Ulrich Magnus and Peter Mankowski*, Brussels I Regulation, 2. Ed. 2012, *Hélène Gaudemet-Tallon*, Compétence et exécution des jugements en Europe, 4. Ed. 2010, and *Burkhard Hess*, Europäisches Zivilprocessrecht, 2010.
3. Concerning the 1998/99 Revision, see *Peter Arnt Nielsen*, Behind and Beyond Brussels I. An Insider's View. 30 Years of European Legal Studies at the College of Europe. Liber Professorum 1973/74 – 2003/04. College of Europe (2005) 241-261.

ply national law in respect of recognition and enforcement of judgments from such States.

Brussels I is in force in all Member States, including the United Kingdom, Ireland and Denmark. In spite of their reservations against judicial cooperation within Justice and Home Affairs, the first two countries decided to participate in *Brussels I* with reference to their possibility to "opt in" in respect of specific legal instruments. Denmark, which does not have such a possibility due to its general reservation towards Justice and Home Affairs, in 2005, entered into a convention with the EU obliging the other 26 Member States and Denmark to apply the provisions of *Brussels I* between them on an international basis.[4]

Generally, *Brussels I* works quite well. However, during 2004 – 2009, the Commission conducted surveys of the application of *Brussels I* in the Member States. First, a team of German professors made an extensive report on the application of *Brussels I* (cited as the *Heidelberg Report*). The Report contains specific proposals for improvements of various provisions of the Regulation.[5] Second, a Belgian professor made a study on residual jurisdiction.[6] Third, Groupe européen de droit international privé (*GEDIP*) proposed amendments to *Brussels I* in order to apply it to "External Situations", that is to say cases where the defendant is domi-

4. The Parallel Agreement of 19 October 2005 and *Brussels I* are in force in Denmark as from 1 July 2007, see Statute No 1563 of 20 December 2006. See also *Peter Arnt Nielsen*, Brussels I and Denmark, IPRax (2007) 506-509. The Parallel Agreement obliges Denmark within 30 days from the adoption of any amendments of *Brussels I* to inform the Commission whether Denmark accepts the amendments and is ready to implement them into Danish Law. If that is not the case, the Parallel Agreement is considered denounced by Denmark according to Article 3 (7) of the Agreement, and *Brussels I* will no longer apply in respect of Denmark.
5. *Burkhard Hess, Thomas Pfeiffer and Peter Schlosser,* Study JLS/C4/2005/03, Report on the Application of Regulation Brussels I, September 2007, available at: http://ec.europa.eu/civiljustice/news/docs/study_application_brussels_1_en.pdf.
6. *Arnaud Nuyts,* Study on Residual Jurisdiction, General Report, 3 September 2007, available at http://ec.europa.eu/civiljustice/news/docs/study_residual_jurisdiction_en.pdf.

ciled in a Non-Member State, and cases where the judgment originates from such a State.[7]

Following these surveys, in 2009 the Commission adopted a Green Paper on the review of *Brussels I*. And, on 26 January 2011, it tabled a proposal for a review of the Regulation (cited as *"the Proposal"*).[8] *The Proposal* is backed up by an impact analysis proving the need for the proposed amendments.[9]

Although the overall objective of *the Proposal* is to "further develop the European area of justice by removing the remaining obstacles to the free movement of judicial decisions in line with the principle of mutual recognition" adopted by the European Council in its 2009 Stockholm Program, that is to say to abolish the exequatur procedure, the Commission also takes up three other important issues.[10] One of them is the efficiency or lack of efficiency of exclusive choice of court agreements.

The Council working party on *Brussels I* is expected to end the negotiations during the first half of 2012. In the following, the Commission's proposal to improve the efficiency of exclusive choice of court agreements is presented and analyzed.[11]

7. *GEDIP*, Proposed Amendment of Regulation 44/2000 in order to apply it to External Situations, IPRax (2009) 283-284.
8. Proposal for a Regulation of the European Parliament and of the Council on jurisdiction and the recognition and enforcement of judgments in civil and commercial matters of 14 December 2010, COM (2010) 748 final/2 is available at: http://eurlex.europa.eu/LexUriServ/LexUriServ.do?uri=CELEX:52010PC0748R(01):DA:NOT.
   The Green Paper on the review of Council Regulation(EC) No 44/2000on jurisdiction and the recognition and enforcement of judgments in civil an commercial matters, COM (2009) 175 final is available at: http://eurlex.europa.eu/LexUriServ/LexUriServ.do?uri=COM:2009:0175:FIN:DA:PDF.
9. Study on Data Collection and Impact Analysis Certain Aspects of a Possible Revision of Council Regulation No 44/2001 on Jurisdiction and the Recognition and Enforcement of Judgments in civil and commercial matters by *Centre for Strategy & Evaluation Services (CSES)*, 2010 (cited as *The Impact Assessment)*. http://ec.europa.eu/justice/doc_centre/civil/studies/doc_civil_studies_en.htm.
10. *The Proposal 3*. The Programme was adopted at the meeting of the European Council held in Stockholm on 10 and 11 December 2009.
11. The author is member of the Danish delegation to the negotiations on *Brussels I*. He was also a member of the Danish delegation to the 1998/99 Revision of the Convention and the working party on Brussels I (1999-2000).

3. Brussels I and Choice of Court Agreements

Art. 23 of *Brussels I* is the key provision for choice of court agreements. According to this provision, where the parties, one or more of whom is domiciled in a Member State, have agreed that a court or the courts of a Member State are to have jurisdiction to settle any disputes which have arisen or which may arise in connection with a particular legal relationship, that court or those courts shall have jurisdiction. Such jurisdiction shall be exclusive unless the parties have agreed otherwise.

Furthermore, the agreement conferring jurisdiction shall be either: (a) in writing or evidenced in writing; or (b) in a form which accords with practices which the parties have established between themselves; or (c) in international trade or commerce, in a form which accords with a usage of which the parties are or ought to have been aware and which in such trade or commerce is widely known to, and regularly observed by, parties to contracts of the type involved in the particular trade or commerce concerned. Finally, any communication by electronic means, which provides a durable record of the agreement, shall be equivalent to "writing".

Contrary to the Hague Convention, *Brussels I* provides for alternative grounds of jurisdiction, for instance for contracts in Art. 5 (1) and for tort and delict in Art. 5 (3). Consequently, in order to avoid parallel proceedings and conflicting judgments, it is necessary to have a lis pendens provision dealing with the situation where proceedings involving the same cause of action and between the same parties are brought in the courts of different Member States.

For such cases *Brussels I*, Art. 27, provides that any other court than the one first seized, shall of its motion stay its proceedings until such time as the jurisdiction of the court first seized is established. Where the jurisdiction of the court first seized is established, any other court than the court first seized shall decline jurisdiction in favour of that court.

The relationship between Art. 23 and 27 is crucial for the effectiveness of exclusive choice of court agreements. The relationship was settled in the Gasser case.

3.1 The Gasser Case

For years, the judgment of the European Court of Justice in the well-known Gasser case has been meet with significant criticism. In this case, the Court decided the controversial issue of the relationship between Art. 23 and 27.

In the Gasser case, a contract had been concluded between an Austrian party, Gasser, and an Italian party, Misat. The contract provided, inter alia, that the Austrian courts should have exclusive jurisdiction to determine any dispute between the parties. However, Misat instituted proceedings against Gasser in Italy under Art. 5 (3) of *Brussels I* claiming that the exclusive choice of court agreement was invalid.

Subsequently, Gasser instituted proceedings in Austria relying on the choice of court agreement, but before the Austrian court Misat claimed that it should stay its proceedings until such time as the Italian court had decided whether the choice of court agreement were invalid, and, in the affirmative, whether the court had jurisdiction under Art. 5 (3).[12]

The European Court of Justice ruled that the Austrian court should stay its proceedings and wait for the decision of the Italian court on its jurisdiction. The Court referred to the fact that the proceedings in Italy were instituted first. Due to the inefficiency of the Italian court system, it would probably take years for the Italian court to reach a decision on its jurisdiction. Meanwhile, proceedings in other Member States should be put on hold due to the lis pendens provision.

The Gasser judgment has created the phenomenon "Italian Torpedoes" meaning that a party can obtain de facto immunity from court proceedings in the Member States of the EU for years, provided that the party wanting immunity manages to institute proceedings first in Ita-

12. Case C-116/02 *(Gasser)*. For severe criticism, see *Trevor Hartley*, Le droit international privé: esprit et méthodes, Mélanges en l'honneur de Paul Lagarde (2005) 322-335, and Richard Fentiman *Case Note on Case C-116/02 (Erich Gasser GmbH v. Misat Srl)*, Common Market Law Review (2005) 241-259.

ly.[13] This is an unacceptable situation, especially where the parties have entered into a choice of court agreement. As the Commission explains:[14]

> *"The efficiency of choice of court agreements needs to be improved. Currently, the Regulation obliges the court designated by the parties in a choice of court agreement to stay proceedings if another court has been seised first. This rule enables litigants acting in bad faith to delay the resolution of the dispute in the agreed forum by first seizing a non-competent court. This possibility creates additional costs and delays and undermines the legal certainty and predictability of dispute resolution which choice of court agreements should bring about."*

3.2 The Commission's Proposal

The consultations conducted prior to the Commission's proposal to recast *Brussels I* showed large support from stakeholders and Member States to improve the effectiveness of choice of court agreements under *Brussels I*. Among the various ways to achieve that objective preference was expressed for granting priority to the chosen court to decide on its jurisdiction.

Such a mechanism would largely accord with the system established in Art. 5 (1) the Hague Choice of Court Agreements Convention from 2005, thus ensuring a coherent approach within the Union and that at the international level were the Union to decide to conclude the Hague Convention in the future.[15]

13. Italian Torpedoes were invented by *M. Franzosi,* Worldwide Patent Litigation and the Italian Torpedo, European Intellectual Property Review (1997) 382. See also *The Heidelberg Report,* 159 and 194-201, characterising the problem as "serious", *Michael Bogdan,* The Brussels/Lugano Lis Pendens Rule and the "Italian Torpedo", Scandinavian Studies in Law (2007) 89, *J. Fawcett,* The Impact of Article 6(1) of the ECHR on Private International Law, International and Comparative Law Quarterly (2007) 1, and *L. Merret,* The Enforcement of Jurisdiction Agreements within the Brussels Regime, International and Comparative Law Quarterly (2006) 315.
14. *The Proposal 3.*
15. *The Proposal 8.* Convention of 30 June 2005 on Choice of Court Agreements, Art. 5. The convention has been signed by the US and the EU and ratified by Mexico.

Consequently, the Commission proposes the following provision in *the Proposal,* Art. 32 (2):

> "With the exception of agreements governed by Sections 3, 4 and 5 of this Chapter, where an agreement referred to in paragraph 1 confers exclusive jurisdiction to a court or the courts of a Member State, the courts of other Member States shall have no jurisdiction over the dispute until such time as the court or courts designated in the agreement decline their jurisdiction."

The Commission's proposal is basically sound. It is a reverse lis pendens mechanism ensuring that the agreed court and only the agreed court can determine the validity of the choice of court agreement if proceedings are instituted before that court. Further, the reverse lis pendens mechanism will not apply to cases involving weak parties under *Brussels I,* Chapter II, Section 3,4 and 5; that is insurance, consumer and employment cases.

The Commission's proposal in Art. 32 (2) ensures that the agreed court has exclusive jurisdiction to determine the formal and substantive validity of the choice of court agreement. This solution, partly inspired by the doctrine of "competence over the competence", is well known and well functioning in international commercial arbitration. It is established, for instance, in Art. 8 and Art. 16 of the Model Law on International Commercial Arbitration.[16]

In the Gasser case, the Commission's solution would lead to the result that the Austrian courts would have exclusive jurisdiction to determine the validity of the choice of court agreement, and that the Italian court would be obliged to stay the proceedings before it at the time proceedings were instituted in Austria in accordance with the choice of court agreement. Finally, the Italian court would only be able to assert jurisdiction if the Austrian court set aside the choice of court agreement.

The Commission's proposal is good. However, the drafting of Art. 32 (2) can be discussed.

First, it should be clarified that the reverse lis pendens mechanism only applies if the chosen court assumes jurisdiction on the basis of the

16. UNCITRAL's Model Law on International Commercial Arbitration, as adopted by the United Nations Commission on International Trade Law on 21 June 1985.

choice of court agreement. The reverse mechanism should not apply where the chosen court sets the choice of court agreement aside, but takes jurisdiction on, for instance Art. 5 (1). In this case, the ordinary is pendens mechanism in Art. 27 should apply.

Second, the proposed Art. 32 (2) should only apply subject to Art. 28 on tacit choice of court agreements, because an express choice of court agreement can tacitly be derogated from.

3.3 Choice of Law for Choice of Court Agreements

The Commission also proposes a choice of law rule for substantive validity of choice of court agreements, see *the Proposal* Art. 23 (1). According to this proposal, this issue is governed by "the law of the Member State", whose courts are granted jurisdiction under the choice of court agreement. Formal validity of the choice of court agreement is still subject to the uniform standard in *Brussels I*, Art. 23.

The proposal for a choice of law rule on substantive validity of choice of court agreements is based on the similar solution in the Hague Choice of Court Agreements Convention, where a chosen court shall determine the validity of a choice of court agreement under "the law of that State".[17] However, the reference in the Hague Convention to "the law of that State" includes the choice of law rules of the Forum State.[18]

It is not clear from the Commission's proposal whether the reference to "the law of that member State" includes the choice of law rules or not, but the intention was that this should be the case. Therefore, the proposal should be redrafted or a recital should be added in order to make it clear that the reference to "the law of that Member State", like the Hague Convention, includes the choice of law rules.

The Commission's proposal for a choice of law rule for substantive validity of choice of court agreements is presented as "a harmonised conflict of law rule on the substantive validity of choice of court agreements, thus ensuring a similar outcome on this matter whatever the court seised."[19] However, in reality this is not the case, because the proposal

17. *The Proposal 8.*
18. *Trevor Hartley and Masato Dogauchi,* Explanatory Report on the 2005 Hague Choice of Court Agreements Convention (2007) 43.
19. *The Proposal 8.*

does nothing but codifying the status quo. At present, each Member State applies its own choice of law rules in respect of substantive validity of choice of court agreements.

The reason for this situation is that neither the Rome Convention nor the Rome I Regulation on choice of law for contractual obligations cover choice of court agreements; see Art. 1 (2) (d) of these instruments.[20] Consequently, choice of law for substantive validity of choice of court agreements is decided differently in the Member States. Some apply lex fori, others apply lex contractus and others a combination of these two laws.

In 2006-2008 during the negotiations on the Rome I Regulation, the Council working party ought to have solved this issue, but it was never really on the agenda.[21] Therefore, the recast of *Brussels I* is an obvious occasion to adopt a real uniform choice of law rule for all Member States.

Considering the overall intention of the recast procedure in respect of choice of court agreements, enhancing the efficiency of choice of court agreements, the choice of law rule should be based on the principle of alternative validity. This principle, well known in the Rome Convention and the Rome I Regulation for choice of law for formal validity of contractual obligations, entails that the agreement is valid, provided it is so under either the law of one particular State or the law of another relevant State.[22]

Consequently, the choice of law rule should be that the choice of court agreement is valid in terms of substance, provided it is so under either the law of the Member State in which the chosen court is (the lex fori), or the law that governs the dispute (the lex causae).

20. Convention of 19 June 1980 on the Law Applicable to Contractual Obligations, and Regulation No 593/2008 on the same subject matter. The Regulation is in force in all Member States with the exception of Denmark.
21. See Ole Lando and Peter Arnt Nielsen, Common Market Law Review (2008) 1687-1725 and in Journal of Private International Law (2007) 29-51.
22. The Rome Convention, Art. 9, and the Rome I Regulation, Art. 11.

4. Conclusion

The Commission's proposal to set up a reverse lis pendens provision for exclusive choice of court agreements is a good proposal, provided the above-mentioned comments and concerns are taken into consideration. Furthermore, the Commission has not considered codifying "the doctrine of separability" in *Brussels I,* Art. 23. According to this doctrine, a choice of court agreement that forms part of a contract shall be treated as an agreement independent of the other terms of the contract, so that the validity of the choice of court agreement cannot be contested solely on the ground that the contract is not valid. The doctrine has been recognised by the European Court of Justice.[23] The recast of *Brussels I* is an obvious occasion to codify the doctrine, which is internationally accepted, for instance in the Hague Choice of Court Agreements Convention, Art. 3 (d).

23. Case C-269/95 *(Benincasa).*

"Primary" Legal Risk Management: Lessons from Claim and Litigation Studies

By

Edward A. Dauer[1]
Denver, Colorado USA
LL.B., M.P.H.

1. Dispute Prevention and Conflict Management

Lawyers throughout the United States and Europe are increasingly familiar with Alternative Dispute Resolution – typically referred to as "ADR" – and with that familiarity have become both adept and comfortable with its use. Conventionally, ADR focuses on after-the-fact dispute resolution. Even when an ADR clause is included in a commercial contract at the outset of the transaction, the clause is most often drafted to be triggered only when there has been a claim or breakdown or impasse or breach. At that point a conflict has become apparent, someone has voiced a complaint or a claim, and the question becomes which of the available devices for resolving that claim would make the most sense, achieving the best result at the least total cost.

Paralleling the development of ADR, though still less well known, is an approach to legal conflict that has been named "Preventive Law" in the US, and "Proactive Law" in the EU – thus in either place we may refer to it as "PL." PL is motivated by the adage that "an ounce of prevention is worth a pound of cure." Its focus is on preventing conflicts and claims from arising at all, rather than on resolving them once they have. While the foundational adage is not always true – that is, elaborate precautions to avoid a small risk of an inconsequential conflict do not always make a lot of sense – it is true often enough to justify attention to prevention at least equally with attention to resolution. This may be particularly so in business activities where the consequences of unresolved conflict can be dangerous to the success of the transaction, as well as costly and disruptive once they emerge. The point is that an effective conflict management approach in almost any setting should consider components of both ADR and PL. We offer in this paper a discussion of the more fundamental elements of that kind of approach.

2. The Principles of "Preventive Law"

Transactional lawyers working in almost any field inevitably develop strategies for protecting their clients' transactions from upset by avoidable conflicts and claims. Much of the work is substantive, as for example drafting contract terms that clearly allocate risk and responsibility when something less than perfect performance happens, or when the context of a deal changes through forces outside the parties' control. Other important techniques include specification of remedies, limitation of post-conflict rights, and other kinds of provisions that would change the outcome in the event of a legal claim and thereby, hopefully, alter another person's propensity to assert one.

Knowing what risks exist and what the workable ways are for responding to them is one of the reasons why transactional lawyers need a background and understanding of their clients' industry and business affairs, in addition to their knowledge of the applicable law. Risks do not arise from unexpected legal rules; they arise from unexpected or untoward facts. And so estate planners know how to avoid potential challenges to their clients' distributive plans by knowing the circumstances under which such claims are likely to be made. Tax lawyers understand the vulnerabilities of alternative structures. Those who form business organizations appreciate the kinds of events that spawn shareholder or partnership disputes.[2] And so on. The challenge for PL, however, has been that of generalizing how preventive law (or better, preventive lawyering) may done across the many fields of practice and across the

2. The foundational work is F. Hodge O'Neal, *"Oppression of Minority Shareholders"* (2d Ed. 1975).

broad swath of trade in which our clients engage. In this need for a more generalized theory of conflict prevention, lawyering is less well developed than it is with respect to conflict resolution.

Some usefully broad principles have, however, been developed. Scanning the literature to date turns up the following:

2.1. When an organization's culture conflicts with the organization's rules, the culture will always win.

If rules are "what we're supposed to do around here," culture is "here's how we actually do things around here." A blood donation and transfusion service publishes clear and imperative rules about recalibrating test equipment. At the same time, it assigns its lab staff deadlines for completing overnight processing that afford too little time for activities that might seem unnecessary, despite the rules. The recalibrations don't get done. A hospital has rules for the interpersonal behavior of its professional staff, but the major producers aren't taken to task when they violate them. The behaviors continue until an explosion becomes unavoidable. In almost any setting, the placards are all about safety and the annual raises are all about efficiency. Efficiency wins, safety loses. Internal memos stress the policy of accuracy and honesty in billing yet instances of "upcoding" (designating a service as some other service which carries a higher reimbursement rate) are known and tolerated. Honesty loses, upcoding wins. Rules are written and posted about disposing of hazardous waste, or about not colluding with competitors; but the employees' rewards dwell on profits and ignore compliance. Rules lose. Culture wins. In all of these and many like instances the better part of conflict prevention requires reshaping the environment, rather than reasserting ever more rigorous rules.

2.2. Legal claims don't always reflect the facts that gave rise to them.

An investigation by Alan Westin,[3] later to become one of the canonical texts in preventive law, revealed that the labeling of legal claims is often unrelated to the real nature of the complaint. The law affords a very limited number of gateways for relief from unpleasant or unbearable circumstances; it doesn't proscribe every kind of noxious behavior there

3. A. Westin & A. Feliu, *"Resolving Employment Disputes without Litigation"* (1988).

is in the world. A problem whose features don't qualify it for one of those gateways cannot command legal attention, and so in the absence of other avenues for relief the claim gets translated into one which the law does allow. The initial study showed this was true for an important fraction of employment discrimination claims based on race or gender or disability. Some employees, for example, have supervisors who are – to use a phrase the study did not use – overbearing jerks. Working under one of these people can be intolerable. But there is no law either national or local offering legal relief to someone whose boss is an overbearing jerk. And so, self-consciously or not, the complainant transforms the grievance into one with a legal gateway – and alleges discrimination on a legally cognizable, prohibited ground. As important as it otherwise is, effective policing against employment discrimination by itself cannot eliminate these kinds of claims, even if it does support a defense when a claim legally pursued. Affording employees avenues for grievance and redress that have functional as opposed to legal gateways might do as much to prevent the claims arising in the first place, if not even more.

2.3. Allocating risk to parties who cannot bear it can be a conflict-producing proposition.

Daniel Ertel, whose work[4] is addressed again later in this paper, listed this among his six admonitions for negotiating successful transactions: "Don't let them overcommit." The "them" in that sentence is the party on the other side of the deal. From a business point of view, deals work when they are capable of actually working, meaning when everyone has a real possibility of living with (and profitting from) what they've agreed to do. Contractually placing the onus of responsibility or the standard of performance on someone who won't be able to bear it may look like a negotiation "win" at the outset, but it undermines the success of the deal once reality sets in. With an untenable burden in place trust begins to fail and the only "out" may be a choice between breach and allegation of breach – because at that point there isn't much to lose. Again, the

4. D. Ertel, *Getting Past Yes: Negotiating as if Implementation Really Mattered,* Harv. Bus. Rev. (Nov. 2004) at 30. This section, summarizing and interpreting Ertel's work, is taken from two sources: the cited Harvard Business Review article, and a book by D. Ertel and M. Gordon, "The Point of the Deal" (2007).

contract may offer defenses if adjudication happens; but the tradeoff is that between the added costs of a workable deal and the dysfunction and costs of a dispute. A health plan, for example, insists on its right to be unconcerned with whether its panel physicians have a mix of patients whose reimbursement rates allow the practitioner to make a profit – that, it feels, is their problem. But the conflicts that emerge from that position become everyone's problem.

2.4. Aligning expectations with reality.

In another early work in Preventive Law[5] Louis Brown observed somewhat prosaically that people bring claims when they experience a feeling of injury; and that feelings of injury occur when people encounter realities that are more painful than what they had expected. A classic case in health care may be a managed care organizations' contractual authority to engage in "rental" systems – effectively allowing non-subscribers access to a physicians' below-market pricing for some of their services while not bringing them the more profitable engagements for their other services. The health plan may have been within its contractual rights to do so, but not every physician understood fully what was in the contract they signed. Neither does it always solve the problem to point out that people who sign contracts should read them first.

On the other side of the contract aisle David Studdert and his colleagues[6] learned that a fair portion of health plan subscribers' claims for services denied can be attributed to misunderstandings about what the subscription contract actually covers. He writes, "Greater transparency about the coverage status of specific services, through more precise contractual language and consumer education about benefits limitations, may help to avoid a large proportion of disputes in managed care." And as Tom Barton points out in a forthcoming work, contract language is a conduit through which the business language of a deal passes but only after being translated into language that only the legal system can

5. L. Brown & e. Dauer, *"Planning by Lawyers: Materials on a Nonadversarial Legal Process"* (1978).
6. D. Studdert & C. Gresentz, Enrollee Appeals of Preservice Coverage Denials at Two Health Maintenance Organizations, 289 JAMA 864 (2003).

process. Assuring effective communication of real meaning may be the reality training that mis-expectations require.

These are a few of the most general principles of PL, typifying the kinds of ideas that distinguish conflict prevention from both conflict adjudication and dispute resolution. We include a number of additional ideas later in the paper, after setting out some additional bits of the structure of PL and conflict management.

3. Primary, Secondary and Tertiary Prevention

Both preventive medicine and public health divide their preventive strategies into three somewhat overlapping but still distinctive layers, called Primary, Secondary, and Tertiary. (Some in medicine would add a fourth – "quaternary" – the objective of which is to prevent further harm from our having too much of any of the others.)

In medicine, primary prevention includes doing those things that can prevent or minimize the onset of injury or disease – using sunscreen, not smoking, maintaining a healthy weight, being immunized, exercising regularly ... Secondary prevention focuses on identifying emerging or incipient conditions that can be managed most effectively if identified and addressed early on – blood pressure screening, periodic tests for colon cancer, mammograms, assays for prostate problems ... And tertiary prevention is applied to keep a bad situation from becoming worse – surgical interventions, medications, and rehabilitation for example.

The three layers are similar in public health, where primary prevention refers to personal or environmental strategies for keeping the origins and vectors of disease from arising – sanitary systems, chlorinated water, swamps drained where malaria-carrying mosquitoes could otherwise breed ... Secondary prevention again denotes early detection, and it applies to dulling the impact of disease vectors once they arise – bed netting to prevent mosquitoes from biting, for example ... Tertiary prevention – which is still prevention – refers to reducing the risk of disease progression or of aggrafating complications.

The analogy to these three layers of care is useful for conflict management as well. We think of *primary prevention* as preventing the causes of conflict from happening. An example is the point just made, about aligning peoples' expectations with their documented legal rights. *Secondary prevention* includes modern conflict *systems*, for example, and other procedures for identifying subsurface conflict and addressing it before friction becomes fire. *Tertiary prevention* includes strategies first applied when a claim of injury or right is voiced and the win-lose mindset has begun to set in. A comprehensive conflict management system will include at the very least consideration of all three approaches, and often a programming elements from each of the three.

What we have referred to as the conventional applications of ADR overlap with tertiary prevention. Certainly arbitration does; and mediation does as well, more often than it should. Because the applications and theories of ADR are already familiar, we will not address tertiary prevention very much here. Our principal focus is on primary; but for reasons that may become clear as we move along, we offer some notes about secondary prevention before getting to primary. The sequence thus moves backwards, or downwards, from the surface of a full-blown dispute through its incipient stages and then to its roots.

4. Secondary Prevention

A dispute has arisen. Recognizing that it might be better to resolve it before it gets worse – or turns into a "claim" – the question is how best to manage it. The reasons for wanting to do so are as numerous as the contexts in which the question arises, though there is one point that may be common to almost any kind of setting. That is, that as conflicts escalate up the pyramid from frictions to lawsuits (or whatever the terminal phase may be) the language in which they are addressed undergoes a change and the ostensible nature of the conflict becomes increasingly less authentic.

An encounter between labor and delivery nurses and attending physicians, for example, starts off with disagreements about when the attending physician will be called. From there it becomes an argument about authority and responsibility, with overtones of care quality and patient safety. And then it goes on to be a major issue regarding the scope of nurses' independent practice. And, though it would be exceedingly unlikely in this example, it might eventually become a legal claim. The point is that the interests of the parties are, at bottom, busy physicians who feel they do not need to be called with every contraction, and nurses who feel they need backup when they become concerned about a patient. We know from the study of negotiation that resolutions work best – and are most easily achieved – when the parties are able to talk with each other about the things that actually concern them (i.e. their "interests"), rather than about the demands they mount (their "positions") in the effort to serve their needs.

As a dispute evolves it is prone to being expressed in other, less authentic voices – until it reaches its crescendo in litigation which is conducted in a language and frame of reference that most often has little to do with what interested the parties in the first place. At that point resolution is impeded by the translation itself. There is a big difference between "Hey, you're sending us butterfly (blood drawing) needles with kinked tubes" on the one hand, and "Three installments this month were in violation of the warranty of fitness under UCC §2-314, allowing us to cancel the contract pursuant to §§2-612(2 and 3)!" on the other. The former is how people think about their problem, and the problem remains the focus. The latter is how the legal system requires litigants (or their lawyers) to talk about the problem, such as why it matters is at risk of getting lost. The parties lose control, the problem takes on a life of its own, and the reservoir of commercial good sense and intelligence about the real problem and its setting become irrelevant. It is like saying the Roman Catholic Mass in Latin rather than in the vernacular.[7] As awe-inspiring as it may be, the translation away from ordinary understanding creates a chasm rather than a bridge. And so the real-world business-based strategies for solving the problem are blown away by the legal missal.

The probability and workability of resolutions is therefore a major reason why it is almost always easier to resolve matters early on – before the authentic language gets lost. Other observations support the same conclusion – it is often less expensive and less disruptive as well. But retaining the authentic voice remains a major objective of "secondary" prevention.

7. E. Dauer, *Justice Irrelevant: Speculations on the Causes of ADR*, 74 So. Calif. L. Rev. 83 (2000).

Some of the standard techniques at this secondary level include staff training and at-the-ready intervention capabilities. Where the context is created by contractual relations, however, there is another – early ADR mandated by private contract. One among many possible examples is the multi-step clause promulgated by the CPR Institute for Conflict Prevention and Resolution[8] in New York: when a dispute [we would prefer it if the trigger were "difference of view"] arises, it must be addressed by good-faith negotiation between the parties' respective project managers; if they do not resolve it in X days it will be addressed by their executive officers; if that fails, then to mediation; and if that fails then to a binding procedure such as arbitration. While it sounds like a bit much, in fact the genius of the system is to put pressure on lower-level managers to resolve matters before they become issues for superiors to be troubled with. By doing that and by keeping the first step within direct party-to-party conversation, the multi-step agreement helps prevent the translation of a problem into a conflict. The first language remains authentic and the focus stays on the problem rather than on the process. That is good secondary prevention.

Another technique of secondary prevention is changing the calculus of conflict. In a purely rational world an injured person may bring a claim against an insurance company, rather than continue to negotiate, when the marginal cost of bringing the claim (the difference between suing and negotiating) is less than the marginal benefit of doing so (the difference between the outcome of a suit and the outcome of negotiation).

To put it into numbers: If the cost of suing is $10,000 greater than the cost of negotiating regardless of the amount of the claim, and if the likely result of suing is $40,000 while the result of further negotiating is likely to be $25,000, then there is a $5,000 advantage to bringing a lawsuit. (The significance of the example can be enhanced by adding a few zeroes to all the numbers.) If the claimant is right, the insurance company will end up paying $40,000 plus its own costs of suit. Suppose now that the company is willing to pay $31,000. The claimant, however, continues to demand $40,000-plus in exchange for a release and is not likely to budge. Should the insurance company pay $31,000 and not insist on a release?

8. CPR's forms and studies can be found on the organizations website: WWW.CPRADR.ORG.

The answer might well be yes, though not every insurance company relishes the idea. If the company does so the amount in dispute – the marginal benefit to the claimant from suing -- will be $9,000 (the $40,000 demanded less the $31,000 paid). But the cost of bringing the suit is still $10,000. A rational claimant would not sue under that circumstance.

There is a more intuitive and therefore more easily generalized way of implementing the same lesson. An injured party's needs are almost always different from their demands. The latter are inflated for several reasons, including the intention to cover the transactions costs of satisfying the former, and the standard mode of negotiation rewards if it does not absolutely require demanding more than one actually needs or expects. Moreover, the intensity of real needs is typically greater than that of acquisitive desires: drawing on Maslow's famous hierarchy, if we can catch all we need to eat, the rest is gravy. People tend to value replacement of losses more than they value equal-sized gains. And other well-documented bits of folk wisdom to the same effect. A staunch defense to a claim leaves both needs and demands unsatisfied, making the prospect of a payoff to claiming all the more valuable. But if the putative claimant's needs are satisfied, the risks and costs of further claiming – compared to the benefits of doing so when all that remains are the supra-needs demands – loom larger. Hence the principle: If we can satisfy a party's needs, we are much less likely to have to respond to their demands. Conflict is avoided and the outcome is fair to boot.

Many of the early-compensation models in health care are based on these observations. In the aftermath of an adverse event a patient may be facing the direct out-of-pocket costs of prolonged care, lost wages due to additional time for healing or correction, a disruption to others of life's plans, and the like. The experiences of the COPIC insurance companies illustrate it well.[9] Young adults with child-care responsibilities, for example, may be seriously disadvantaged by an extended hospital stay or a period of rehabilitation that limits their ability to care for others. The need may be that simple. Satisfying it, in COPIC's experience, typically removes the threat of claims for incremental demands. And both parties are better off – each received what it needed.

9. Reports of the COPIC "3Rs" Program can be found at http://www.callcopic.com/home/resources-tools/newsletters/copics-3rs-program/.

5. Primary Prevention - The Human Factor

Primary prevention is, again, focused on keeping disputes from arising in the first place. Some of the strategies are obvious: clear contracts, goods that always conform to the contract specs, adequate capability for performance on every side, and a world in which the unexpected never happens. In this section we address another technique, albeit one that may lie as much on the cusp with secondary prevention as within the realm of the primary.

The concept is straightforward: to prevent disputes we need to predict the circumstances under which disputes are likely to occur, and then we take steps to manage those causative circumstances. We begin with the notion that disputes are the results of decisions taken by people; and that when a person is prodded with an irritating stimulus some reactions will be more dispute-causing than others. The working hypothesis is this: *People* engage in conflict when they *perceive* that the *benefit-to-cost ratio* of conflict is better than that of adjustment, compromise, or "exit."

The word *people* refers both to individuals acting as individuals, *e.g.* consumers, patients, suppliers, partners, shareholders, doctors, nurses, and others; and to organizations or firms. Though the latter may be more complex, at some level the behavior of firms is of necessity directed by the decisions of people. The preventive strategies therefore apply to both.

The word *perceive* is also key. Unlike strictly economic theories of organizational behavior which assume a modicum of rationality, or accuracy in assessing the financial consequences of alternative strategies unalloyed with subjective factors, the preventive approach assumes that what matters is not what is, but what people see it as. That does not mean errors; it does mean that the calculation includes multiple factors beyond the strictly economic, and it means that how those factors are weighed is a matter not of fact, but of perception.

The idea of a *benefit-to-cost ratio* is likewise richer than the numerical calculus of dollars pro and con. As one expert mediator once quipped, "Everything everybody does makes sense to them somehow. The mediator's job is to figure out what sense it's making." Some decisions about disputing may well be driven by the cold arithmetic of financial risk and reward; but those factors are often beyond the ability of anyone else to control. We focus, therefore, on the rest of it – those parts of the environment surrounding the event that might affect the subjective aspects of the assessment.

Students of disputing behavior have built their work on two foundational ideas, which we can refer to as *transformation* and *attribution*.

The transformation model stems from the seminal work of Felstiner, Abel and Sarat.[10] Drawing on studies of dispute behavior known through the date of their writing, these authors postulated that the way an injurious event becomes a dispute is through three transformations, the outcome of none of which are predetermined. The sequence is *naming, blaming,* and *claiming*.

The first transformation ("naming") is the realization that something happened that was in fact injurious. An adverse event or unsuccessful outcome of a surgery might be objectively injurious but need not necessarily be perceived that way. The patient might see it as an injury, or might see it as the predictable next step in the condition or disease. As Felstiner *et al.* themselves said, asbestosis became an injury only after it was recognized as a disease rather than as the inevitable shortness of breath that follows installing insulation for ten years. A pat of the hand on the body of another might be an injury if it is recognized as an unwelcome or sexually motivated touching; while the same pat by a close friend might be perceived as an act of friendship or support and thus not an injury at all.

The second transformation ("blaming") turns the perception of injury into a grievance by attributing it to someone else and labeling it as a wrong. It has been well said that "even a dog knows the difference between being tripped over and being kicked," but the same foot in the ribs and the same pain that follows could be either a trip or a kick depending less on the extent of the injury than on the precursors and conditions surrounding the event. Whether the kicker gets bitten in response depends on whether the dog undergoes this second transformation.

The third step ("claiming") includes two parts – someone who perceives an injury as wrongful articulates the wrong and asks for a remedy.

10. W. Felstiner, R. Abel & A. Sarat, *The Emergence and Transformation of Disputes: Naming, Blaming, Claiming,* 15 L. & Soc'y Rev. 631 (1981).

The claim, the authors say, "is transformed into a dispute when it is rejected in whole or in part."

Hence a dispute emerges from an event through the three stages of naming, claiming, and blaming. Each of these transformations is subjective, each is malleable over time, and each depends at least in part on the immediately pre- and post-event behavior of the others, including both the actor and the others with whom the affected person communicates. Thus we know, for example, that one of the critical factors in the assertion of medical malpractice claims is how physicians respond to their patients in the immediate aftermath of an adverse event (in addition to the quality of the relationship before it); and we know that the advice of other physicians, family members, even lawyers, contributes to the patient's transformation at each of the three stages.

The data generally fit the model. Kritzer's work[11] for example, done ten years after Felstiner, Abel and Sarat's, analyzed the differences in claiming rates between, principally, England and the United States. Holding all other things constant, Kritzer demonstrated that the second transformation – now blended with a parallel literature on "attribution" – was significantly determined by differences in the cultures of the two countries. As he put it, "... the American links adversity with recompense while the Englishman or woman accepts adversity as a routine part of life." The key is expectations, and expectations are culturally determined.

Kritzer's work is expanded by other aspects of attribution – i.e., by the process through which an injured person attributes blame or wrong to someone else. As Lloyd-Bostock[12] has it, the entire environment is involved – social as well as cultural factors, relationships, the known surrounding "rule systems," even the availability of forums for the making of claims. And for that reason, Lloyd-Bostock adds, the process is untidy and non-linear: attribution of fault can follow from the process of claiming.

11. H. Kritzer, *Propensity to Sue in England and in the United States of America: Blaming and Claiming in Tort Cases,* 18 J. L & Soc'y 400 (1991).
12. S. Lloyd-Bostock, *Propensity to Sue in England and in the United States of America: The Role of Attribution Processes,* 18 J. L & Soc'y. 428 (1991).

What we know about the emergence and management of medical malpractice claims supports the attribution and transformation models, and leads us directly into the realm which neither the transformation nor the attribution scholars address: How can these insights assist in the practical challenge of *preventing* conflict? Details and practical guidelines are addressed next. To state the principle in a general way, however, it is this – we should try to craft the environment of predictable events in such a way that people acting within it are more likely to perceive the net costs of disputing as greater than the net costs of the alternatives. Or, to say the same thing in a positive way, arrange the environment to make the benefits of resolution seem greater than the benefits of conflict.

The practical applications may be drawn from two bodies of data. One is medical injury claiming. The other is the litigation propensities of commercial firms. We address each separately and then suggest how combining them yields a richer picture of why disputes begin – and therefore, how they might not.

5.1. Medical Malpractice – Why Do People Bring Claims?

The literature of individuals' "claiming behavior" is both substantial and diverse, including among others studies of divorce, employment discrimination,[13] personal injury and torts in general, small claims, class actions,[14] and corporate whistle-blowing.[15] For a number of reasons, much of the best of it deals with injured patients and families making claims following an unexpected medical injury or adverse event. Medical malpractice claiming is both well understood and typical of the many contexts in which individuals elect conflict, or the voicing of legal claims. As one author [Relis] points out, a common denominator of all of the studies is that claimants' behaviors are almost uniformly responses to their adversary's having in some fashion "added insult to injury."

The message is not hard to understand, yet it too often falls to be heeded. One malpractice insurance company, for example, had two

13. P.A. Morgan, *Risking Relationships: Understanding the Litigation Choices of Sexually Harassed Women,* 33 Law & Soc'y Rev 67 (1999).
14. S. Meili, *Collective Justice or Personal Gain: An Empirical Analysis of Consumer Class Action Lawyers and Named Plaintiffs,* 44 Akron L. Rev. 67 (2011).
15. Many of the recent studies are collected in T. Relis, *It's Not About the Money: A Theory on Misconceptions of Plaintiffs' Litigation Aims,* 68 U Pitt 701 (2007).

house rules regarding its insured physicians, applicable once a patient injured or disappointed by an outcome began making noises that sound like an incipient conflict or claim. Rule number one: "The physician may not speak about a claim with a patient until the company appoints counsel." Rule number two: "The company will appoint counsel once a formal claim has been filed." For quite some time the company resisted the idea that its house rules were producing litigation which it might very easily – and far less expensively – have avoided. The empirical data on medical malpractice claims explains why and how avoiding those claims is possible.

Hickson and his colleagues[16] at Vanderbilt did the first of the modern studies in 1992, inquiring of families that had recently suffered injuries to their child during birth why they brought their claims and what they hoped to accomplish by doing so. Contrary to the then-prevailing view that patients become plaintiffs in order to win money, Hickson found that his respondents – some of whose babies had died, some of whose babies faced a lifetime of medical challenges – were moved by a much richer set of needs. Only 24% reported that they sued for the money needed for long-term care. Another 24% said they brought a claim because the physician was not honest with them in the aftermath of the events. Some 20% said "we realized the baby has no future;" and the same proportion sued simply to "find out what really happened." A like proportion – 19% – acted from the desire for accountability, in this case a blend of deterrence (to be sure it never happens to anyone else) and revenge.

Two years later Vincent and colleagues[17] published a similar study in England, asking their respondents – all of whom had brought claims for medical injuries in the more rigorous tort system of the U.K. – what motivated them to do so, and what the defendants might have done that could have avoided their bringing the claim. The distribution of answers to the first question is worth repeating in full. The numbers in the table indicate the percentage of all respondents who agreed with each of the statements:

16. G. Hickson et al, *Factors That Prompted Families to File Medical Malpractice Claims Following Perinatal Injuries,* 267 JAMA 1359 (1992).
17. C. Vincent et al., *Why do People Sue Doctors? A Study of Patients and Relatives Taking Legal Action,* 343 Lancet 1609 (1994).

So that it would not happen to anyone else	91.4
I wanted an explanation	90.7
I wanted the doctors to realise what they had done	90.4
To get an admission of negligence	86.7
So the doctor would know how I felt	68.4
My feelings were ignored	66.8
I wanted financial compensation	65.6
Because I was angry	65.4
So that the doctor did not get away with it	54.7
So that the doctor would be disciplined	47.6
[I]t was the only way I could cope with my feelings	45.8
Because of the attitude of the staff afterwards	42.5
To get back at the doctor involved	23.2

The relative rankings are striking. While the desire for money is higher, at 65.6%, perhaps because all of Vincent's respondents had brought lawsuits rather than just claims – lawsuits in which the only remedy a court can give is money – and because of the possibility of agreeing with an unlimited number of factors, the message is consistent with Hickson's. The desire for money ranked seventh on the list, well behind deterrence, explanation, apology, and other non-financial motivations and needs. Strikingly, "because I was angry" ranked equally with "I wanted financial compensation."

When asked "What could have been done to prevent your bringing this claim?" Vincent's respondents made the point even more clearly:

Explanation and apology	37
Correction of mistake	25
Pay compensation	17
Correct treatment at the time	15
Admission of negligence	14
Investigation by drug company / hospital	3
Disciplinary action	4
If listened to and not treated as neurotic	5
Honesty	4

Both Vincent's and Charles' findings were based on post-event surveys of people who had brought claims following a medical accident. On the one hand this may strengthen the message that financial motivations are not the driving force of claims-making, since all of the responses were from people who had brought claims – presumably those who did not have needs or motivations which they believed the claiming process could not have met. On the other hand, surveys of post-event behavior are subject to important criticisms. One is the suspicion that people answering a survey have a need, no matter how anonymous the answers may be held, to appear to be "good people", *i.e.* people who did not sue just for the buck, but for the betterment of their fellows through deterrence, accountability, or punishment.

It is difficult to say how much, if at all, that factor distorted the results. But other studies of similar phenomena support the general lessons in ways that are not subject to the same methodological critiques. Hickson's later analysis[18] of claims against obstetricians was one. It was well known that most malpractice claims are asserted against a small proportion of all physicians. What distinguishes the high-claim physicians from the others? Hickson's research explored the correlation between claims risk and patients' satisfaction with care. But the respondents were not women who had brought claims against their doctors. Rather the study isolated those OBs who were in the high-claim group; and then inquired of a cohort of recent mothers, most of whose labor and deliveries were uneventful, about their experiences with their physicians. Descriptions of the patient-doctor encounters were then matched to the physicians' prior malpractice claims histories – with significant result. Patients of high-claim OBs reported, for example, that they felt rushed during visits, that they were ignored or left uninformed during their labor, that their doctors would not listen to them or that they perceived a lack of concern or respect. The largest category of complaints about the high-claim group were related to communications. Doctors in the low-risk group were seen as "concerned, accessible, and willing to communicate." Those in the high risk group were seen as "hurried, uninterested, and unwilling

18. G. Hickson et al., *Obstetricians' Prior Malpractice Experience and Patients' Satisfaction With Care,* 272 JAMA 1593 (1994).

to listen and answer questions." "Claiming," Hickson concluded, "does not appear to be random."

Perhaps more directly, a study done in New Zealand in 2006 reached findings similar to those of Vincent and Hickson, in a way that did not rely on surveys. In New Zealand there are two places an injured patient might take a complaint. One, the Accident Compensation Corporation, is the only place where money compensation can be won. The second, the Health and Disability Commission, has no authority to award compensation but does entertain complaints, resolve disputes, and extracts learning (hence prevention) from collected complaints submitted by patients and others. Bismark and colleagues[19] had access to the HDC complaints – the very documents, written by the complaining patients (almost always without legal counsel), in which the individuals stated what they wanted the HDC to do. These were all performative documents rather than explanations taken through surveys after the fact. The results of the study's coding were remarkably similar to what Hickson had found in 1992. Organizing the HDC claims into four categories, the complaining individuals sought the following:

Sanction (discipline or punishment of the doctor)	12%
Restoration (intervention in care or compensation)	22%
Correction (review of competence and system change)	51%
Communication (explanation, apology, taking responsibility)	41%

If more proof is needed it lies, as the saying goes, in the pudding. Across the United States leading hospitals and insurance companies have been putting into place early intervention systems, built around full disclosure, apology where appropriate, statements of actions taken to correct the flaw for the future, and satisfaction of an injured patients' immediate needs (financial and otherwise) without cavil. Among the published results are those from the Veterans Administration (hospitals adopting disclosure programs went from the top quartile in claims to the fourth within nine years), the COPIC Insurance Company (payments in its "3Rs" program averaging just over a scant $5,000), and the University

19. M. Bismark et al., *Accountability Sought by Patients Following Adverse Events From Medical Care: The New Zealand Experience,* 175 CMAJ 889 (2006).

of Michigan (a 73% reduction in total claims costs and claims frequency after beginning its program, and a 41% reduction in the numbers of paid events).[20]

The Toro lawnmower company found similar results with a similar program, suggesting that there is nothing unique about medical malpractice. Ditto for class action lawsuits, employment discrimination claims, and every other aspect of individual claiming behavior studied so far.

We add just one more note to round out the data: "whistleblowers."

Whistleblowers are generally insiders who go public with claims and evidence against their own employers' alleged crimes or fraud. With the exception of the federal and state false claims acts, which include statutory compensation for successful claimants under the *qui tam* doctrine, most whistleblowers gain nothing financial for their efforts. Even under the false claims acts very few ever succeed, and those that do suffer personal and financial tolls typically out of proportion to their rewards, which come – if ever – after a substantial part of the complainant's lifetime. The motivations are psychic, not fiscal – personal integrity, altruism, a sense of justice, vindication and sometimes self-preservation. Beyond these features, all redolent of the malpractice studies, we underscore one thing more: in nearly every case of an insider who brought a whistleblower claim the claimant tried first to have the problem addressed internally, by taking it to a superior in the organization. Only then, after rebuff or inattention, did the claimant go outside.[21] To cite Hickson again, "Claiming does not appear to be random."

5.2. Business Conflicts – The Human Factors

Before drawing additional lessons from these facts about individual claiming we sample what is known about conflict and claiming among business firms. Economic theorizing about the behavior of firms abounds, some of which is mentioned in the text below; but of greater interest is the empirical information about the circumstances under which firms

20. A. Kachalia et al., *Liability Claims and Costs Before and After Implementation of a Medical Error Disclosure Program,* Ann Int Med 2010: 153(4); 213.
21. A.S. Kesselheim et al., *Whistle-Blowers' Experiences in Fraud Litigation Against Pharmaceutical Companies,* NEJM 2010: 362(19) 1832.

resort to formal conflict rather than to informal resolution of business-to-business disputes.

The starting point is, as it must be, the seminal work of Stewart Macauley, written in 1963.[22] Macauley learned that in the manufacturing industry, where deals are ubiquitously papered with written contracts, "Disputes are frequently settled without reference to the contract or potential or actual legal sanctions." Though he described his work as preliminary, outlining questions for study rather than offering any certain answers, his interviews among business executives and business attorneys produced notable suggestions for answers to his question. Of greatest interest are two – first, that the style with which a business manager analyzes the available strategies for dealing with a conflict or breakdown depends significantly on the society of others who would be affected or involved. That means, in effect, the audience, and the personal relationships among its members. Second, that within business there are near-universal non-legal "norms": "Commitments are to be honored ... one does not welsh on a deal." And "One ought to produce a good product and stand behind it." The expectations created by these norms bring forth other forces, such as the loss of future business, that replace the discipline which contracts might in other circumstances provide. It would not go far beyond Macauley's data, however, to add that going-to-law happens when those norms are not observed – as Louis Brown observed, when expectations are disappointed – and that full and voluntary accountability for errors can make up for a lot of imperfect widgets. Very much like what patients demanding full disclosure seek in the aftermath of a medical accident, and very like the responsiveness – or lack of it – that motivates whistle-blowers when an insider sees a resistance to fixing corporate wrongdoing.

Other authors have followed Macauley's path, filling in the gaps with empirical information about the conditions under which legal claims are made, vs. those in which claiming does not occur. The lessons are, not surprisingly, consistent with the lessons gleaned from the studies of disputing by individuals, albeit expressed here in the language of organizational theory.

22. S. Macauley, *Non-Contractual relations in Business: A Preliminary Study,* 28 Am. Soc. Rev. 1 (1963).

Gerson,[23] for example, divides firms' post-event (post loss, post breach, post disappointment ...) behavior into two styles: "End-game norms" or EGNs and "relationship-preserving norms" or RPNs. The premise is that relationships between businesses or between business operators are assets of the sort economics can model. Thus, although RPNs have value as the lower cost routes for working out most business problems, accommodation and compromise have their costs as well. The movement from RPN behavior to EGN behavior on any given day is inhibited by the longer-term value of the *relationship*. When the relationship has low potential value, or when its "substitution cost" is low (the cost of finding a new trading partner), other factors in favor of the end-game strategy can come to predominate.

How do relationships gain high value? For one, relationships are worth preserving when there is either high "asset specificity" (following Williamson) or high "party specificity" – i.e., when an upfront investment cannot easily be moved to another relationship either because some *thing* matters greatly or because some *persons* do. For another, game theorists, as Gerson notes, have shown that repeated interactions between people tend to foster future cooperative behavior. That, it is reasonable to suspect, happens as trust and the belief in future reciprocity build over time. Gerson tested his hypothesis empirically, and found it to be sound and significant – over 50% of business claiming behavior could be predicted on the basis of these "substitution" costs alone.

A later study by Gersen and Cheit[24] added detail to the relationship-value model. That work used the concept of "anonymity," for practical purposes the opposite of "relationship." As the authors observe, businesses that engage in "long-term contractual relationships" are by definition not anonymous. Both theoretical and empirical investigations have shown, to underscore it again, that "an extended horizon of future interaction" results significantly more often in cooperative behavior and informal conflict resolution than it does in formal legal claiming. The phenomenon breaks down when anonymity is high.

23. J.E. Gersen, *Markets and Corporate Conflict: A Substitution-Cost Approach to Business Litigation,* 24 Law & Soc. Inq. 589 (1999).
24. R.E. Cheit, & J.E. Gerson , *Why Businesses Sue Each Other: An Empirical Study of State Court Litigation,* 25 Law and Social Inquiry 798 (2000).

Heightened anonymity can result from either endogenous or exogenous factors. An industry populated by large numbers of small firms, for example, permits business to operate anonymously, without the cost of investing in relationships. Rapid changes in markets create uncertainties which can also increase the importance of short-term gains over long-term connections. And some kinds of transactions are more inherently anonymous than others – the 19th century sale of a horse from one stranger to another, for example, compared with the long-term relationship of manufacturers and dedicated component suppliers. Brief market interactions create fewer incentives to avoid conflict; and recurrent transactions operate to the contrary. The key is, again, the value of the personal, perhaps even more than the business, relationship.

A major feature in the preceding discussion of individual claiming, or disputing, was the contextual dimension of perceptions and attributions. Hickson's study of obstetricians, for example, showed unambiguously that components of a relationship unrelated to the proximate cause of an injury affected how the facts of an injury become operative. Later work by Robbennolt[25] and others has shown that the relational dimensions (in Robbenolt's study, expressions of apology and regret) can affect perceptions of injury at the cognitive and not just the evaluative level.

A parallel set of concepts operating in the business-to-business world has been described as "thematization." [26] Business firms tend to place their transactions within one or another frames of reference – assignments which both carry presumptions about the meaning of events, and which predispose the flow of communications in response to them. Thus two managers seeing the same percentage of defective widgets in the carload may both perceive and respond to the same fact in different ways, depending on the "theme" in which the transaction is dressed.

The variables which inform that thematiztion are rather different from those which the law regards as significant. What matters to the law, when contemplating defective widgets, are the contractual antecedents and commercial consequences of the defects – degree of conformance with

25. J. Robbennolt, *Apologies and Legal Settlement: An Empirical Examination,* 102 Mich. L. Rev. 460 2003).
26. B. Blegvad, *Commercial Relations, Contract, and Litigation in Denmark: A Discussion of Macauley's Theories,* 24 Law & Soc'y Rev. 397 (1990).

contractual specifications, previous and cumulative nonconformance, timing vis-a-vis forward commitments, the availability of substitutes in the market, reliance costs already invested and consequential losses flowing from the defects, and the like. The authors of the "thematization" idea find that other variables may create themes, or predisipositions even to these – variables such as the business manager's role within the firm, their ideology, their experience, and the management structure around them, as well as the legal and economic cultures of the business and its market.

One set of thematizing variables is of particular interest: how the transaction is governed. The authors adopt Williamson's taxonomy of unilateral (one party in control, resulting in ready resort to contract), bilateral (governed interactively by the participants), or trilateral (adjustments provided by a third entity such as an external arbiter.) Not surprisingly, the empirical data suggest that discrete transactions are assigned a unilateral character and resort to contract-based behavior is frequent. Long-term relationships involve bilateral or trilateral governance structures, and a legal voice is seldom employed. Some of the assignations seem immutable – debt collections, for example, tend to be highly contractual, while quantity adjustments tend to be afforded a bilateral governance structure and its concomitant theme.

"The success of bilateral governance depends on the firms' organizational ability to manage risks involved in building a continuing relationship with another firm,"[27] and that in turns depends on a number of factors including the internal structure of the firm and the way in which it allows transactions to be managed: access to direct communications between the directly affected managers, for example, and the intensity and ease of two-way flows of information and advice – both of which conduce to a mutual understanding of the terms of the relationship and a theme built on bilateral governance.

The point of these several sets of findings about business firms' responses to breakdowns and failures is twofold. First, while some of the conditions affecting the emergence of actual conflict cannot easily be changed in any identified transaction – *e.g.* external economic conditions that affect transactional horizons – some can be. And second,

27. Op. cit.

that the factors affecting "attribution" and thereby shaping responses to conflict-potential events among individuals have strikingly close parallels among business which are, after all, managed by people. What are some examples, then, of how these malleable components can be put to good preventive use?

6. Two Concrete Illustrations: Partnering, and Negotiating

One of the bullet points which emerges most clearly from this review of the claiming literature, both business and individual, is that the subjective "affect" of the transaction really matters. That affect, or theme in business, or attribution process among individuals, is shaped and colored by the whole history of the interaction within which the conflict-potential event takes place: the antecedents, the surroundings and the access to alternative routes for resolution, the presumption derived from history, and the flow of information and responses at the moment of the immediate event. While secondary prevention means rushing a crash cart to the site of the arrest (or referring to clear language in a contract), and while tertiary prevention means saving the dying with last-ditch resuscitation machines (or voicing a claim of right for external adjudication), primary prevention draws the focus to managing the context in advance. The present section offers two abbreviated illustrations, drawn from two different literatures, about how that can be done.

6.1. "Partnering"

Partnering is a conflict prevention process widely used in the construction industry, though its basic lines are applicable to any transaction with an extended future. It emerged in the 1980s as the synthesis of two movements then gaining currency – total quality management, or "TQM," and ADR. One of its earliest expositors, James Groton, summed it up[28] this way:

28. J. Groton, *"Dispute Prevention in the Construction Industry,"* paper in the author's files.

> When used on a transaction-specific basis, partnering is usually instituted at the beginning of the relationship by holding a retreat among all personnel involved in the transaction who have leadership and management responsibilities, in which the participants, assisted by an independent facilitator, become acquainted with each other's objectives and expectations, recognize common aims, develop a teamwork approach, initiate open communications, and establish nonadversarial processes for resolving potential problems.

The underlying notion is a recognition that when a problem arises in an ongoing transaction or project, there is a tendency for each side to begin its response by identifying its sole interest implicated in the question, and acting in a way meant to protect it. With each doing the same, but in opposite directions, what may have been a manageable challenge becomes a more difficult to manage conflict.

The procedure can be varied to suit the circumstances, but the most essential objectives and circumstances are straightforward. The process begins, when best applied, with an agreement made in advance to adopt the process from the outset of the relationship and throughout, as the circumstances require. Although in some elaborated forms it may employ a neutral facilitator and a "team-building" approach, neither is strictly necessary. Small projects neither justify nor require an outside facilitator; and some parties have little time (or taste) for team-building fun and games, perhaps especially so in time-sensitive industries such as health care. The objectives are to assure a common or at least compatible understanding of the project (or relationship, or transaction), to create pathways for informal communication, to identify expected challenges and bumps in the road, and to establish a problem-management plan identifying where and to whom problems go and in what order. Trust and familiarity are built as the process goes forward – and with these investments the relationship acquires value.

Groton identifies a "kick-off" meeting, pursuant to the agreement, and that is customary at the very outside. The participants may include not only the contracting parties, but others whose contributions – or expectations – are significant as well. Under some plans the kick-off results in a "Charter" – a list of common goals, a commitment to a collaborative process, and a schedule of future events. After the kick-off most projects add periodic (monthly, quarterly, annually depending on the transaction) meetings of the same group, where the accomplishment of identified goals is assessed, new issues are put out for discussion, and commitment to the process is reconfirmed. More detailed schedules and sample workplans are available from any of a number of sources. [29]

While partnering as originally conceived is as much a conflict resolution tool as it is a method for preventing disputes, it fits well within the models discussed above. At its core it provides a frame of reference – a thematization, to recall that concept – within which unanticipated sources of conflict and potential injuries or losses are perceived, weighed, and assessed. It injects value into a relationship, thereby affecting the fight-or-resolve calculus; it reduces the access cost of alternatives to conflict by making a system for resolution a standing part of the relationship rather than a special procedure that has to be travelled-to or brought in from outside when something flares up. And it destroys anonymity and adds to party specificity – all to the good of changing dispute-response behaviors.

6.2. Negotiating the "Point of the Deal"

"The product of a negotiation isn't a document; it's the value produced once the parties have done what they agreed to do."[30] So Danny Ertel closes an analysis of deal-making which begins with the observation that too many negotiators (especially lawyer negotiators) mess up deals by doing what they believe they are supposed to do. More precisely, negotiators too often fail to recognize the difference between deals that are all present and no future, begun and finished in a stroke such as the transfer of an asset from seller to buyer each of which has no concern for ever seeing the other again, and those deals in which value is created for each side over the course of time and through the success of the parties' working together. "Winning" the negotiation for the former means getting the best immediate deal possible, with price and terms as favorable for the negotiator's client as they might be. These negotia-

29. See, e.g., F. Carr, *"Partnering: Aligning Interests, Collaboration, and Achieving Common Goals,"* CPR Institute for Conflict Prevention and Resolution, available online at www.cpradr.org.
30. Op. Cit.

tors, Ertel says with only a slight touch of caricature, "couldn't care less about launching a relationship." One of the many succeeding problems is that negotiating towards a favorable contract, rather than towards a workable future, leaves the people who will actually be doing the value-creating work as strangers, with no appreciation of what the negotiators had in mind or how the contract was meant to handle a happening it never addressed. And neither side experienced the background with the other that could have created the trust that smoothing friction requires. In the terminology previously described, the resulting transaction has a high degree of anonymity, and the asset value of the respective managers' relationship starts at zero. Far better, Ertel suggests, to negotiate as if "*implementation* really mattered."

Ertel was writing about strategies for negotiation, from a business profit point of view. His prescriptions, however, are easily embraced within the principles of conflict prevention, even if it were only the case that a deal that produces conflict is the opposite of a deal that produces value.

Ertel's principles are six in number:

First, from the outset of a relationship intended to create value for both, such as those that characterize much of health care – hospitals and doctors, doctors and nurses, payors and providers – the deal-making should keep on center stage what each side will actually need to create value for itself. The right individuals need to be teed up, and the way they get into the deal should reflect the way they'll interact with each other after the ink on the contract is dry. Good business means understanding that A won't succeed, in the longer run, unless B can succeed as well. Talk about what that might take. Surprises and gotchas are OK for selling horses in the Old Wild West; but not where the deal is expected to have a future.

Second, "consult broadly." Involve the people who will lead the deal in the making of it. It may be the habit of physicians' groups to have their business manager negotiate a capitation arrangement with the business manager of a major health plan. Better, Ertel suggests, to include in the writing of it the people who will act in the play after it's written. Doing so creates buy-in, promotes understanding, identifies pitfalls, and – maybe most important of all – enhances the asset value of relationships.

Third, use the deal-creating process as a way of establishing the styles of interaction that might be necessary when frictions do break out in the future. If extensive, voluntary, sharing of information will be needed then, do it now. If resort to creative solutions to future problems will be more important than standing on well-known rules, use just that approach to designing the arrangement. If collaborative rather than re-active responses to bumps in the road are the better way in the future, negotiate that way from the outset. Here, it seems, the "experience" variable in the process of thematization.

Fourth, "Air your nightmares." On the one hand, as Arthur Leff once put it, the lawyer's job is to think about things that aren't going to hap-pen. On the other, there is too often a fear that raising the "what'll we do if …" question creates risks that the deal might founder on a contingency that probably won't occur. The balance is a matter of judgment but the advantages to airing your nightmare, in Ertel's phrase, are significant – workable allocations of risks can be addressed, preventive steps might be designed to forestall or minimize the disruptive consequences of the nightmare, conflict-management strategies might be designed … i.e., making secondary prevention primary.

Fifth, and a point already made at the beginning of this paper, neither party in a long-term deal benefits in the longer term if the other party takes on a risk or responsibility it won't be able to bear. I suppose I could win a negotiation with my wife by getting her to agree to change the oil in the family airplane whenever it's supposed to be changed. But it won't work. She doesn't know what engine oil is, much less what it does or how frequently it has to be changed. I am not sure it would matter that it was her fault, when the engine seizes up at altitude. All risks can be expressed as costs; and the point of a win-win negotiation is to cre-ate value by trading gains and losses where they have different values to each of the negotiators. Party A should be willing to take on a risk it might otherwise insist B take on, if A can bear it more cheaply and if B reciprocates with something of value that it can do better than A can.

Sixth and finally, think about the handoff. No less than medication reconciliation in health care, or any other aspect of care transitions, a joint and explicit handoff can avoid a good deal of trouble from laps and gaps and misunderstandings and miscommunications. "OK, here's what we mean by this, and the first thing we'd like to see is that …"

Bear in mind Louis Brown's earliest admonition: people make claims when they experience a sense of loss, and a sense of loss comes from a disappointed expectation. Get the expectations lined up and the losses might not be perceived.

The confluence between Ertel's prescriptions and the preceding discussion of variables that guide and shape responses to conflict-potential events is striking. Among them: high party specificity reduces formal claiming; relationships are utilized in lieu of claiming when the relationship itself has positive prospective value; claiming is seldom engaged in when transactions are governed bilaterally; and the subjective "affect" of personal contact provides the "theme" that colors the very perception of injurious events.

Whether a dog feels it has been tripped over and kicked, and whether it bites the nearest ankle or just goes back to sleep, depends on all that has come before, as well as what happens at the moment. None of it happens in isolation. Dispute-making seems not to be random.

The Usefulness of Legally Useless Clauses – Proactive Law and Strategic Perspective

By

Hugues Bouthinon-Dumas[1]
Associate professor of law at ESSEC Business School, European Centre of Law & Economics

Antoine Masson[2]
Référendaire at the European Court of Justice, European Centre of Law & Economics (ESSEC Business School)

"If it goes without saying, it would go better by saying it."
(Talleyrand)

1. Introduction

Many contracts contain not only useful clauses, but also legally useless clauses, i.e. clauses which produce no specific legal effect. From a legal point of view, this phenomenon seems bizarre since especially in French law a contract is legally defined as an agreement entered into by two or more parties who agree to perform obligations under particular conditions which form the substance of the clauses of the contract. However, the insertion of so-called legally useless clauses in the contracts is very common. The fact that this has become *common* practice seems to indicate that useless clauses may not be completely useless… If they *were* completely useless, they would have been removed from the contract, not least because any superfluous element in a legal document costs time and money.

1. Leading author. bouthinondumas@essec.edu.
2. antoine.masson@essec.edu.

In practice, the question as to the usefulness of useless clauses often arises in the context of long-term contracts. It is in this context that parties – both firms and individuals – will have to refer to the clauses of their contract. Indeed, often useless clauses are to be found in a wide range of contracts, such as lease contracts, distribution contracts, employment contracts, articles of association and, more generally, relationship-specific contracts (cf. the transaction cost theory: R. Coase, O. Williamson, etc.). These clauses may have been drafted by all the parties or by one of them only, negotiated at arms-length by the parties or merely accepted by one of them, read in full by the parties or only signed.

Whether a clause is useless from a legal point of view depends on the legal system that governs the contract. In our presentation, we will take the example of clauses governed by French Law. However, the effects that these clauses are likely to produce will be the same in other legal contexts. Our analysis can thus be applied generally, even if the rules governing contract drafting and styles of contract drafting vary from one legal system to the other.

The usefulness of useless clauses seems to present us with a paradox, but the paradox is only in our minds. It lies in perceiving a phenomenon which is not only legal from a legal point of view. Of course, the value (and ultimately the usefulness) of terms and conditions in a contract is primarily assessed by lawyers. However, clauses (and, indeed, the contracts themselves) are also linguistic phenomena, in other words "speech acts" (Cf. J.R. Searle, *Speech Acts: An Essay in the Philosophy of Language*, Cambridge UP, 1969; J.L. Austin, *How to do Things with Words*, OUP, 1962). And the psycho-sociological effects of legal documents are not limited to the legal effects. Consequently, a clause may appear useless from the perspective of a contract lawyer but at the same time useful from the point of view of the parties. These legally useless clauses may matter for the "contractual relationship" which goes beyond the legal agreement (cf. I. MacNeil's theory about relational contracts).

From a strictly legal and traditional perspective, clauses which produce no legal effects do not have a *raison d'être* in a contract and must accordingly be considered useless. For this reason, they have not been – so far – a topic for academics (except the « boilerplate clauses » – Cf. E. McKendrick, *Contract Law*, Oxford University Press, 2000). When lawyers show an interest in the uselessness of legal provisions, it is usually to draw attention to the decline in the quality of statutory instruments. Lawyers are keen to criticise badly-written laws for having become "wordy". This problem is associated with the "legislative inflation" phenomenon: statutory instruments and regulations (and their provisions) are becoming increasingly lengthy and numerous. Much of this legislation is therefore considered "useless". The lawyers' dream of concise statutory instruments (based on principles rather than detailed provisions…) is not new (Cf. J.E.M. Portalis, , *Discours préliminaire sur le projet de Code civil,* 1801: « We do not need useless laws. They weaken necessary laws and compromise the certainty and majesty of legislation»). Economy and temperance are virtues expected from rule-makers. They should also be expected from contract-drafters.

In this context, why claim that useless clauses can be useful? To understand the paradoxical usefulness of so-called "useless clauses", we need to go beyond a purely legal approach and adopt a multi-discipline approach, taking into account the cognitive, sociological and economic effects of contractual speeches on the impressions created in the minds of the parties to a contract. Contracts can produce non-legal effects. They have a psychological and behavioural impact on the parties, which is not strictly related to the normative effect sought and generated by the contract.

These non-legal effects of useless clauses are important for analysing contract performance from a proactive perspective. Insofar as useless clauses contribute to the prevention of misunderstandings, tension between the parties and opportunistic behaviour and, subsequently, to avoiding time-and-money-consuming litigation, they can facilitate contractual relations. The legal obligations generated by the contract are just one component of contractual relations. Therefore, we have to pay attention to the other components of those relations, especially the useless clauses that may generate significant non-legal effects.

It should be mentioned here that useless clauses can also produce the opposite effect by causing problems instead of improving good feeling between contracting parties. Useless clauses may not only really be useless, they may even be detrimental. It is thus necessary to examine the usefulness of useless clauses in order to determine to what extent and under what conditions they can contribute to proactive contract law and thus increase the mutual benefit for both parties to a contract.

We will investigate the concept of useless clauses and create a typology of the different categories of useless clauses (I). Then, we will analyse the effects of these clauses and their usefulness for contracting parties (II) because they are the foundations of legal strategies based on useless clauses (III).

2. The different categories of useless clauses

Different theories of clauses have been proposed by lawyers specialising in contract law. Some have distinguished clauses according to their nature: the ones which are key elements of the contract (*essentialia clausa*), obligations resulting from key elements (*naturalia clausa*) and particular conditions (*accidentalia clausa*) (Cf. J-R. Potier, *Traités sur différentes matières de droit civil*, 1773-1774); others according to their function (clauses determining the power of the parties in the contractual relationship, clauses defining the bargain expressed in the contract and clauses dealing with the mechanics of dispute resolution (Cf. Geneviève Helleringer, *Les clauses contractuelles. Essai de typologie*, doctoral dissertation, Paris 1 Panthéon-Sorbonne, 2010)). But no criteria have ever been proposed for distinguishing between useless and useful clauses. It is thus necessary to clarify this distinction and to explore the concept of useless clauses in relation to better known kinds of contractual terms. There may be many reasons why a clause does not produce legal effects: some clauses are without normative value (A), some clauses are a copy of rules deriving from the law and thus superfluous clauses (B) and, finally, some clauses are illegal clauses (C).

2.1 Clauses without normative value

A contract states, in a written form, the terms and conditions agreed by the parties. Therefore, clauses express the undertakings of the parties and the conditions under which those undertakings will be performed (Cf. S. Whittaker, "On the Development of European Standard Contract Terms", *European Review of Contract Law* 2006, n°1, p. 51.). Certain clauses are common and may be expressed in a standardised form, others are more specific and drafted *ex nihilo*. In all cases, clauses are supposed to contribute, directly or indirectly, to the legal determining of the contracting parties' behaviour, since they define those parties' obligations and powers. But when phrases in the contracts do not contribute to legally determining what the contracting parties are obliged to do or what they are authorised to do, they are useless clauses.

The concept of useless clauses is difficult to define in French law. Indeed, in French law, as in many other legal systems, there is a (non-binding) principle of contract interpretation which states that a clause should be interpreted in a way that gives it a useful effect (Code civil, article 1157: *Where a clause admits of two meanings, one shall rather understand it in the one with which it may have some effect, than in the meaning with which it could not produce any)*. It is only exceptional (and those exceptions are to be strictly interpreted) that a clause will be regarded as without effect. More generally, the dividing line between a useful clause and a useless clause depends on the interpretation rules in contract law. Hence, we can distinguish the clauses which only appear to be legally useless (false useless clauses) from those which are truly useless because they do not have a normative value (true useless clauses).

First, certain clauses seem to have only a "virtual usefulness" because they will apply only if a set of particular conditions are met – conditions which appear very improbable at the time of signing the contract. These clauses are typically used to give "completeness" to a long-term contract which is necessarily subject to uncertainty. These clauses are useful because they look ahead and help deal with uncertainty in the economic environment.

Other clauses appear to be useless because they are standardised and are simply mechanically inserted into contracts, with the result that parties – and even, on occasion, drafters – do not pay any real attention to them. Lawyers know them as "formal clauses" ('clauses de style'). However, a clause being standardised is not sufficient to establish that this clause is useless. Contract law presumes that contracting parties have included each clause in order to achieve a particular purpose. It is only exceptional that such a clause will be without effect. For example, in case two clauses are conflicting, a judge will give precedence to one of them on the basis that it better expresses the common intention of the contracting parties.

Moreover, it is difficult to support the claim that a clause is useless just because it contradicts another one. For example, in the case of plurality of debtors, contracts frequently stipulate that debtors will be held "jointly and severally" liable ('conjointement et solidairement'). However, those terms are contradictory under French law. If they are considered separately they have a normative value, but taken together they cancel each other out. Therefore, a contradicted clause is not a clause without normative value, but more precisely a clause without normative effect in the specific context of a contract.

Clauses in a contract can also appear to be useless because they are not fully relevant with regard to the particular transaction the contracting parties wish to make. Some parties seeking to standardise their contractual practices may draw up contractual conditions which can be applied to various situations (irrespective of the nature of the relationship between the parties or the law governing the contract). This leads, for instance, to general terms for sale or purchase. However, in order to draw up all-purpose contractual documents (also called omnibus contracts) of this kind, drafters are inevitably obliged to include clauses in the contract which are usually irrelevant. For example, clauses related to sale of goods (clauses reserving property, etc.) will not be relevant if the contract is being used to provide a service. These clauses are not useless *per se*, but they have no legal effect in the particular context in which the contract has been used.

Clauses which are apparently descriptive can have an indirect normative effect. Certain clauses contained in contracts aim at describing facts or situations rather than creating obligations. For this reason, we can oppose an explicitly normative clause to an apparently informative clause. However, we cannot conclude that only the former is legally useful, whereas the latter is useless. Indeed, many clauses look like descriptive notes (they indicate what is – the *Sein* – and not what should be – the *Sollen*) but these clauses nevertheless contribute to the normative substance generated by the contract. For example, when a clause describes what "force majeure" is, listing the assumptions which correspond to that situation, that clause has a genuine normative effect. Indeed, as the occurrence of force majeure is an exemption from contractual liability, defining this concept helps to define the debtors' liability itself.

Some clauses seem to be purely descriptive. This is the case when a clause states that a specific piece of information has been given. These informative clauses can be regarded as useless because they apparently have no normative effect. However, if this statement is required by law (for example, doctors must fully inform their patients about the risks involved in any proposed medical procedure or treatment), then this informative clause has a legal effect because it is a proof, given by the contract itself, that the debtor has fulfilled its duty of disclosure.

Frequently, contracting parties mention the context in which the contract has been concluded, what they had in mind and what objectives they were pursuing. Such phrases are generally placed in the introduction or the preamble to the contract. Most of the time, these indications do not have a normative value. This is particularly true when the statements deal with former relations between the parties. Under French law, the reasons which have led parties to enter into an agreement are (in theory) not taken into consideration by judges. Only if the contracting parties wish to put their motivation for drawing up the contract and the context in which the contract was made into the legal substance of that contract can that context and those motivations be taken into consideration by a judge in order to assess how the parties should perform their obligations.

Sometimes, contracts may also include figures of speech and incantation formulas. From a legal point of view, appeals to God or any other deity, along with swearing a mediaeval oath or invoking spiritual or supernatural powers, are useless in modern contract law. Under French law, the binding effect of a contractual agreement comes from the State and is enforced by public officers (Code civil, article 1134-1: *Agreements lawfully entered into take the place of the law for those who have made them)*. Such old-fashioned practices seem to be irrational and ridiculous. However, current contracts frequently include useless phrases, such as 'lu et approuvé' (read and approved).

Lastly, certain elements of the contract, sometimes considered "clauses", are just practical guidelines. For example, a contract frequently contains, on its first page, a number or other means of identification. Obviously, this type of information does not have any normative value.

2.2. Superfluous clauses

Among legally useless clauses, the ones that appear most often are those which do not have any usefulness because they are redundant since provisions contained in statutory instruments are applicable to the contractual relation. They are equivalent to "terms implied in law".

The legal rules that contracting parties must comply with are not only those laid down in the contract itself (express terms of the contract), even if we consider all the contractual documents (additional, general terms, endorsements, etc.), but also (by virtue of Article 1135 of the French Civil code: "*Agreements are binding not only as to what is therein expressed, but also as to all the consequences which equity, usage or statute give to the obligation according to its nature*"), the obligations resulting from all sources of law higher than the contract. This includes legislations, regulations, collective agreements and standard terms, as well as legal precedent and business practices. The contract, and hence the contractual relationship, is simultaneously governed by the clauses seen in the contract and by invisible legal provisions.

Concerning statutory provisions, French law makes a distinction between imperative rules ('règles imperatives'), also called public order rules ('règles d'ordre public'), which are compulsory (from which the parties cannot derogate), and default rules ('règles supplétives') which apply in so far as the parties have not agreed otherwise. Consequently, under French law it is pointless to copy imperative rules into a contract, except in – extremely exceptional – cases where the law requires parties to copy such provisions (e.g. Code de la consommation, L. 121-23 7°) into their contracts for informative purposes. It is also pointless to copy default rules because they automatically apply in the absence of clauses to the contrary. Ultimately, only clauses derogating from default rules need to be stipulated.

It is only in limited circumstances that copying the law can be of legal interest. For example, in the event that the law governing a contract is amended (due to circulation of the contract or evolution of the law), the contractualisation of the original relevant legal provision can sometimes help to maintain its applicability to that contract. This assumes that the former provision does not conflict with the public order provisions of the new legal system which is now governing the contract. This – highly hypothetical – situation does not explain why so many drafters copy in the statutory provisions applicable to a contract. It is much more reasonable to think that this exercise of copying can be explained by the drafter's need to justify his or her work (and the accompanying remuneration!) and by the non-legal effects that useless clauses can produce.

2.3 Obviously illicit clauses

The third subcategory of useless clauses deals with illicit clauses. This may seem surprising. However, if we consider that a useless clause is a clause which does not produce a legal effect, we need to include illicit clauses in this category. Indeed, as illicit clauses are against the law, they are deprived of effect by law through various mechanisms: they can be considered as illegal, invalid, unenforceable, as if they were not written, etc. In all these situations, if one party requests the application of an illicit clause, it will not be able to enforce it.

French law deprives illicit clause of effect for several reasons: unfair clauses, unlawful clauses, clauses abusively restricting the basic obligations of the contracting parties, etc. (L. Merland & J. Mestre, « De quelques risques d'invalidité des clauses contractuelles en droit français », in *Regards comparatistes sur le phénomène contractuel*, PU Aix-Marseille, 2009, p. 123).

However, only clauses which are obviously illicit can be considered as useless. When a reasonable person can doubt a clause's compliance with the law, it is not a useless clause. It is just a risky clause or a disputed clause.

3. The useful effects of legally useless clauses

Useless clauses exist and we should ask ourselves why. Two possible reasons may explain the existence of useless clauses in a contract. Either they have been inserted accidentally, or due to the laziness of drafters who have copied from inappropriate templates or are unaware of the uselessness of the clauses. Or the useless clauses have been inserted willfully, because of the non-legal effects that at least one of the parties has perceived.

In this paper, we will explore the second option. First, we will list the different positive or negative effects that useless clauses can produce (A), then identify who can draw benefit from them and, consider the level of awareness that drafters and parties have of that uselessness (B). This point will determine how clauses will be used, especially, as a resource for legal strategies.

3.1. What kinds of usefulness can useless clauses have?

Clauses that are unlikely to have legal effects can still produce other types of effects, which we will state without denying their potential adverse effects. At this stage, it is important to note that useful clauses can also produce the same sort of effects as useless clauses. Our focus here is, however, on the latter, rather than the former.

3.1.1. Informative effects

The main effect of useless clauses is to convey information to the parties reading them. Although these clauses have no normative content, they form a medium through which the drafter of the contract can transmit a large range of information such as references or dates relating to the situation or the state of mind of the parties when they agreed upon the contract, information about the context in which the contract is intended to produce an effect, and so on.

However, the potential informative effect of useless clauses needs to be discussed carefully. Most legally useless clauses do not contain any relevant information. Even when they contain relevant information, useless clauses may actually reduce the parties' level of information by inundating them with a surfeit of data (too much information kills information). An excessive use of details is likely to divert the parties' attention from key elements of the contract. The main purpose of the contract must prevail if the parties want to maintain good business relations.

Useless clauses may even produce bad informative effects (cf. A. Masson, «Essai de théorie des stratégies juridiques », *Revue de droit prospectif*, avril 2008, p. 443-452). First, the information contained and conveyed by useless clauses may be inaccurate. Therefore they may make the parties more confused. They may create erroneous representations of the contract and mislead the parties in their contractual behaviour. Of course, this confusing effect may be what one party has deliberately sought. In this case, we see that a useless clause can be used to manipulate a legally naïve party.

Secondly, an excessive use of useless clauses can make a contract harder to negotiate. Negotiators can meet difficulties when it comes to agreeing on certain clauses, for example deciding whether Clause X expresses a mandatory rule or is a reminder of a legal provision. On the other hand, vagueness has its own virtues. It can help to make a contract an acceptable compromise, each party having the impression of getting what it wanted, even if, in this situation, difficulties have just been taken out, disguised and then replaced.

3.1.2. Cognitive effect

In addition to their informative effect, useless clauses can affect the parties' minds. In other words, useless clauses may produce cognitive effects, modifying the parties' perceptions of the contract. Cognitive effects can be positive as well as negative.

The cognitive effect of useless clauses can help contracting parties to finalise a contract when they best express the intention behind that contract or help the parties to perform their obligations spontaneously. In this respect, useless clauses may play a positive role if they promote trust between the contracting parties, foreseeability regarding the contractual relationship and coordination between economic actors. The relationship between the parties can bear fruit far beyond the performance of the obligations explicitly expressed in the contract.

But some useless clauses can also produce negative effects. The cognitive effect of such clauses will significantly depend on the context of the contractual relationship. Indeed, useless clauses carrying misleading information can be a source of mistrust and disputes. For example, if a contracting party proposes an over-detailed contractual document, including many elements which are legally ineffective or irrelevant; this unusual document will be perceived with suspicion by other parties with whom he has previously had business relations.

3.1.3. Symbolic effect

Useless clauses may also have symbolic impact. As noted, many clauses included in a contract are not legally relevant. Such is the case for instance with the title "contract" and with the "choice" of the law governing the contract (when there is in fact no real choice available, or when the choice of the law does not need any expression of will). It is the same when contracting parties refer to external and superior forces, such as the Law, the State, etc. Despite the fact that these references are legally useless, they help to add, in the minds of the parties, to their awareness of being involved in a legal process that can have serious consequences. Simply lengthening a contract can contribute to its symbolic significance. The symbolic force of typical legal terms and phrases, perhaps more than the legal consequences and remedies attached to a breach of contract in some cases, encourages parties to respect their promises.

From the same perspective, we should emphasize that useless clauses can also act as phatic expressions and therefore facilitate negotiations. The phatic language is made up of small-talk, clichéd phrases – such as "Have a nice day", "hello", "you're welcome", etc. – which are used to establish or maintain contact. According to Roman Jakobson (Cf. R. Jakobson, "Linguistics and Poetics", in T. Sebeok, ed., Style in Language, Cambridge, MA: M.I.T. Press, 1960, pp. 350-377), the purpose of the phatic expression is for speakers to reaffirm their status and indicate their respective identities and social positions. Thus the phatic communication fulfils an identity need. Contractual communication is not an exception in this respect. Certain useless clauses have a phatic function. They are used to reassure the parties of their legal status and their capacity to understand the law, because it seems to be made understandable.

Let us for example take the phrase "read and approved". Under French law, this phrase has no legal effect. However, this phrase is so deeply rooted in popular legal culture that if this handwritten phrase is not used in a contract, that contract may be perceived by some consumers with suspicion. One might ask oneself what the legal value of a contract which does not include the legal formula *par excellence* is! Even the French Conseil d'Etat, which is the Supreme Court for administrative matters, uses this useless handwritten phrase alongside the addressee's signature in some of its acts.

3.1.4. Economic effects

Finally, useless clauses can have an economic effect.

Irrelevant clauses can make contracts more flexible and therefore likely to apply to a greater number of situations. This solution is likely to decrease the transaction costs related to the developing and validating process. Standardisation of a contract can be more expensive.

Mentioning a large number of mandatory rules in the contract gives its reader an overview of the entire law applicable to the contractual relationship. Thus the contracting parties can avoid wasting time, because they will not have to check the statutes, case-law, etc., that interact with the contract. For this reason, useless clauses may save time and money.

Useless clauses can facilitate the creation of templates, or at least routines, for the administration of contracts by legal departments (design, archival, classification, etc) and by non-legal departments (risk management, audit, etc). However, an excess of useless clauses can be counterproductive. Indeed, an excessively lengthy contract is difficult for a layman to understand. Useless clauses may thus increase legal risk.

In addition, the economic value of useless legal clauses is limited by the fact that the insertion of any clause is costly, because it consumes paper, ink, and above all the time and expertise of people who develop these over-completed contracts.

Useless clauses can produce contradictory effects. For example, too many supposedly informative clauses lead to overlong, costly, confusing contracts. But if the combined effect of useless clauses is ambiguous, we should then consider this question: who are useless clauses useful to?

3.2. Consciousness of the usefulness of useless clauses

To explain the existence of useless clauses, it is not enough to observe from our academic perspective that such clauses can nevertheless be useful. It must be added that this usefulness needs to be perceived by the contracting parties themselves if they want to use them successfully.

The psychological and socio-economic effects of useless clauses can be perceived in different ways by contracting parties. This has strong implications when we assess the role of useless clauses.

First scenario: these effects are not perceived, consciously or unconsciously, by the contracting parties. In this case, the parties will not try to take advantage of them. Only external observers, in particular psychologists and sociologists, will be able to identify and possibly measure these effects. Interest in the study of useless clauses will remain mainly theoretical.

Second scenario: the parties have perceived the interest of useless clauses, but this perception remains confused. They feel (rather than observe) that the insertion of useless clauses in contracts tends to facilitate the contractual process (negotiation and execution of the contract). Consequently, they will develop the habit of including clauses which appear satisfactory or advantageous to them in their contract, but without assessing for each contractual relationship whether the specific effects produced by those clauses are useless.

Third scenario: the parties are clearly aware of the advantages which can be gained from the insertion of certain useless clauses into their contracts. The useless clauses are considered a paralegal instrument for achieving business objectives, in particular maximising the contract's value, sometimes to capture value illegitimately from other parties, depending on whether the usefulness of useless clauses is shared between parties or used unilaterally.

Indeed, useless clauses may be beneficial to all the parties or only to one. This determines to whom useless clauses may ultimately be useful. Useless clauses may be of interest to all contracting parties and therefore may be useful to the contract itself. When contracting parties exchange information via informative clauses, they increase their level of knowledge and their mutual trust. All of this will increase the quality of the contract and therefore create more value for contracting parties who will be able to share this surplus. Useless clauses, including illegal clauses, may only be of use to one party, who may try to use them against the other party. In this case, the usefulness of useless clauses is not shared but unilateral. Of course, such clauses do not fit with the concept of collaboration, but rather with an opportunistic perception of the contractual relationship.

Useless clauses can be one of many legal weapons in the array of legal strategies that are drawn up and implemented by social actors, in particular businesses (Cf. A. Masson et M.J. Shariff (ed.), Through the Legal Looking Glass: Exploring the Concept of Corporate Legal Strategy, Eur. Bus. Law Rev., vol. 22, 2011, p. 51; L. Lopucki et W. Weyrauch « A Theory of Legal Strategy », Duke L.J., vol. 49, 2000, p. 1405; R. Bird, « Pathways of Legal Strategy », Stan. J.L. Bus. & Fin. Vol. 14, 2008, p. 1; C.E. Bagley, *Winning Legally: How to Use the Law to Create Value, Marshal Resources and Manage Risk*, Harvard Business School Press, 2005, p. 50; C. E. Bagley, Winning Legally: the Value of Legal Astuteness, Acad. Mgmt. Rev., vol. 33, 2008, p. 378; A. Belcher, Corporate Risk Management and Legal Strategy, *in* A. Masson et M. Shariff (ed.), *op. cit.*, p. 247). Useless clauses are thus a resource which can be exploited by businesses to get a competitive advantage.

4. The strategic use of useless clauses

Nowadays, businesses consider law an important part of their business strategies. It is a relatively new field of interest for scholars (Cf. Constance Bagley, "What's Law Got To DO With It? Integrating Law and Strategy", *American Business Law Journal* 2010, 44/7, p. 587). The Research Centre of ESSEC Business Schools is one of the places where this kind of research is done. Law is often considered by business people as a source of risk (and costs) that limits their freedom of action. But some business people perceive that law is also a key resource for achieving commercial, industrial and financial objectives. The Law & Management approach aims to analyse the legal performance of a business, taking into account the internal legal organisation of that business, together with the specific legal strategies that the business implements in order to take advantage of its fellow contracting parties and harm its competitors.

In the Law & Strategy or Law & Management approach (Cf. Antoine Masson and Hugues Bouthinon-Dumas, "L'approche 'Law & Management'", *Revue trimestrielle de droit commercial* 2011, n°2, p. 233), legal strategies can be defined as strategies implemented by economic actors who use legal tools in order to achieve specific objectives such as developing the business, outperforming competitors or capturing value. This approach is based on a disruptive vision of the law, seen as a resource for business people and not as a neutral constraint. Law can provide a competitive advantage for those who are aware of the specific help and power it can give. Legal strategies can be drawn up with a very wide range of legal or even paralegal tools: the choice of a suitable legal regime, the designing of an efficient set of rules through flexible law (contract law, etc), optimisation of legal structures and processes, well-organised legal management in-house or by external legal practitioners, etc.

We will now analyse useless clauses as the key elements of particular legal strategies. Legal strategies depend on a specific context where market operators are provided with legal resources but also with the cognitive, organisational, economic and financial resources which those legal resources interact with. To analyse those legal strategies, it is important to show how all of these different resources are used and combined to achieve a specific objective in a particular environment.

Thus, we would like to highlight the role that useless clauses can play among the resources mobilised for legal strategies. In addition, we would like to note that some of the legal strategies based on useless clauses fit into the perspective of proactive law, but not all.

It is necessary to make a distinction between collaborative strategies based on useless clauses that converge towards a proactive law approach (A), and opportunistic strategies that are inconsistent with a proactive law approach and deserve to be criticised (B).

4.1. Collaborative strategies based on useless clauses. A contribution to proactive law.

Useless clauses can be used to build a mutually beneficial relationship between parties (1) and to improve businesses' contract management (2).

4.1.1. Collaborative strategies involving all the parties

From a typically proactive perspective, we can argue that the quality of a contractual relationship closely depends on the understanding by each contracting party of the situation and objectives of the other party. Deep mutual understanding is an essential requirement for ascertaining, clearly and accurately, the purpose of any contract. On this basis, the contracting parties can build a contractual relationship that should create extra value because they thereby minimize the post-transaction costs related to disputes, litigation and enforcement. Regardless of the strictly legal transaction costs, a good understanding of the individual and mutual expectations relating to the transaction is likely to improve the quality of coordination between the contracting parties. Therefore, performing the contract will be as time-and-resource-efficient as possible. The economic impact of contractual good feeling must not be underestimated. That is why a proactive contract can create value for both parties.

Following this view, useless clauses can be used, along with other means of informal communication (a common education, belonging to the same community, etc.), by the contracting parties as very efficient tools for fostering mutual understanding. Useless clauses that convey indications of information and involvement seem highly appropriate. Useless clauses which have a positive informative effect can improve the contracting process and facilitate negotiation.

Firstly, useless clauses can be used by parties as a reference point, helping them to understand the nature of the obligations on which they have to agree and to organise their contract accordingly.

Secondly, useless clauses can be used to give other contracting parties the information that they need to gain assurance and thus to accept the contract. Confidence has a decisive effect: the more the economic actors trust each other, the more they are willing to exchange goods and services with each other. Moreover, if a person feels the other party is trustworthy, the precautions that he will need to take to guarantee the transaction – precautions which have a cost – will be reduced. Therefore, trust reduces the transaction costs. But to trust the other party, a party must be able to evaluate its own likely exposure to risk. By making visible the invisible, useless clauses enhance the performance of the contract.

In addition to the written contract, which formalises the rights and obligations of the parties, a psychological contract is formed between those parties, based on their beliefs, perceptions, and expectations (Larry DiMatteo, "Strategic contracting: Law as a source of competitive advantage", American Business L.J., vol 47, winter 2010, pp. 781-783). In this respect, useless clauses can be used to reduce cognitive bias in the parties' perception of the contract and thus, disappointment, misunderstanding and mistrust which can lead to the dissolution of the contract.

The value of this legal strategy depends on the balance between the pre-transaction costs involved in using these useless clauses, on the one hand, and the post-transaction costs thereby avoided, on the other hand. Therefore this form of proactive contracting based on useless clauses seems suitable for relational contracts. It refers especially to relational contracts agreed between larger independent businesses in order to arrange a long-term cooperative relationship aimed at reducing economic uncertainty in a complex and changing environment.

4.1.2. Collaborative strategies involving all the stakeholders of a contracting body

Useless clauses play a role not only in the relationship between contracting parties but also in the teams who are involved with each of those contracting parties. Actually a contract is not only an agreement between legally independent actors, but also a roadmap that each party must implement. In addition, contracting often involves the cooperation of different people from different departments within a company: business people such as engineers, business executives, managers, etc., on the one hand, and lawyers, auditors, compliance officers, etc., on the other. Members of the former group usually initiate any negotiations relating to the contract and are responsible for implementing it once it has been finalised. Members of the latter group have to ensure and confirm the legal correctness of the contractual documentation and integrate the contract with the information, decision-making and accounting systems and policies of the business. The quality of the cooperation between these actors is a key element in the success of the contract and its capacity to create full value for the organisation.

Again, useless clauses can facilitate understanding of elements in a contract and interest in that contract and can enable all stakeholders to communicate effectively. They can help to make the contract understandable for "average Joes". First, as has been emphasized previously, certain phrases in a contract are useful for facilitating its management. Most laymen recognise a contract only if it is presented as such (Cf. G. Berger-Walliser, R.C. Bird, et H. Haapio *Promoting Business success Through contract visualization,* page 62), and useless clauses – such as the title "contract" – remove any potential ambiguity in this regard. Secondly, useless clauses can facilitate implementation. Once signed, a contract must still be accepted by those implementing it.

In their article on this subject, entitled *Promoting Business Success Through Contract Visualization,* Gerlinde Berger-Walliser, Robert C. Bird and Helena Haapio, have emphasized that contracts should not be made by lawyers for lawyers: it is important that all stakeholders in a contract (i.e. those who will write, negotiate and apply it) understand its key elements (Ibid, p. 66). Making a contract readable by reducing its hidden parts (the rules which apply to the contractual relationship despite being not laid down in the contract, for instance), reduce the risk of misinterpretation and consequently of incorrect execution. If a contract is self-explanatory, its implementation will be easier. In order to achieve this objective, useless clauses are helpful to make contracts clear for non-lawyers, who do not have enough time or geeky interest to read the statutory instruments and all the legal background related to the contract. Similarly, useless clauses have a useful pedagogic effect as they can increase non-lawyers' awareness of the legal risks attached to contract law.

4.2. Opportunistic strategies based on useless clauses

As contractual behaviour is influenced by useless clauses, useless clauses can be used in a contract to create value for both parties. However, in the context of a unilateral strategy aiming at squeezing an advantage out of the other contracting party, in the negotiation process (1) or even in the enforcement process (2), useless clauses can also be a resource which is only at the disposal of one party.

4.2.1. Strategic use of useless clauses in the negotiation process

During negotiation, the parties may use various tactics to obtain concessions from their interlocutors (Cf. William Ury & Roger Fisher, Getting to Yes: Negotiating an Agreement Without Giving In, Random House Business, 2003 and Alain Lempereur, Aurelien Colson, Michele Pekar, *The First Move. A Negotiator's Companion*, John Wiley & Sons, 2010). Among these tactics, one party may exploit the emotions or perceptions of the other contracting party (Cf. R.M. Kramer, E. Newton & P.L. Pommerenke, (1993) "Self-enhancement biases and negotiator judgment: Effects of self-esteem and mood". Organizational Behavior and Human Decision Processes, 56, 110-133; B. Barry, I. S. Fulmer & G.A. Van Kleef, (2004) *I laughed, I cried, I settled: The role of emotion in negotiation*. In M.J. Gelfand & J.M. Brett (Eds.), *The handbook of negotiation and culture* (pp. 71-94). Stanford, CA: Stanford University Press; M.N. Davidson, & L. Greenhalgh, (1999) "The role of emotion in negotiation: The impact of anger and race". *Research on Negotiation in Organizations*, 7, 3-26). A party is more willing to accept a compromise if he/she has a positive perception of its interlocutor. But this perception can be ill-founded because it is the result of a manipulation.

First, outlining in a contract an obligation which is prescribed by a mandatory rule, can give the impression to the other contracting parties that the contract offered is generous. For example, most businesses, in order to appear concerned about their employees' well-being, emphasize in their employment contracts advantages which are in fact already provided by employment regulations. The employer's apparent generosity is, therefore, artificial.

Second, some useless clauses are only included in the draft of a contract in order to be used as bargaining chips in negotiation: the party which has drafted the proposed contractual document will offer to delete them in exchange for real sacrifices on the part of the other contracting party. In this case, the desired result is achieved without incurring any substantial costs and without risking amending the general structure of the contract. Useless clauses in a contract can thus be the unscrupulous person's means of part-payment.

Third, clauses which are useless because they are superfluous can be used during negotiation to divert the attention of the other contracting parties from a key element of the contract. A surfeit of clauses in a contractual document discourages parties from reading them. If a contracting party wants to present an impressive and unattractive contract, it can be useful for him/her to insert a number of useless clauses among the useful clauses. Intimidating contracts of this kind are frequently presented to consumers, especially as far as online contracts are concerned.

Ultimately, this sort of legal strategy is based on the insertion of useless clauses which actually serve as traps and lures. They involve an unscrupulous contracting party exploiting an inattentive contracting party.

4.2.2. Strategic use of useless clauses in the enforcement process

Useless clauses also may produce effects once contracts have been exchanged. Contracting parties may seek to take advantage of the contract to the detriment of the other party, using the third category of useless clauses. Illegal clauses are not likely to have an effect in court because any lawyer can easily see that they are contrary to law or to judicial practice, according to the definition we have adopted. Nevertheless, contracting parties might seek to have a significant influence on the other party by employing useless clauses if the other party does not know that those clauses are illegal. The bad influence of this kind of useless clause may exist at two stages.

Illicit clauses can influence a person who reads a contract that s/he has not written. But the kind of contracting party who gives his/her consent before reading and understanding the implications of a contract, as many consumers do, is likely to take that contract to be a genuine binding document. For many people, any piece of paper which is drafted in a typically legal style is considered a legally valid document. Thus that party will presume that that document is legally binding. Most of the time, contracting parties do not even suspect that the contract and the clauses thereof might not be valid. As they do not have the legal background and knowledge that would enable them to suspect and confirm that one – or several – of those clauses is illegal, those clauses spontaneously affect the behaviour of the more vulnerable contracting party. For instance, they may agree to pay money to the other contracting party, even if payment is not due from a strictly legal point of view.

In many cases, contracting parties do not even read the contract. The unscrupulous contracting party who has inserted illegal clauses may bring up those clauses when the vulnerable contractor expresses his dissatisfaction with the contract. Perhaps he feels uncomfortable with the contract or even considers that the contract is unjust. Accordingly, he brings a complaint. However, in many cases this complaint is expressed outside of court and there is very little chance that the vulnerable contracting party will decide to sue. That is why, when that party complains, the unscrupulous contracting party may try to manipulate him or her. He may do so by bringing up a clause which gives him a right or some form of legal protection or which deprives the other party of a legitimate right, even though the unscrupulous party knows perfectly well that that clause should not be used. This strategy is based on the fact that many contracting parties are legally naïve. This phenomenon goes beyond the imbalance of legal awareness. It has to do with the spontaneous attitude of contracting parties to a contract.

5. Conclusion

Useless clauses are double-edged swords. They may be useful or detrimental to one party or to all contracting parties.

Iterative Contracts as Proactive Law Instruments

By

René Franz Henschel
Associate professor, Department of Law, Aarhus University

The purpose of this article is to analyse the use of proactive law in contracts illustrated by the use of a particular type of contract within the IT industry, the so-called iterative contract. This type of contract has its root in a special software development process called iterative and incremental software development. In contrast to traditional IT project methodologies, where the product development takes place in a sequential design process, the iterative process is characterized by the software being developed through a series of repeated cycles in smaller portions at a time. This software development process has driven the need for a new contract design that fits the product life cycle better than the traditional contracts. As will be shown in the analysis, the iterative contracts represent important legal innovation and can be categorized as a proactive law instrument that has the potential to create more business success. However, empirical research still needs to be done in order to confirm that these types of contracts are better at securing business success than traditional contract forms.

1. Introduction

1.1. Purpose of the article, methodological and theoretical starting point

The purpose of this article is to analyse the use of proactive law in certain types of contracts called iterative contracts named after the software development process they support.[1] By analysing this particular type of contract used within the software development industry, it is described how new proactive contract forms are developed in order to improve business success, and how these types of contracts defer from traditional contracts.

The article uses freely available empirical contract data, in the form of certain standard contracts, developed and published in a book by lawyers working for law-firms specialised in IT law.[2] The article does not investigate other types of iterative contracts, or other types of industries, which could be seen as a flaw in the research design. Consequently, the analysis in the article may represent information and conclusions that cannot be generalised. However, the purpose is not to conduct such a broad comparative-analytical investigation of different types of contracts within different industries, but merely to illustrate the concept of proactive law, as illustrated by examples of a particular contract type in a particular industry. Furthermore, the article does not analyse the actual result on business success of using these new types of contracts. Future research should therefore be directed towards investigating this.[3]

1. It is sometimes seen, that iterative and incremental software development are described as identical to agile software development. However, there is no unanimous agreement of this. In an agile project the core values are often expressed with reference to the so-called Agile Manifesto, see http://agilemanifesto.org/. The core values in such a project are: Individuals and interactions over processes and tools; Working software over comprehensive documentation; Customer collaboration over contract negotiation; and Responding to change following a plan. These core values are shared by the iterative and incremental approach.
2. © J. Langemark, Claus F. Sørensen and N. Dragsted: Iterative projektmodeller og kontrakter (2009), published by the Danish law-firms Dahl Advokatfirma (www.dahllaw.dk) and BvHD (www.bvhd.dk). The book can be downloaded from www.k02.dk. The book distinguishes between the iterative contract named 01i, which is designed for projects of a shorter development period, and the contract named 02i, which is designed for a longer development period. The analysis in this article is primarily based on the contract called 02i.
3. See also critical as to the documented benefits of agile software development methods, H.P. Breivold, P. Wallin and M. Lindgren, Impacts of Introducing Agile – A Literature Survey, available at http://www.mdh.se/polopoly_fs/1.26583!Peter_Hongyu_Markus_FinalReport.pdf, and on critical success factors in agile projects, T. Chow and D-B. Cao, A survey study of critical success

In order to analyse whether or not the chosen contract could be categorised as a proactive law instrument that defers from traditional contracts, it is necessary to first provide a brief definition of the theoretical framework upon which the article is based. It is not the purpose of this article to analyse the concept of proactive law more thoroughly, however interesting this might be. The author is well aware of the dangers the theoretical and methodological foundations of the article poses to the results of the analysis.

In this article, proactive law is generally defined as an approach to law in which the focus is on how to secure success rather than on mitigating damages caused by failure, which is characterized as a reactive approach. This definition is overall in line with the definitions proposed in literature,[4] as well as in recent communications from the European Union.[5]

It is quite obvious, that in order to promote success, the parties need to take initiatives, which promote and strengthen the factors that drive success, including legal initiatives.[6] Seen in a legal context, this means that in proactive contracts the parties need to take *contractual* initiatives and actions, which promote the factors that drive success. Thus, in order for a proactive contract to be called a proactive law instrument, in the

factors in agile software projects, Journal of Systems and Software, Vol. 81, Issue 6, June 2008, p. 961-971.

4. For an overview of the development of proactive law, see G. Berger-Walliser, The Past and Future of proactive law: An overview of the Development of Proactive Law, in: K. Østergaard (ed.), Proceedings of the 2nd European Proactive Law Conference, Copenhagen, 5-6 December 2011 (2012) On proactive law in contracts, see e.g. H. Haapio, Business Success and Problem Prevention through Proactive Contracting, in P. Wahlgren (ed.), A Proactive Approach, Scandinavian Studies in Law, Volume 49 (2006), p. 150-194, and S. Pohjonen and K. Visuri, Proactive Approach in Project Management and Contracting, in H. Haapio (ed.), A Proactive Approach to Contracting and Law, Turku University of Applied Sciences, Course Material 38/IACCM (2008). These articles have been an inspiration for the analytical framework in this article.
5. See generally the Opinion of the European Economic and Social Committee on "The Proactive law approach: a further step towards regulation at EU level" (2009/C175/05).
6. See Opinion of the European Economic and Social Committee on "The Proactive law approach: a further step towards regulation at EU level" (2009/C175/05), paragraph 5.4.

author's opinion, the actions have to materialize themselves as proactive legal components in the contract. In this way, they have a clear legal-contractual nature, and not only e.g. a managerial nature, like contract management processes outside the contractual framework that may improve the possibility for success, however important this may be.

However, this does in no way rule out that the contractual components may be of a managerial nature as well, e.g. project management tools and tools that build collaboration and trust. This is no contradiction; it is simply an emphasis on the need to think innovative and interdisciplinary as a lawyer when drafting contracts, which is also in line with economic and management theory on contracts.[7] Used in the right way, proactive law can then be used to gain a competitive advantage,[8] by aligning the contract design and the contract clauses with the attributes of the transaction.[9]

Furthermore, the contractual components have to actively and positively affect the possibility for creating success. Otherwise, there will be no difference between a traditional and a proactive legal instrument.

This can be illustrated by an example of a particular division of the nature of contract clauses. In a traditional contract, the contract clauses are sometimes divided into what is called active and passive clauses.[10]

7. See e.g. H. Haapio, Innovative Contracting, S. Pohjonen and K. Visuri, Proactive Approach in Project Management and Contracting and T. Cummins, Taking the Law out of Contracts – and putting Lawyers into the Contracting Process, all published in H. Haapio (ed.), A Proactive Approach to Contracting and Law, Turku University of Applied Sciences, Course Material 38/IACCM (2008), p. 105-152, p. 75-96 and p. 97-104 respectively. On law and economics, and relational contracts see e.g. R. Cooter and T. Ulen, Law and Economics (2012), p. 299-306. See also K. Vitasek with J. Crawford, J. Nyden and K. Kawamoto, The Vested Outsourcing Manual (2011), especially p. 1-42, explaining many of the connections between economic theory, trust, collaboration, risk management and better contracting.
8. See further G.J. Seidel and H. Haapio, Using Proactive Law for a Competitive Advantage, American Journal of Business Law, Vol. 47, Issue 4, 641-668, Winter 2010.
9. See further N. Argyres and K. J. Mayer, Contract Design as a Firm Capability: An Integration of Learning and Transaction Cost Perspectives, Academy of Management Review, 2007, Vol. 32, No. 4, p. 1060-1077.
10. Se e.g., T. Cummins, M. David and K. Kawamoto, Contract and Commercial Management, The Operational Guide (2011), p. 366.

Active clauses are clauses that define certain actions that have to be taken, e.g. to deliver the goods on a certain date at a certain place. Passive clauses are clauses that do not explicitly demand certain actions to be taken, but regulate what happens, if a particular action is *not* taken, e.g. liability in case of late delivery. What then, differentiates proactive clauses from active and passive clauses? This may be seen in the way certain contract clauses are now categorized, e.g. ADR clauses.

An ADR clause could be called active, in the sense that it directs certain activities to be conducted, if disagreement occurs, but it could also be called passive, e.g. in the way it defines the applicable law and procedural rules to be applied. At the same time, ADR is very often categorized as being a proactive measure, as a means to avoid litigation, and solve the problem while needed.[11] In this way, ADR better secures business success, and is consequently proactive when related to traditional litigation. But can clauses and contracts be even more proactive than this illustration? Can they interfere directly in the actions needed to secure success?

In the author´s opinion, proactive initiatives which are integrated into the contract need to be clearly connected to the factors that drive business success. If the initiatives are not or only indirectly connected to the key business success factors, they can hardly be called proactive in the sense described and defined above. In the author´s opinion, initiatives that are not directly connected to the factors that drive business success belong to traditional risk management.[12]

Traditional legal risk management is often more focused on how to avoid risks and not so much on how to avoid losing opportunities or secure success.[13] Consequently, in this article the focus is not on traditional legal risk management,[14] but rather on factors and legal instruments

11. See e.g. G. Seidel and H. Haapio, Proactive Law for Managers. A Hidden Source for Competitive Advantage (2011), p. 143 et seq and T. Salmi-Tolonen, Proactive Law and Alternative Dispute Reolution Mechanisms, in K. Sorsa, Proactive Management and Proactive Business Law. A Handbook (2012), p. 85 et seq.
12. On legal risk management se e.g. J. Iversen. Legal Risk Management i Private Virksomheder (2007).
13. On this see further R.F. Henschel, Managing Crisis Through Contracts, Revista da Faculdade de Direito Milton Campos, Volume 18, 2009, p. 129-144.
14. However, the so-called risk log in the iterative contract 02i is described below section 3.

that drive success, and therefore can be seen as the very core of proactive law. This, however, does in no way imply that traditional legal risk management is not and cannot be proactive, e.g. when designing legal procedures that secures the validity of liability disclaimers, or which tries to secure that delivery will be timely, e.g. by rights of inspection of production facilities, regular meetings etc. Consequently, traditional legal risk management and proactive law are closely interlinked.[15] However, it is not the aim of this article to go further into the relation between traditional risk management and proactive law.[16]

In order for a contract to be a proactive law instrument as defined in this article, firstly the key business success factors have to be clearly identified, and secondly, these key success factors have to materialize themselves as contractual tools, e.g. a particular contract design and/or contract clauses.

In the following section, the process of identifying the key success factors will be identified. In the next section, it will be described how the contractual design and the contract clauses are adapted to the business goals and the product life cycle in a way that legitimizes the categorization of the iterative contract as a proactive law instrument.

2. Identifying key factors for business success

In order to identify the key business success factors, obviously the parties in the transaction and their legal advisors first of all have to have a deep understanding of the particular business they operate in, e.g. the IT industry. Secondly, the parties – based on extensive experience – have to be able to identify the key factors that drive not only business failure,

15. See e.g. R.F. Henschel, Proactive Risk Management, in K. Sorsa, Proactive Management and Proactive Business Law. A Handbook (2012), p. 243 et seq.
16. Further on this, see T. Mahler, Legal risk management. Developing and evaluating elements of a method for proactive legal analyses, with a particular focus on contracts. PhD thesis, University of Oslo, 2010.

but also business success and design the legal response accordingly.[17] Analysing not only the failures but also the success stories can help the parties to achieve this.

An example that illustrates how this is accomplished is the emerging of agile and iterative project models in IT development projects. Companies discovered that by using new IT project development methods they created more success in the final outcome.

When starting to develop new software, companies often choose to make use of sequential project methods, which where originally developed for use in the hardware manufacturing industry, e.g. like the "waterfall model" known from software development projects.

When using a sequential process companies first of all invest a lot of time and money in analysing their needs, and then based on this analysis, develop a detailed request for delivery. This request is then integrated into a detailed specification and attached or integrated into a contract, which consequently often gets to be very detailed and static.

According to the waterfall model, the supplier after signing the contract develops the software and delivers it on the day agreed with the customer. The software is then received and tested by the customer, and accepted if satisfactory or rejected in non-conforming. This type of delivery is often called a "Big Bang" delivery, as failure or success depends on whether or not the supplier has been able to understand and meet the customer's needs and expectations, as specified in the contract and other relevant documentation, including meetings etc.

If the customer finds out that he was not able to accurately describe his needs, this will have to be addressed in a detailed amendment to the contract and paid for, unless the supplier should have taken this into consideration. If the supplier finds out during the development that the

17. See further on this: E. Van de Leutgarden, J. Jansen and M. Jansma, A Proactive Approach for Lawyers, in K. Sorsa, Proactive Management and Proactive Business Law. A Handbook (2012), p. 127 et seq., and on the value-chain perspective, K. Sorsa, Proactive Contracting in Value Chain Management, in K. Sorsa, Proactive Management and Proactive Business Law. A Handbook (2012), p. 211 et seq., and T. Salmi-Tolonen and K. Sorsa, Proactive Contracting, in K. Sorsa, Proactive Management and Proactive Business Law. A Handbook (2012), p. 179 et seq. I would also like to thank C. Wissink, Lawyer, Ferens Legal (www.ferenslegal.com) for many good conversations in regard to proactive law and the product life cycle and value chain perspective on contracts.

project can be better fulfilled by using another design or functionality than described in the contract etc., this is not necessarily something which will be communicated or benefits the customer, unless otherwise agreed. Consequently, the customer may miss opportunities that could have created more business success.

Furthermore, the customer runs a great risk, if the project is not delivered on time and/or according to specifications, as this is usually not to be discovered until the software has been delivered and tested. In that case, the customer has no other choice than to allow the supplier to remedy, unless there is a fundamental breach and the supplier wants someone else to deliver the required software. This, however, is often connected to great cost and risk also, and therefore the parties in practice are often locked into the contract.

Finally, if the project runs over a longer period, the customer risk that the delivered product is "out of date" when delivered, although confirming to contract specifications, because new technology has been developed in the meantime which was not taken into account at the design and contract closure phase.

Consequently, the "waterfall model" and similar models often imply a great deal of risk of not getting business success. But how can this be changed?

The companies facing these problems first of all considered whether or not the entire project model where was appropriate for the business' needs and risks. This meant that the project process had to be redesigned in order to fit the product lifecycle stages.

The new project model, the so-called iterative project model, is a model where the software development takes place in a series of repeated development phases called iterations. Each phase can be described as a mini-waterfall development phase, however with much greater interaction between supplier and customer and with other characteristics.

An iteration project runs over a pre-defined timeframe, usually 1 or 2 weeks, and usually at an agreed pre-defined cost, and a general overview of the functionality and goals of the iteration.

The supplier will develop as much functionality and business value within the iteration phase as possible in close cooperation with the customer. If the customer gets a new idea, which often happens right after the first demonstration, once the customer has the first working software in his hands, he can ask the supplier to develop the software accordingly. Similarly, if the supplier discovers ways to improve or simplify a process, change the design etc., he can propose it without recourse. This is not necessarily a change request – it is simply an embedded agile and flexible development process. Both parties know how changes affect the iteration, and thus, the bottom line. There is generally no relying on the old concept of a "change-order", and the project form allows for a rapid-feedback-loop securing what is being developed by the supplier is exactly what the customer want.[18]

New iterations are based on the experiences of the former iteration, and so the product is gradually developed. The illustration below shows the development model:

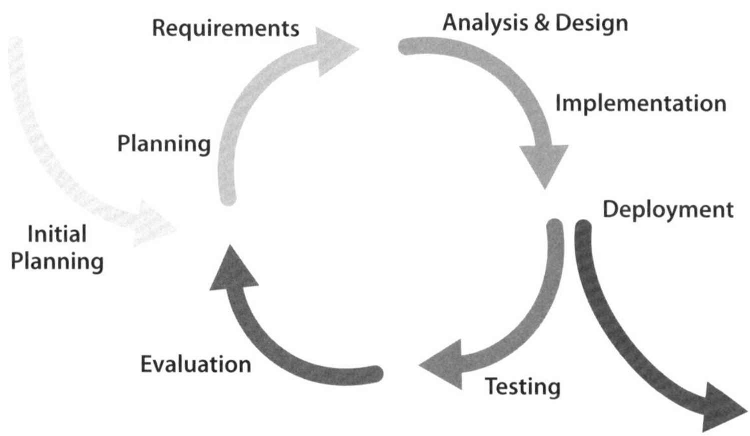

Illustration taken from WIKIPEDIA (COMMONS LICENSE)

Consequently, in the iterative project model, the focus is on the what, not the how, on the business needs and output, and on how to get the project to work in collaboration between the supplier and the customer, in contrast to waterfall models or similar models, where the business value is supposed to be delivered in the end all at once ("Big Bang"),

18. See further on this example, K. Sorsa (ed.), Proactive Management and Proactive Business Law. A Handbook (2012), p. 188 et seq.

and based on a well-defined contract with exact specification of requirements of the to-do's and how's.

Consequently, the type of contract needed should closely reflect the project process and the product lifecycle and the collaboration needed between the customer and the client. This means contractual focus on project management, the methodology to be used on the development phase, the advice that needs to given and the resources both parties have to supply in order for the project to be a success.

The following section will show how iterative contracts have been developed which take this new project methodology into account.

3. Developing the proactive contractual tools

As indicated above, the iterative project form requires a new collaborative working method in order to succeed. Consequently it would be illogical to use a form of contract where all the responsibility was put on one party only and keeping the relation on an "arms-length". Furthermore, as the success of iterative development projects is closely connected to the process and methodology of the development of the software, this needs to be addressed in the contract. Finally, the contract has to balance the flexibility of the project model with the need to have some sort of control over resources invested and the result which will be achieved.[19] In the following sections, these characteristics as reflected in the iterative contract developed by the law firms will be described more thoroughly.

3.1. Description of the customer's business case and the choice of an iterative project

The first step is to describe as accurately as possible the customer's business case. This business case must describe why the iterative project model has been chosen, in comparison to a more traditional project model, e.g. the waterfall model. Only in this way are the parties sure that they are both aware of the special requirements such a project de-

19. J. Langemark, C.F. Sørensen and Nicolai Dragsted, Iterative projektmodeller og kontrakter (2009), p. 28.

mands, and whether this choice supports the customers business case.[20] Furthermore, the business case should describe the key business success criteria and be made part of the contract, by use of an appendix to the contract or similar technique.[21]

In an iterative project, the iterations are not only used to develop the IT programs (programming, testing etc.), but also to analyse the business case if necessary, clarify business needs and articulate the specific needs for the relevant business processes and consequently, the software that has to be designed. [22]

3.2. Specification of the customer´s business needs and related business processes

The next step is to specify more accurately, but not more accurately than required by the flexibility required in the iterative project form, which business needs, the software delivery is addressing and which business processes it supports. Focus is on the "whats" and not the "hows".[23] How to fulfil the business needs will be developed in collaboration between the supplier and the customer throughout the project period. However, the supplier will usually describe the overall design of the solution, before the contract is entered into.[24] A more detailed description will then be developed during the project.[25]

3.3. Frames and constraints of the project

Although an iterative project does not operate with a very detailed specification of how to accomplish the project, the iterative projects do operate with certain frames and constraints in order to address the relevant risks and secure business success. These fundamental frames and constraints,

20. J. Langemark et.al op.cit p. 9.
21. J. Langemark et.al op.cit p. 96. (Definitions, Business Case).
22. J. Langemark et.al op.cit p. 9-10.
23. In the 02i contract, consequently the so-called Requirements Specification (Kravspecifikation) is replaced by a Needs Assesment (Behovsopgørelse). See also article 2., in 02i.
24. J. Langemark et.al op.cit p. 31, 55 and 98.
25. J. Langemark et.al op.cit p. 31.

e.g. in relation to time and price, are made a part of the business case and should also be specified in a description of the delivery.[26]

Usually, the frames and constraints relate to time, price, technology, process and business-related frames. The price is usually agreed on a price-per-hour charge, however with a maximum price within which the supplier obligates himself to deliver certain minimum requirements described in the customer's business case. It is the responsibility of the supplier to plan, control and adjust the resources in the project so that these goals can be fulfilled within the frames and constraints of the project. [27]

Consequently, in an iterative contract, the obligation of the supplier is more that of a specialist advisor, consultant and project manager than in a traditional waterfall-based contract model, where the contract often looks more like a traditional manufactured goods contract.[28]

3.4. Project management, collaboration, flexibility and the parties' maturity level

In the iterative project model, the parties should be working closely together in order to obtain the goals of the project. This collaborative working form is closely matched by the contract design.

First of all, the iterative phases are described as: I) the clarification phase, II) analysis, design, development and implementation phase, and III) testing and overall approval of delivery.[29] These phases also reflect the overall contractual design.[30]

The close collaboration form in iterative projects is addressed by establishing a common project organisation called "Collaboration Organization".[31] It is specified in the contract that the employees participating in this common organisation must supply a CV, and that no project manager may be replaced without the other party's consent, unless for very particular personal or other relevant reasons. The new

26. J. Langemark et.al op.cit p. 10.
27. J. Langemark et.al op.cit p. 10.
28. J. Langemark et.al op.cit p. 10-11.
29. J. Langemark et.al op.cit p. 89 et seq.
30. J. Langemark et.al op.cit p. 29 and 02i, article 3.
31. See 02i, article 26.

project management must have at least the same qualifications as the person being replaced.

However, it is important to note, that it is the supplier who has the responsibility to conduct the project management and who has the overall advisory role in the project.[32] It follows e.g. from the contract that the supplier must secure that there is always detailed and updated time- and work plans for the next 20 days of the project, which must be approved by the customer. These plans are quite detailed, e.g. they must have information about what the customer is expected to contribute with, on what time and with which employees and/or competences.[33]

During the project management, the supplier is obligated to focus on pursuing the activities and to achieve the functionality that supports the realisation of the customer's business case and any minimum requirements specified by the customer.[34] In short, the supplier must pursue maximum "value for money" for the client. [35] If this is not possible, the supplier must be aware of this and propose the necessary changes.[36]

A special feature is also seen in article 2.3.7 of the iterative contract called 02i according to which the customer may increase its participation in the contract with 20 days of notice to the supplier. If this has consequences for price or other important factors, this must be made into a request for change. If the parties cannot agree on this, the dispute is immediately escalated to a so-called Steering Group where senior project management is able to address the dispute. There is also a particular process established for "change orders", cf. article 5 in 02i.

Also the customer may freely ask for a re-prioritization of the project deliverables, unless this affects time and economy of the project. If this is the case, there must be a change request.[37]

The supplier also has a duty to warn if there is a danger that the project might be delayed or otherwise not performed according to the agreed terms.[38]

32. J. Langemark et.al op.cit p. 31, and 02i, article 2.3.
33. See 02i, article 2.3.1 i.f.
34. See 02i, article 2.3.2.
35. J. Langemark et.al op.cit p. 35.
36. See 02i, article 2.3.3.
37. See 02i, article 5.10.3.
38. See 02i, article 2.3.8.

The supplier also has to maintain an updated risk log, where all risks that might endanger the successful performance of the project are mapped and online accessible for the customer. The Steering Group monitors the risk log at least on a monthly basis.

As the iterative development process also requires certain skills from the customer, the contract also specifies how the customer is expected to participate in the project.[39] Equally important, the customer as well as the supplier must fill out a "Maturity Level Questionnaire" before the contract is entered into, and this questionnaire is made of the contract as an appendix.[40]

3.5. Other characteristics of the iterative contract

During the project, there will be a continuous testing of the software developed so far. However, this continuous testing should not be compared with the final testing. In the iterative contract subject to analysis, this distinction is called non-contractual, measure-point or milestone testing versus contractual testing.[41] The difference is based on the need to work collaboratively in the iterative development projects.[42]

Furthermore, the contract differentiates between so-called "observations" and non-conformity issues. An "observation" is something that has to be addressed in the next iteration in order for the business output to be fulfilled, while a non-conformity issue is something that has to be remedied within the specific iteration where a part of the functionality is delivered.

The customer also has a right to request "audits", in order to discover risks for delays or non-conformity. The supplier may also audit the

39. See 02i, article 9.
40. See 02i, article 10.
41. J. Langemark et.al op.cit p. 33.
42. See also the preamble to 02i: "The parties agree to cooperate with a positive, profession-al and responsible attitude throughout the project and promises to provide a considerable effort in order to obtain the best result possible. The parties should exhibit reasonable and usual flexibility when performing an iterative project like the present one. The parties must continuously inform each other about any issue that might be estimated to have relevance for the appropriate fulfilment of the contract. The must loyally exchange information, data and documentation to the extent this is relevant for the fulfilment of the contract" (authors translation).

customer´s maturity level as required by the contract. An independent third party appointed by the Danish Arbitration Institute conducts the audit. If nothing is wrong, the party requesting the audit will have to pay the costs.

If the customer is able to avoid the contract, he is only able to avoid with effect "ex nunc" and not "ex tunc". This is based in the nature of the iterative project, where the supplier delivers and charges by the hour in the iterations of the project. Consequently, the customer is also able to keep the deliverables up until avoidance.[43]

Finally, as a response to the possibility of the project not being able to fulfil the expectations of the customer, the customer has an option to step out of the contract with a notice of 20 working days.[44] This is not to be considered avoidance as in a case of breach of contract. However, the contract also includes such traditional remedies, e.g. avoidance in case of breach and liability for damages.[45]

4. Conclusion

The iterative contracts analysed above reveal a contractual design and a range of contractual tools especially designed to fit the transaction. Many of the features are innovative in comparison to traditional contracts, e.g. the ability to adapt and change the contract according to the circumstances. These differences can be explained by the fact that the underlying product life cycle requires new contract models to be implemented in order not only to mitigate risks, but more importantly to try to promote and strengthen the factors that drive success.

This is done by focusing on the factors that are critical for business success in iterative projects, e.g. describing the "what´s" and not the "how´s", establishing best practice project management, documenting and observing the maturity levels of the parties, maintaining and monitoring risk logs, and by implementing instruments that are directed

43. J. Langemark et.al op.cit p. 40 and 02i, article 20.2.
44. See 02i, article 5.5.
45. See 02i, article 17-19.

towards securing flexibility, so that changing business needs can be met within reasonable limits by the other party.

In short, the iterative contract is an important legal innovation, which tries to address the factors which are critical for success by implementing certain active governance forms in the contract. From a theoretical point of view as well as from a common business sense practical point of view this seems to have a lot of merit. Therefore, this author does not hesitate to conclude, that these iterative contracts can be seen as proactive law instruments.

However, further research should be conducted in order to confirm the observation that iterative contracts have the intended positive effects on business success.

Selective Distribution – A Proactive Perspective

By

Kim Østergaard
Associate professor, Ph.D.
Law Department – Copenhagen Business School

1. Introduction

When a manufacturer uses a distributor as a means to market and distribute the products made by the manufacturer, the manufacturer basically has three main options with respect to distribution form. The manufacturer can either use selective distribution, mass distribution, or exclusive distribution. If a manufacturer decides to use selective distribution as a way of marketing and distributing the products of the company, the manufacturer is traditionally highly focused on how the product is marketed and sold by the distributor. Furthermore, the manufacturer who has chosen to use a selective distribution system limits the number of distributors within a territory and the distributor within the territory has no exclusive rights. Thus, selective distribution is different from mass distribution where the manufacturer pursues a distribution strategy, where the contract products are distributed to as many distributors as possible and different from exclusive distribution, where the distributor gets exclusive rights to distribute the contract products within the territory or in a geographical area.[1]

1. If the manufacturer uses mass distribution as a means of distribution, the contract between the manufacturer and the distributor will normally amount to sales and delivery conditions, while the contract in conjunction with exclusive distribution is more comprehensive like a contract used in conjunction with selective distribution.

In accordance with Commission Regulation No. 330/2010[2] article 1 (e) selective distribution is defined as follows with my accentuation:

> *"Selective distribution system means a distribution system, where the supplier undertakes to sell the contract goods or services, either directly or indirectly,* **only to distributors selected on the basis of specified criteria and where these distributors undertake not to sell such goods or services to unauthorized distributors** *within the territory reserved by the supplier to operate that system;"*

In accordance with the definition, the distributor has to accomplish specified criteria in order to become a distributor within the selective distribution system. Such criteria are traditionally linked to the complexity of the contract goods and/or the brand value of the selective distribution system which the manufacturer has already achieved or strive to achieve.

Selective distribution is often applied to goods or services that are complex from a technical point of view and thus need specific services by a qualified staff, including instructions about the use and non-use of the products in question. Manufacturers of brand products, especially high-end brand products often choose selective distribution in order to protect and increase the value of the brand. In some cases the manufacturer might have different product lines resulting in a differentiated distribution strategy where the distributor in question only has the right and obligation to resell a particular product line, whereas another distributor has the right and obligation to resell all product lines. Such a differentiated distribution strategy can for instance be justified due to the complexity of the product lines, exclusivity level of the product lines, educational requirements to the staff, and the physical location belonging to the distributor.

From an economic point of view, many of the manufacturers of luxury goods have chosen to use a selective distribution system in order to

2. Commission Regulation (EU) No 330/2010 of 20 April 2010 on the application of Article 101(3) of the Treaty on the Functioning of the European Union to categories of vertical agreements and concerted practices.

protect and hopefully increase the value of the brand, which in turn should result in a higher long-term profit.

Thus, the manufacturer has a keen interest to secure that the distributor does not resell the contract goods to unauthorized distributors outside the selective distribution system. The contract between the manufacturer and the distributor will in most cases, I presume, contain a provision whereby the distributor is prohibited to resell the contract goods to a distributor outside the selective distribution system.[3] Such a provision must be considered a reactive provision and in accordance with the goal of the article, there is no need to discuss this issue any further, besides stating that a contract comprising a selective distribution system will consist of both reactive and proactive provisions.

The crucial questions are how the use of proactive provisions in the contract can support the protection of the brand value created by the manufacturer, whether the brand value is based on the complexity and/or the exclusivity of the contract goods? Before I turn to this question in paragraph 2 of this article, I would like to turn the attention to the interaction between law and economics. If a manufacturer has decided to use selective distribution as the distribution strategy, the basic question in mind is how the contract can be used strategically to support this distribution strategy and especially how the use of proactive provisions in the contract can create a further advantage to the manufacturer from an economic point of view.

The figure below illustrates the interaction among the elements which must be taken into consideration, once a manufacturer has decided to use a selective distribution system, and the contract with the distributor has to be written.

3. In general, most manufacturers running a selective distribution system pursues to limit price competition using provisions in the contract which prohibit the reselling of the contract goods to others than authorized distributors and consumers.

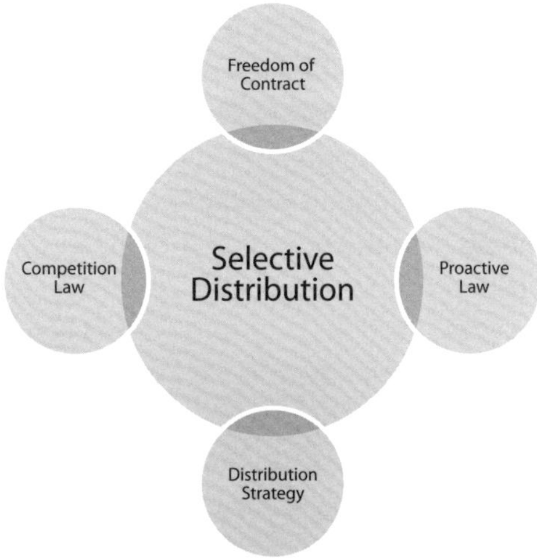

Most legal systems have a principle of freedom of contract, which in this context implies that the parties to the contract, the manufacturer and distributor, can enter into a contract which serves their interest in the best possible manner. This is also the starting point between the manufacturer and the distributor. However, at least two legal systems have acts restricting the freedom of contract. This is the case in Belgium and Denmark, where the law in different manners seeks to protect the distributor from the manufacturer.[4]

The proactive provisions in the contract must, as mentioned above, support the distribution strategy of the manufacturer. In order to do so, the manufacturer has to make sure that the perceived value of the selective distribution system is in no way diminished or in the worst case simply destroyed.[5] Thus, the proactive provisions should at least

4. In Belgium, see bill from July 27th 1961 which was revised in April 13th 1971 which comprises distribution contracts in general. For further reading in Danish, see Ole Lando, Elisabeth Thuesen, Christina Tvarnø & Kim Østergaard, Udenrigshandelens Kontrakter, 5th edition, 2006, pp. 283-286. In Denmark, see bill no. 234 June 6th 1985 about gas distributor contracts and ibid pp. 265-266. The bill does not apply to other distribution contracts besides gas distributors.
5. Counterfeits are for many manufacturers of high end brands a serious threat to the brand value.

maintain the value of the selective distribution system but even better further the value of the selective distribution system.

While the three aforementioned elements are "possibilities" (which) the manufacturer can take into consideration, competition law on the other hand might create some constraints from the manufacturer´s point of view. Competition law might limit the freedom of contract which might be advantageous for the manufacturer from an economic point of view. Even though the parties have a choice of law provision in the contract, whether it might be a national or an international contract, (then) the parties might risk that the contract is violating competition law where the contract has effect. If the contract violates competition law the risk is that the contract as a whole or in part becomes void.

Within the European Union a selective distribution system is considered a vertical contract, which is comprised by (the) TFEU (Treaty on the Functioning of the European Union) Article 101. TFEU Article 101 prohibits agreements have as their object or the effect the restriction of competition. If the contract for the selective distribution system fulfills the conditions set out in TFEU Article 101 (3), it may benefit from an individual exemption. Otherwise there might a possibility to get an exemption in accordance with the block exemption in Regulation no. 330/2010.

The European Court of Justice has dealt with a number of cases concerning selective distribution systems. The most recent case[6] dealt with a manufacturer of cosmetics and personal care products. In accordance with the contract, the distributor was required to have a qualified pharmacist present at the physical sales point which de facto prohibits the authorized distributors from any form of internet reselling.[7] The European Court of Justice stated that the previous block exemption Regulation no. 2790/1999 is not applicable to the selective distribution system in question.[8] However it is possible to get an individual exemption in accordance with TFEU Article 101 (3), if the requirements are fulfilled. The European Court of Justice did not address this question, since the national court had not posed such a question. However, it seems very unlikely to get an individual exemption, since there is no reason to require

6. Case C-439/09 Pierre Fabre.
7. Ibid para 37.
8. Ibid para 59.

a fully certified pharmacist considering the character of the products sold by the manufacturer. Thus, it seems impossible to justify any sort of improvement of distribution by using a fully certified pharmacist in accordance with TFEU Article 101(3).

In general, the manufacturer has to take competition law into consideration when drafting the contract, since competition law could create some constraints to the content of the contract depending on whether the manufacturer chooses to comply with the law as a part of the company´s strategy or not.[9]

2. The proactive contract

In this paragraph, a number of suggestions for proactive provisions in the contract are presented. The suggestions do not present an exhaustive list of proactive provisions aimed for the selective distribution contract, but the suggestions are examples of provisions which to a great extent must be characterized as being proactive rather than reactive.

Since the selective distribution system presumably evolves over time it has to be kept in mind that the content of the proactive provisions cannot be considered static. Even the proactive provisions have to evolve over time.

2.1. Business goal

The contract should contain at least one provision dealing with the goal of the selective distribution system. Thus, the selective distribution must be described in such manner that the brand value created by the manufacturer is clear to the distributor in order to maintain and hopefully enhance the value of the selective distribution system in the corporation between the parties. In my opinion, such a provision in the contract

9. See Constance Bagley, What´s Law Got to Do With It? Integrating Law and Strategy, American Business Law Journal, Volume 47, Issue 4, 587-639, Winter 2010, p. 608 ff.

should create a legal and an economic framework in which the parties intertwine their mutual interests.[10]

The provision could contain information about the background of the manufacturer. For instance information about when and where the company was founded and the number of countries in which the manufacturer operates the selective distribution system etc. A description of the product lines produced by the manufacturer, including but not limited to information about the creation and the unique character of the design, the complexity of the products, and why it is essential that the distributor has sufficient knowledge about the products in order to market and resell the products.

Furthermore, such a provision should set out the obligation of the distributor to act loyally at any time and in every manner in order to maintain and further the fundamental values created by the manufacturer.

2.2. Selective distribution

It must be stressed that the manufacturer operates a selective distribution system in order to maintain and further the brand value created, where the distributor must comply with requirements set out by the manufacturer. Otherwise a distributor cannot be part of the selective distribution system. As mentioned in paragraph 2.1. in fine, the distributor must act loyally within the selective distribution system, but it must be considered essential that the manufacturer on a continuing basis contributes to the selective distribution system in order to make sure that the distributor benefits from being a part of the selective distribution system.

Considering the reselling of the products, the distributor should normally be entitled to resell the contract's products to consumers, depending on the market on which the manufacturer operates. However, the distributor might be entitled to resell the contract products to other authorized distributors within the selective distribution system, provided however that the other distributor is entitled to resell the contract products. The wording of such provision is quite important in cases where the manufacturer has different product lines, but where the distributor

10. Furthermore, such provision might reduce the risk of a violation of the competition rules within the European Union. See for instance paragraph 29 in case C-59/08 Christian Dior.

in question is only entitled to sell a certain line of products.[11] This is closely related to the distribution strategy of the manufacturer.

The distributor should possess knowledge of the particular trade relating to the product lines in order to support and become part of the selective distribution system. The distributor might only carry the goods produced by the manufacturer, and if the distributor is entitled to carry other goods such goods must have the same standard as the manufacturer's This is particular crucial to manufacturers of high-end goods.

2.3. Physical location and website

The contract has to deal with the physical location and the website belonging to the distributor.[12] Once again such a provision is crucial in order to maintain and further the brand value in the selective distribution system.

Considering the physical location belonging to the distributor, the manufacturer will to a large or lesser extent have a keen interest in securing that the contract goods will be resold in a certain manner. In general, the distributor must have the obligation to display the contract goods in a manner corresponding to the quality level and reputation of the manufacturer. For instance this might include the obligation to use certain display cabinets and show cards (logo) provided by the manufacturer.[13] The use of such display cabinets could be very important

11. A violation of such provision in the contract will often constitute a fundamental breach of the contract which in case will imply the right of the manufacturer to terminate the contract and claim damages from the distributor. Such a provision is of course a reactive provision.
12. There is hardly any doubt that electronic commerce creates different challenges to the manufacturer. This is a challenge particularly with respect to the pricing of the contract goods to be resold, since electronic commerce implies a higher degree of transparency where the consumer or other distributors at least to some extent have the possibility to compare prices. The manufacturer might have an interest to be able to withhold price differentiation depending on the market where the contract goods are sold. Furthermore, price differentiation can be a violation of competition law.
13. The manufacturer might lend or sell the display cabinets to the distributor. In case the distributor borrows one or several display cabinets from the manufacturer, the manufacturer must secure a title to the display cabinets since the display cabinets might represent high value. In accordance with Danish law, it should be sufficient to place a sticker on each of the display cabinets where it

in order to present the contract goods in the best manner to maintain the exclusivity of the contract goods. Thus, other goods resold by the distributor must not be displayed in the display cabinets provided by the manufacturer.

If the distributor is entitled to resell the contract goods through the website belonging to the distributor, the manufacturer must, like the requirements to the physical location, set out the requirements to the website in question.[14] Such requirements will differ compared to the requirements to the physical location. The contract could for instance contain a provision requiring that the contract goods are shown in a special section on the website belonging to the distributor. The distributor should only be allowed to use pictures, logos etc. provided by the manufacturer on the website in order to secure the perceived value of the brand. The distributor should not be allowed to use any trademarks, pictures, names, or domain names belonging to the manufacturer as part of the distributor's own business name, trademarks, or domain names either on the internet or any other electronic communication platform.[15] Furthermore, the manufacturer could require that the distributor is en-

is stated the display cabinet belongs to the manufacturer. The contract should also contain a provision about this issue. In my opinion, it is necessary to deal with this issue in order to secure the economic interest of the manufacturer if the distributor goes bankrupt or if somebody is pursuing to levy execution to the display cabinets. Furthermore, if the display cabinets are lent to the distributor the contracts need to be taken into consideration if any harm is done to the display cabinets, if the display cabinets are destroyed, and the use of the display in order to minimize any claims by any third party. So once the display cabinets are returned to the manufacturer for whatever reason, the distributor must be held liable if the display cabinets are in a state beyond normal wear.

14. There is hardly any doubt that ecommerce causes major challenges to the manufacturer of high end brands, including but not limited to the pricing of the goods (lack of price differentiation?) perception of the goods, and the increased transparency in the market place.
15. It has to be kept in mind that the manufacturer and the distributor are two independent legal entities. The distributor acts for one´s own name and for one´s own account and risk.
    Thus, a distributor is a different intermediary compared to a commercial agent. For further reading in Danish, see Udenrigshandelens Kontrakter, Ole Lando, Elisabeth Thuesen, Christina Tvarnø, and Kim Østergaard, 5th edition, 2006, chapter 3.

rolled in an accreditation scheme where the distributor has the physical location of the store.[16]

2.4. Changes

The contract between the manufacturer and the distributor is traditionally a long-term contract. From an economic point of view this makes sense, since both parties to the contract are having active specific expenditures. Thus, it is very likely over the years that the distributor would like to change physical location or increase/decrease the number of physical locations from where the contract goods are resold. Furthermore, the distributor would perhaps like to expand or decrease the product lines the distributor is entitled to resell.

These issues have to be taken into consideration in the contract. In a situation where the distributor, for instance, wants to change the physical location and the contracted goods are considered high-end products, the manufacturer has a keen interest in securing that the new physical location in terms of protecting the brand value of the manufacturer is situated in a neighborhood which is perceived in accordance with the value of the brand. Otherwise, it might diminish the brand value associated with the selective distribution system. In order to do so, the manufacturer must have the right to approve or reject the suggested physical location.

A change in product line might require additional training of the distributor and his employees if the production line in question is very complex, sophisticated, requires certain information[17] and perhaps "storytelling" once the contract goods are resold to the consumers. If the manufacturer has different product lines which are perceived differently, considering the brand value of each product line, the manufacturer must take into consideration whether the highest perceived product line should be sold by the distributor. In such a case the physical location of the distributor might play a part in this kind of decision.

16. In Denmark, see http://www.emaerket.dk/in-english.aspx.
17. Case C-439/09 Pierre Fabre.

2.5. Reporting

Even though the manufacturer sells the contract goods to the distributor and the contract contains an obligation to buy a certain quantity during a specific period, the manufacturer can still have an interest in getting certain information from the distributor on a frequent basis.

An obligation to pass on information to the manufacturer could include the turnover rate of contract goods, how the local market is developing and future predictions about the local market, and if the customers are requiring goods which are not produced and sold at the time of reporting.[18]

2.6. Marketing

In order to protect the value of the selective distribution system, the manufacturer has a keen interest in the manner of which the contract goods are promoted in the market place. There might be some differences depending on the media chosen to promote the contract goods, but in general the manufacturer would like to control the way logo(s), text, and pictures are used in conjunction with the promotion of the contract goods.

Thus, the manufacturer can require some sort of approval process of any promotion initiatives which the distributor wants to pursue. However, it must be kept in mind that any such approval process implies transaction costs between the parties, why it is necessary to establish an approval process which causes the least transaction costs.

If the contract goods are perceived as high-end brands it would be obvious to have a provision requiring that contract goods are only to be sold in the original packaging provided by the manufacturer, since the packaging in many cases is a crucial part of the whole product. Take for instance high-end cosmetic products, where the costs of promotion and packaging amount to a substantial part of the total price of the product. The manufacturer might even require that damaged packaging has to

18. It must be kept in mind that this kind of reporting system creates transaction costs to both the manufacturer and the distributor. Thus, it is essential if such a reporting system is established where the information provided actually creates value in order to maintain and further the selective distribution system.

be replaced before the contract goods are resold, provided the contract goods are not harmed.[19]

2.7. Relation maintenance

The parties will in most cases have decided upon the applicable law to the contract (choice of law provision) and jurisdiction (choice of venue provision), once a conflict arises, but most contracts do not deal with the issue about how to handle that a conflict with a certain magnitude is not taken to court. However, mechanisms to avoid conflicts and/or maintain and enhance the relation between the manufacturer and the distributor are seldom, to my knowledge, formalized in the contract between the parties.[20]

The parties can include a provision in a contract which states the obligation to a physical meeting between the parties. For instance every six months. By doing so, the parties can mutually discuss the obstacles but naturally also the possibilities within the selective distribution system. The parties could for instance discuss a new future physical locations belonging to the distributor or the distributor could provide the manufacturer with information about the local market which goes beyond the written reporting as mentioned in paragraph 2.5. Having such physical meetings implies transaction costs. However, it must be kept in mind whether the benefit created from these meetings is higher than the transaction costs. This will in most cases be very difficult to measure. An alternative could be to hold such meetings electronically in order to reduce the transaction costs or only have this provision with key distributors.

Even though the contract contains the aforementioned provision about the obligation to have meetings with a certain frequency, a conflict

19. If the contract goods have been delivered to distributor, the distributor carries the risk if the contract goods are harmed or destroyed before the contract goods are resold and delivered typically to a consumer. Between the manufacturer and the distributor, the parties might use one of the clauses in INCOTERMS 2010.
20. I guess the argument in this paragraph is applicable to almost all long term contracts. To my knowledge, no survey has been conducted to investigate how parties in long term use contract provisions in order to maintain and even better to enhance the relationship and the business between the parties.

might arise. In such cases, the provision concerning conflict solution can be carried out in three stages. At first, the parties have the obligation to settle the conflict in an amicable manner. In order to prevent that any of the parties tend to speculate on withdrawing the process, the provision should contain a fixed number of calendar days by the end of which he conflict has to be solved, once one of the parties has given written notice in accordance with the provision. If the parties are not able to solve the conflict in an amicable manner, then the next step in the conflict provision is the obligation to use a mediator to help solving the conflict between the parties.[21] [22] The mediator will typically focus upon the interests of the parties in order to solve the conflict. The interest of the parties is in most cases focused upon the economics instead of pure law. Thus, the keen interest is to investigate whether it is possible to reach a common understanding between the parties, which in most cases require a rider to the original agreement or (perhaps) even a completely new agreement to replace the original contract.[23] Once again, the parties should settle a number of calendar days during which the conflict has to be solved through the mediator. Otherwise the conflict is relocated to the final step in the conflict solution process, whether that might be a court or arbitration depending on the content of the provision. Once the court or the court of arbitration has passed its verdict it is very unlikely there is any relation between the parties.

This three-step provision concerning he conflict solution process between the parties should hopefully provide a basis to maintain the contract between the parties and reduce the risk of conflict ending up in court or arbitration. Furthermore, such a provision should reduce transaction costs ex post even though the transaction costs are increased ex ante. But as a whole, the transaction costs should in total be reduced.

21. To my knowledge no research, at least in Denmark, has been performed in order to investigate to what extent the use of a mediator reduces the likelihood that a case is taken to court or arbitration.
22. Alternative Dispute Resolution (ADR) could also be an option.
23. See R.H. Coase, The Problem of Social Cost, The Journal of Law & Economics, Vol. III, 1960, pp. 207-240. The author shows among other things that the pure legal solution is not necessarily economically efficient which creates an incentive to do otherwise.

2.8. Termination

As mentioned in the introduction, the contract between the manufacturer and the distributor is usually a long term contract. However, at some point of time the contract will end. Either of the parties has given notice of termination in accordance with the contract or one of the parties declares the contract avoided, since the other party has breached the contract which is considered a fundamental breach of contract.

Even though the proactive provision serve as a "tool" to avoid termination, the manufacturer still has to take into consideration what has to happen upon termination of the contract for whatever reason. Considering the contract goods the manufacturer acts as seller while the distributor acts as buyer of the contract goods. Upon termination of the contract the manufacturer has to take into consideration what should happen to those contract goods which are already sold and delivered to the distributor, but not yet resold by the distributor. The contract should contain an option to the manufacturer, where the manufacturer is entitled to rebuy the contract goods upon termination. Such an option helps the manufacturer to avoid the reselling of the contract goods in a manner not consistent with the no longer existing contract and perhaps at a price which might cause harm to the perception of the selective distribution. It must be kept in mind that there is a risk that the distributor will act on an opportunistic basis against the manufacturer, once the contract has ended. Thus, from an economic point of view, there is a strong argument to use a provision where the manufacturer has the option to rebuy the contract goods upon termination in order to protect the selective distribution system

Furthermore, the distributor should have the obligation to return, at his own expense and risk, visual merchandising provided by the manufacturer.

3. Conclusion

Even though the suggestions for proactive provisions discussed in paragraph 2 are not exhaustive, there seems to be an indication that the proactive provisions in the contract for selective distribution system is closely related at least from the point of view of the manufacturer to preserve or even further the value of the brand created by the manufacturer himself or/and in collaboration with former or current distributors within the selective distribution system.

The proactive provisions, suggested, can be seen as a means to support and further the distribution strategy and business goals set out by the manufacturer where the distributor plays a crucial part in the fulfillment hereof.

Empowering Contracting Parties – Proactive and dialogic contracting in public procurement

By

Soile Pohjonen

Katja Koskelainen

Abstract

In this article we analyze contracting competence in public procurement especially through the influence of legal thinking over contracts and contracting competence as part of business capabilities. Both public procurement and contracting suffer from an image of rather harming than enhancing business. Seeing contracts as legal documents has overshadowed their role as collaboration tools to be created and used cross-professionally. One of the aims of the European public procurement regulation is to support competition and, along with it, the competitiveness of European supplier companies. In some respects this target might well be reached, but the demand that tenders usually have to correspond exactly to invitations to tender does not develop tendering skills. The image of contracts in many discourses is to represent formality and self-interest. They are seen to hinder trust and cooperation which are essential business partnership ideals. This may have as a consequence that contract competence is not developed and contracts continue to be left for lawyers to handle as purely legal documents and legal contracts are drafted for legal interpretation disputes. Proactive contracting aims at business success and sees contracts as collaboration instruments. This viewpoint sets quite new requirements for contract documents which could be tackled with e.g. visualization. We argue that proactive contracting builds foundations for trust and cooperation. But in order to do that, contracting competence has to be developed first. It most probably will not be if its value as an essential part of business capabilities is not admitted. Many companies are starting to realize the potential of contracting in developing their competition skills, in building their image as attractive partners and in creating common responsibility with contract mechanisms which encourage to that. The same realization begins to apply to procurement authorities.

1. Introduction

The economic value of procurement is huge both in the public and the private sector and the more the public sector outsources, the greater the role of procurement will be. Nevertheless, procurement capabilities have traditionally not been widely appreciated. The focus in business is usually in selling. Same lack of appreciation applies to contracting competence. Both public procurement and contracting are often seen as legal formalities. Substance of procurement contracting is dwarfed by legalese.

European public procurement regulation is based on the belief in competition. The regulation aims at developing business capabilities of European companies by the tendering process. Our focus is on open procedure procurement process which is the most commonly practiced procedure in Finland. Its practice seems to show that what the system strengthens is the capability of tendering exactly what the buyer demands in the invitations to tender. In business a good seller tries to sell a buyer the best possible solution to fulfill the buyer's needs. To offer something more suitable than what the buyer was even able to ask for is welcomed warmly. The buyer is happy and willing to continue the relationship. In public procurement this kind of "normal behavior" usually leads to rejection of the offer. To succeed in public tendering, sellers need to learn away from this behavior. Tendering is part of contracting competence. Contracting competence is often not recognized as part of business cooperation capabilities.

Contracts are often seen as harming business and contradicting its logic. Cooperation and trust are seen as the more or less naturally existing circumstances in doing business. This harmony is considered to be destroyed by contracts when contracts are seen as the opposite of common good and trust. But is this so? We argue that the image of contracts and the corresponding practice is caused by having allowed legal interpretation logic to invade realms which it in theory denies to reign. The aim of contracts has become to secure success in litigation. If we instead see contracts according to Proactive Law and Proactive Contracting, trust and good collaboration are goals, not already existing starting points and contracts are tools to build cooperation and trust as well as to reach the desired goals.

In this paper, we explore the influence of legal thinking over contracts particularly in public procurement and how this affects contracting practice and its development. Dialogic[1] and proactive legal thinking produces a different kind of attitude towards contracts and contracting.

2. Theoretical background: The image of contract as an outcome of the image of law – towards dialogic law

The goddess of law is illustrated as *blind-folded*. She delivers justice based on some divine or natural source or on norms interpreted by legal logic. She is a neutral mediator, a separate entity. She is not aware of the perceptions her law is made of. She is not responsible for creating laws or for their implementation. She is responsible only for the coherence of her logic. Based on Cartesian influence[2] the goddess has been alienated from other sources and has become more of an interpretation machine.[3] She has likewise begun to see humans as thinking machines without any other characteristics. The results of the reign of this goddess hiding behind formality are here to be seen.

1. We refer to the so called bohmian dialogue, see David Bohm, *On Dialogue* (L. Nichol ed., Routledge: London, New York 1996/1999) and William Isaacs, *Dialogue and the art of thinking together* (Currency: New York 1999).
2. With this is meant the influence of René Descartes's dualism on Western thinking: the rational mind has been emphasized at the expense of embodied emotions. Even if this dualism has been widely criticized, main stream science is still much embedded in it.
3. Sherwin has emphasized this aspect and the need for the sublime and mindfulness, Richard K. Sherwin, *Visualizing Law in the Age of the Digital Baroque, Arabesques and entanglements* (Routledge: London and New York 2011).

But what if we had instead *a goddess who sees*, who is conscious of herself, who is aware of her subjectivity, who sees and takes responsibility of her influence on creation of laws and on their implementation, who understands human nature and reasoning?[4] She would see law as a continually-developing process. Her law would be sensitive and self-reflexive. This goddess would see the variety in the world and know that it cannot be managed with monolithic methods. She would know that there are no straight ways and no steady goals to reach or find. She would know that everything is infinitively becoming. She would know that everything changes continuously and attempt to manage processes of uncertainty and choice[5]. She would know that in a world of dissimilar human minds everything is fragmented - the universal wholeness is possible only beyond the mind.

The object of law is commonly seen as being justice. Justice of *the blind-folded goddess* is found in already existing texts when they are applied transparently and predictably according to legal logic. This is how the blind-folded goddess is seen to protect autonomy of people against despotism. *The seeing goddess* knows that justice and autonomy are nowhere to be found and protected, but are instead goals. Justice of the seeing goddess is time and context bound, internalized ways of thinking and feeling. Her task is to be involved in a process of co-creating a system where norms, their interpretation and implementation would together promote justice and autonomy. Her task is to be aware of her influence on these other spheres and what perceptions she adopts from other spheres and disciplines.

Like protecting autonomy, *the blind-folded goddess* sees herself as a protector of the will of the contracting parties. Contracts are expressions of will. Law is seen to protect the realization of will according to its own

4. Moral conceptions, perceptions of human nature, philosophical understandings, experiences and "self-evident" insights of the actors to name a few, all have influence in legal thinking but it is not in the core of jurisprudence to reflect the choices of its sources. Belief in objectivity increases subjectivity. Many discussions, like feminist jurisprudence, have emphasized the inevitable subjectivity of human thinking increasing possibilities to a more objective law.
5. Management of uncertainty and choice are examples of terms used at present to describe the inevitability of change and its positive aspects as offering new possibilities.

interpretation norms in litigation. Her ideal contract is final: the will has been frozen to bring stability through legal interpretation. 'Contract' has become a legal document drafted by lawyers for legal disputes. Thus, the interests of the parties appear rather opposite than common. Contract relationship is a rational, impersonal relationship which aims at executing a transaction.

In the world of *the seeing goddess*, contracts are developed in collaborative networks and are used to manage the target-oriented cooperation. Contracting is a process which balances between freezing and flowing, between bringing stability and managing choice. Will is rather a continuously becoming goal than an already existing perception. Co-creation in contracting networks is based on communication skills which are based on understanding about human behavior, human mind and emotions. Ideal contracts are user-friendly instruments for co-creating, expressing and realizing the will of the parties. The seeing goddess sees herself as an enabler of achieving the goals parties aim at. She sees contracting as a cross-professional collaboration process.

Public procurement contracting, through the logic of *the blind-folded goddess*, concerns impersonal sales where the buyer seeks to find the cheapest seller. The goal is to give equal opportunities to tender in publicly financed sales. Discrimination is believed to be abolished and transparency achieved with formal procurement regulation and application. Around the blind-folded goddess an attitude of self-limitation spreads, to be on the safe side. Around *the seeing goddess* the goal is good procurement for the benefit of European companies and for the benefit of the public sector – for us all. From the viewpoint of this goal, self-limiting fear is an irresponsible attitude.

The law of *the blind-folded goddess* is a dialectic and rational process created by legal professionals. The law of *the seeing goddess* is also in dialog with Others. In order to co-create and communicate with others she needs to be aware of her own characteristics and perceptions. The more hidden her own nature is to her, the more it contorts her understanding. Besides understanding herself she needs to: respect the perceptions of others and listen to them actively, understand the functioning of human beings as well as embrace communication and collaboration skills. The domain of *the blind-folded goddess* of law is a tribunal where offences and disputes are addressed. *The seeing goddess* wants to promote successful function where tribunals are not hopefully needed or may be replaced by dialogic mediation. The seeing goddess admits that legal interpretation logic influences outside her domain and she needs to be responsible for that influence and simultaneously empower other actors to take back their power when it has been conquered from them by law.

The language of *the blind-folded goddess* is an introspective, professional language for legal professionals who are obliged to master it. Her focus is on rational texts. *The seeing goddess* sees herself through the eyes of society, as a part of a target-oriented and context-bound process. She sees herself as one player in a common game. Rules of the game should be co-created and the game played together. People playing the game are both rational and emotional. Language of the common play needs to be, besides rational, also communicative, tempting and inspiring. Her language goes beyond words. Her goal is collaboration where understanding is shared through various channels, like contracts and laws. Her success depends on the ability of these channels to cross the boundaries between people and organizations.

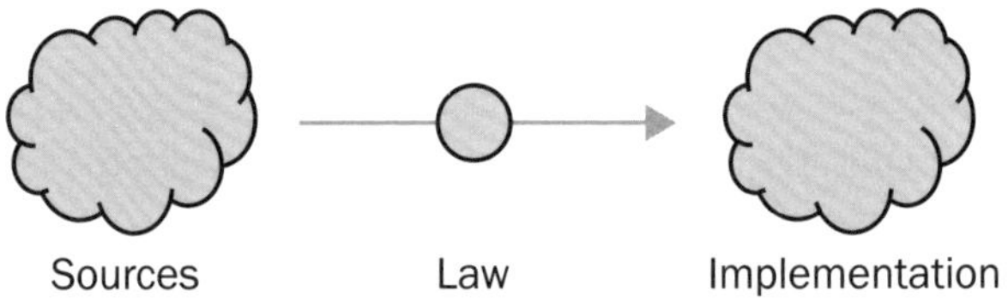

Picture 1: Self-understanding of **law** as a 'neutral mediator' from legal **sources** (like legislation and precedents) or contracts towards **implementation**.

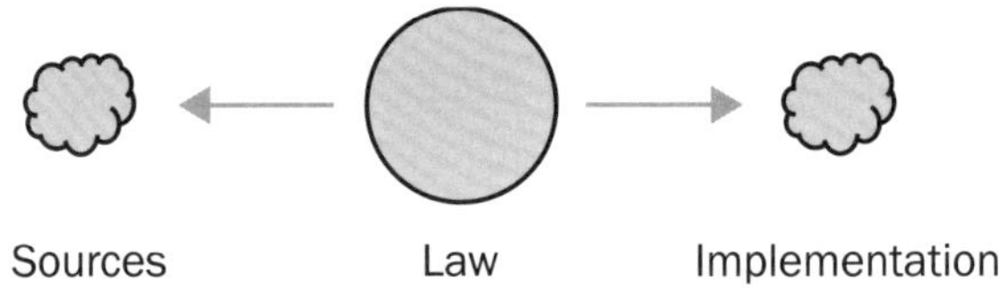

Picture 2: In practice **law**/legal interpretation logic dominates legislation/contract/**source** making and administration/**implementation**.

3. Case method and data description

Our cases consist of open procedure procurement processes of municipalities in Finland. The research approach in our study is a combination of case study and action research. We conduct process simulation projects according to SimLab business process simulation method[6], focusing on developing networked public procurement practices and related contractual processes. Process simulation reveals what really happened in the process in question. The actors involved are able to see the whole picture and their own role in it, reflecting what they could do to diminish problems and enhance working methods. This follows - on a case level - the logic of dialogic law: actors become aware of their own suppositions and perceptions surrounding them, begin to reflect their own operation and interaction with others and hopefully take responsibility for amelioration. In legal discussions a somewhat comparable idea has been called legal autopsy.[7] If lawyers would see the ending up in court as a consequence of unsuccessful lawyering, they could use it as a learning experience which reveals deficiencies in the preceding legal work. Even today, the idea of this kind of learning is not very common among legal profession.

The data collection and analysis methods used are qualitative including semi-structured theme interviews, observation of group discussions, participation in workshop working, and the analysis of transcribed interviews and group discussions. We interviewed procurement professionals, field professionals and suppliers. Secondary written documentation, such as contracts, invitations to tender, tenders and internal procurement guidelines were analyzed. Besides, we have studied the procurement function in general based on databanks, literature and expert discussions. We have among other things arranged expert network meetings where particular themes concerning public procurement have been discussed. In our data analysis we apply the iterative process of

6. Riitta Smeds, Miia Jaatinen, Antero Hirvensalo and Anna Kilpiö, *SimLab Process Simulation Method as a Boundary Object for Inter-Organizational Innovation*, 10th International Workshop on Experimental Interactive Learning in Industrial Management, Trondheim, Norway June 11-13 2006.
7. Louis M. Brown, *Legal Autopsy*, Journal of the American Judicature Society, Vol. 39, 2/1955, 47-49.

considering theory and empirical data following the grounded theory approach presented by Strauss and Corbin[8]. Our viewpoint to the procurement contracting process is based on Proactive Law and Proactive Contracting approach.

Our first research question in data analysis was to find out how the procurement process in itself had affected the end results received by the process, i.e. the number and quality of tenders. Strict and complicated formalities and definitions in competitive tendering decreased the number of tenders available. Some suppliers didn't tender at all, some tenders had to be rejected. Sometimes only one tender remained to be chosen. The quality of the product bought is affected by the demand that successful suppliers have to tender exactly what was demanded for in the invitation and not what they consider to be the best option for the buyer. In this paper we analyze the prerequisites for success in procurement contracting processes.

4. Proactive Law and Proactive Contracting

Proactive Law belongs to approaches born out of real-life needs to balance the prevailing legal logic.[9] In Proactive Contracting, contracting is considered a cross-professional process to promote success. The approach has been developed in cross-disciplinary co-creation between researchers and experts in business-to-business contracting practice. In business contracting, Proactive Contracting focuses on helping the parties to reach their business goals and identifying possible sources of problems before damage has occurred. It looks at contracting from the perspective of individual contracts as well as the whole contracting system of an organization and the implementation of the contract by

8. A.L. Strauss and J.R. Corbin, *Basics of Quality Research: Techniques and Procedure for Developing Grounded Theory* (Sage Publications: Newbury Park, CA 1990).
9. See on Proactive Law and its history in George J. Siedel & Helena Haapio, *Using Proactive Law for Competitive Advantage,* 17 American Business Law Journal 2010, 641 and Proactive Law in relation to legal thinking in general in Soile Pohjonen, *Proactive Law in the Field of Law,* in A Proactive Approach 53-70 (P. Wahlgren ed., Scandinavian Studies in Law, Vol. 49, Stockholm Institute for Scandinavian Law: Stockholm 2006).

different employees. Further, it understands contracting as an essential part of business management and strategic planning. The emphasis is on value-generating. Contracting is enhancing knowledge sharing and knowledge co-creation,[10] securing that all parties know what they are supposed to do, creating methods to prepare for changes, promoting the desired attitudes, and so forth. Contract visualization is at present one of the most important emerging interests.[11] If contracts are supposed to be expressions of will and if the will more often than not remains unclear, the most obvious key to improvement is to ameliorate knowledge sharing where infographics is an efficient tool.

The orientation of Proactive Contracting is to the future, whereas the traditional legal focus is on the past, related mainly to legal disputes. Since court decisions have constituted the core interest in legal thinking, the most common future-oriented element in legal discussion has been the anticipation of those decisions. Contract law is mostly about dealing with contract failures. Proactivity differs from reactivity in that it emphasizes consideration how one can create the preconditions for achieving goals oneself in a manner that does not contribute to unnecessary problems. Therefore, it is not about simply reacting to something that has happened or is happening. Rather, it is about self-reflection and responsibility. The Proactive Law's goddess of law is the dialogic seeing goddess mentioned above.

10. The term knowledge co-creation used here is a combination of knowledge creation by I. Nonaka and H. Takeuchi, *The Knowledge-Creating Company* (Oxford University Press 1995) and co-creation by V. Ramaswamy and F. Gouillart, *The Power of Co-Creation* (Free Press: New York 2010).
11. See for example Passera, Stefania & Haapio, Helena, *User-Centered Contract Design: New Directions in the Quest for Simpler Contracting,* in Bringing together academics and practitioners to promote research and best practice in Contracts and Commercial Management 80-97 (R. F. Henschel ed., Academic Forum for Innovative Research and Practice, International Association for Contract and Commercial Management IACCM: Ridgefield 2011) and Gerlinde Berger-Walliser, Robert C. Bird & Helena Haapio, *Promoting Business Success through Contract Visualisation,* 17 The Journal of Law, Business & Ethics 2011, 55. On legal visualizing in general see Colette R. Brunschwig, *Visualisierung von Rechtsnormen – Legal Design* (Zürichen Studien zur Rechtsgesichte, Vol. 45, Rechtswissenschaftliche Fakultät, Universität Zürich, Schulthess Juristische Medien: Zürich 2001).

Proactive Contracting approach aims at the development of contracting competence. Traditionally contracting competence is seen as a dominantly legal skill where the emphasis is on preventing and allocating legal risks. In Proactive Contracting, contracts are not seen as primarily legal documents, but rather as business plans which clarify what has been agreed upon. The most important task of proactively drafted contracts is not purely to prevent legal risks, but rather to enable business goals. A proactively oriented lawyer should be able to create functional legal frameworks for the particular business goals and perceive potential legal risks in that particular business context and how these risks could be prepared for legally. In order to be able to understand the business, its goals and the significance of potential risks, she needs to collaborate with other professionals. That requires proper tools to enable knowledge sharing and co-creation. Contracts are at present rarely made for that purpose. Contract competence is not developed if we do not believe that contracting has potential to benefit business instead of being "pure law".

5. Does public procurement regulation counteract development of business capabilities?

EU strives for creating a single European market where open and fair competition reigns and desires access to world procurement markets. In public procurement this is supposed to mean choice from a larger market both for contracting authorities and supplier companies. One objective is to strengthen the competitiveness of European suppliers. But what are the effects of the EU regulation on the competition capabilities of the European companies?

From the viewpoint of that question, the emphasis is different from what it would be if the focus were on another goal of the EU public procurement policy like on abolishing favoritism and corruption in public procurement. European Commission has pointed out that additional guarantees for this would often increase administrative burdens for procurers and suppliers. The balance between the two goals - fight against unsound business practices and simplification of the procedures – must be carefully weighed[12].

Public procurement regulation faces challenges on various levels. 1) Quality of regulation and awareness of it: Some of the troubles said to have been caused by the regulation are in fact caused entirely or partly by false assumptions about the regulation while some really are caused by the regulation. 2) Compliance: On the one hand the concern has been noncompliance. On the other hand the compliance, especially the overly cautious compliance, causes complications. 3) Solutions: Some of the complications caused by the regulation cannot be solved without reregulation while some of them can be unraveled with contracting competence.

The effectiveness of the public procurement regulation has been a widely discussed topic. In the green paper from 1996[13], the Commission sees that the results "achieved on the transparency front are highly encouraging" but "problems still remain in terms of the practical effectiveness of the legislation" (3). It is pointed out in the paper that larger companies manage bidding for public contracts [14] whereas small and medium-sized enterprises (SMEs) face greater difficulties (29-33). SMEs would need assistance and training in the tendering process. "The opening-up and simplification of contracting authorities' practices through the training of procurement offices" is suggested to "make it easier for SMEs to bid for contracts" (32). Concern about SMEs continues in the green paper 2011[15].

In the European Parliament resolution on new developments in public procurement (A7-0151/2010), the European Parliament deplores that the simplification of procurement rules has not yet been achieved and calls on the Commission to simplify the public procurement procedure

12. Green paper on the modernization of EU public procurement policy Towards a more efficient European procurement market (COM 27.1.2011 15 final), 49.
13. Green paper, Public Procurement in the European Union: Exploring the way forward (COM 27.11.1996), 583.
14. The number of contracts won by firms based in other Member States was noted to have remained small with the exception of larger firms who can submit tenders through their local subsidiaries or via consortia.
15. Green paper 2011, *supra* note 12, 3.1., Better access for SMEs and Start-ups, 27-30.

(point 1). Existing regulation is pointed out to be complicated and confusing which creates serious legal problems (point 2). Moreover, public procurers often have to prioritize legal certainty above policy needs and award the contract in question to the cheapest offer instead of the most economically advantageous tender. The Parliament is afraid that this will weaken the EU's innovative base and global competitiveness (point 3). It emphasizes that simplifying the procedures will facilitate SMEs access to public contracts and supports the admission of alternative bids (points 20 and 22).

In the Commission Staff Working Document (23.2.2007), a guide which provides proposals to develop a public procurement policy that promotes innovation, in chapter 4 "Let the market propose creative solutions" (8-9), accepting variant bids and arranging design contests are suggested. "What to do" paragraph crystallizes two tasks: "Give companies room to propose ideas and be open for alternatives" and "Ask for a solution, do not prescribe it".

In the studied open procedure cases the mostly used criterion was the lowest price and variants were not authorized even if the criterion had been the most economically advantageous tender when it would have been possible. There seems to be a present tendency in Finland to prefer the lowest price criterion. It is easy to compare and desired quality criterions may be included as minimum requirements. Scoring-based competitive tendering has been seen to lead more easily to complaints in court compared to lowest price award[16]. On the other hand, including all prerequisites in minimum requirements furthers the risk of receiving too few or too many tenders[17]. Using the most economically advantageous award instead of the lowest price would enable a decreasing of the problem of strict calls for tenders.

The demand to strictly follow the invitation has two consequences: 1) Public procurers need to be very well informed of the markets in order to draft an intelligent invitation. 2) Tenderers have to tender exactly what

16. Fredrik Waara, *Mitigating contractual hazards in public procurement: a study of Swedish local authorities*, Construction Management and Economics 26, February 2008, 137-145, 141.
17. Fredrik Waara, *Mitigating contractual hazards in public procurement: a study of Swedish local authorities*, *supra* note 16, 143.

was asked for in order to get their tenders accepted even if they would be able to provide a much better solution or product.

Public procurers should, thus, be not only intelligent but super-intelligent customers.[18] The high demands are even aggravated by false assumptions. Public procurers in Finland have often been overcautious about their contacts with the market in fear of being accused of favoring.[19] Thus, they have not been able to benefit the supply of the market and the assistance available. This has not supported the development of their procuring capabilities.[20] The regulation does not forbid contacts with the market as long as they are open and non-discriminative. Public procurers would need to know the market even better than private procurers because they usually have to stick to the content of the invitation. Moreover, the public procurement market may at least partly be semi-competitive as the suppliers who find the tendering system too complicated or expect the price level to be too low do not tender. Some municipalities are hard-pressed to receive any tenders at all.

As suppliers have to learn to tender whatever is demanded for in the invitation, the system does not nurture their general tendering capabilities i.e. learning to satisfy the real needs of customers. The situation is not improved by the above mentioned possible lack of hard competition. The strictly formal application of the system abolishes at least partly the positive effects of opening up of the market i.e. everyone having the opportunity to tender. The role of public procurement in promoting competitive markets is a wide topic in need of many-sided further research.[21] In this paper our viewpoint to competitiveness is purely and simply competence concerning tendering.

18. See Commission staff working document Guide on dealing with innovative solutions in public procurement, 10 elements of good practice (Brussels 23.2.2007, SEC 2007), 280 on remarks and suggestions to become an intelligent customer.
19. If a not selected tenderer appeals against a procurement decision Market Court process will delay the procurement. Besides, many procurers experience an appeal against their decisions as a failure.
20. Public procurers face many challenges, one of them being cooperation with substance experts of the product to be procured. User authorities do not always find it as their task to participate in the defining process even if they are the ones who will use the product.
21. Nigel Caldwell, Helen Walker, Christine Harland, Louise Knight, Jurong Zheng, Tim Wakely note in their article *Promoting competitive markets: The Role*

In private business, a tendering process may be a preparing phase for an actual contract.[22] Tenders may offer new information and ideas which ameliorate the preliminary plans. In addition, contracting and contract law discussions have emphasized the dynamic nature of contracts during their currency on many levels.[23] The significance of this phenomenon is different if the focus is legal interpretation of contracts or preparation of functioning contract cooperation. Change of circumstances is proactively taken into consideration in contracting, for example by creating change management instruments. In public procurement, contract amendments to the provisions would usually require a new competitive procedure if the provisions differ materially from the original contract[24]. Amendments are considered material if for example the new conditions would have allowed the participation or success of other tenderers. Accordingly, the main rule is that tenders have to correspond to the calls even if contracting authorities may authorize tenderers to submit variants where the criterion for award is that of the most economically advantageous tender (Article 24)[25]. This option has to be indicated in the tender as well as the minimum or specific requirements to be met. Directive 2004/18/EC brought some concession to tendering procedure

of public procurement, Journal of Purchasing & Supply Management 11, 2005, 245-251 that the role of public procurement in promoting competitive markets is in its academic infancy. Besides, there are many perceptions of 'competitive'.

22. In public procurement call for tenders is preceded by a contract notice, but as these two are usually more or less the same, we do not mention in the text the notice to compare more clearly public and private contracting.
23. See on the relation between business contracting and contract law Soile Pohjonen, *Law and business - successful business contracting, corporate social responsibility and legal thinking,* Tidskrift utgiven av Juridiska Föreningen i Finland (JFT) 3-4/2009, 470-484.
24. Green paper 2011 *supra* note 12, 2.5. Address concerns relating to contract execution, 24-25, includes also case-law of the ECJ. In the paper a question, if a more flexible competitive procedure following an amendment would be justified, has arisen.
25. Directive 2004/18/EC of the European Parliament and of the Council of 31 March 2004 on the coordination of procedures for the award of public works contracts, public supply contracts and public service contracts.

by creating the possibility to Competitive dialogue for particularly complex contracts (Article 29).[26]

What increases formal and cautious attitudes is the complexity of the public procurement regulation. Its logic and rules are not well internalized. On the contrary both authorities and suppliers are often quite vaguely acquainted with the system. This leads people to act on the basis of the perceptions they have acquired whether these are suppositions, simplified truths, educated guesses or facts. The opportunities the system would offer are not used. Fear of ending up in Market Court which delays the procurement strengthens the caution. As mentioned above, public procurement regulation would offer opportunities to interact with the market and request alternative bids, but in practice these options or procurement procedure options are not often exploited. If we look at this phenomenon from the viewpoint of a procurer, who wants to procure products smoothly through the competitive tendering process, lowest price criterion may be a very understandable choice: easy to compare and the decision probably will not be appealed against. But as a prevailing habit, this creates the situation where formality and tendering exactly what is called for, prevails. In this kind of culture procurement capabilities of neither public procurers nor their suppliers flourish. In addition, ignorance may induce that authorities neglect the rules and suppliers fail or feel reluctant to adapt them.

One could ask if court procedure is the best method to ensure the goals of the public procurement directive. As the attention in court is focused on formal interpretations, the attention of procurers is accordingly drawn to that direction. Some companies add on to this development by appealing whenever they have lost the competition. A dialogic, policy-oriented instrument would most probably be more suitable to guide procurement praxis towards enhancing good procurement. It could possibly have authorization to forward serious discrimination cases to court.

In this article, our focus is on contracting in the prevailing circumstances, which means that we do not emphasize reregulation needs (*de lege ferenda*), but concentrate on ways how public procurers could cope

26. Also some other purchasing systems like dynamic (Article 33) contain some options for tender modification. Projects may be proposed outside of the strict terms of reference in design contests (Articles 66-74).

in the present reality. Besides requiring alternative bids and arranging contacts with the market, procurers could unprompted clarify contracting documents and processes in order to make it easy for suppliers to participate in the competitive procedure.

6. Do contracts counteract business?

Above, we emphasized the public procurement part of the phenomenon public procurement contracting. Now, it is the turn of the other part i.e. contracting. If public procurement is seen as purely the competitive tendering phase - as a bureaucratic legal nuisance - the image of contracts is more or less the same: from the viewpoint of business, they have been seen as useless documents drafted for legal purposes only.

What is a contract? To put it simply, it is an agreement where two or more parties commit themselves to something, at least on an intention level. To realize this commitment or intention, the contract should be somewhat clear in order to be of any use. If people agree to do something, but define this intention vaguely it is more than likely that all the parties have different perceptions of the aim of the contract and end up quarreling and mistrusting each other. The parties should be able to estimate on realistic grounds whether they are willing and capable to commit themselves. If their participation rests on misconceptions their commitment and performance will suffer. When contracts are seen as plans for committed cooperation, their aim is to enable success. Contracts should balance between building up security and flexibility. Change management is an essential instrument towards success in real life circumstances.

Companies are contracting networks. Business projects are often very complicated networks and clarification of the aims is no easy task. Cross-professional expertise is usually needed. Technical frames and solutions, feasibility calculations, legal frames and shields and so forth, have to be planned. Contracting competence includes an ability to combine the different areas of know-how to form a functioning whole. If the core of the collaboration is based on technical expertise, financial calculations have to be based on understanding the costs and profits of these particular technical solutions in these particular circumstances. The same applies to legal instruments: they have to support the goals wanted and enshrine from the risks probable in those circumstances. For example liabilities and damages are tightly connected to the work definitions and timetables as well as the planning of resources available. Legal shields are not generalizable clauses which do the trick in every situation, no more than technical solutions are suited to all situations. Besides, careless contracts may give the other party unintended opportunities to demand damages. In addition, there are many other prerequisites for contracting success or in other words business success like communication and knowledge sharing between organizations and inside them, not to mention the input of interest groups such as end users.

However, the above described perception of contracts is not the prevailing one. In our Western world business contracts are usually seen as legal documents which are drafted by lawyers who know the law. The aim of contracts is thus to prepare for legal risks i.e. disputes to be won in courts or in arbitration according to the law. Even if disputes were negotiated or mediated, the shadow of law usually has its effects on one's bargaining power. Ideal legal contracts have traditionally been seen as stable. The will of the parties has been frozen in the document, however unclear and dependent on changing circumstances it may in reality have been. In contract law, will is mostly viewed through the image of a rational human being who knows what he (the image is a "he") wants. The liberal concept of free will presupposes human autonomy, for will is viewed as being free if it is not hindered. The legal interest concerning freedom of will is usually in protecting people from being forced, manipulated or exploited. In protecting the free will in solving court cases, the legal system fills the gaps in contracts, which business partners may not realize and even less, how these gaps are filled. Nevertheless, the will of a human being is a complicated internal and organizational process. To take autonomy as the aim, rather than as an existing starting point, increases assurance that expressions of the will do reflect the real will of the parties. Besides, traditional contract law is based on the image of a contract relationship as a one-shot transaction and not that of a cooperation network. The same applies to public procurement regulation: it is most suitable for buying bulk goods. This description is not the whole truth of contracts in practice but far from unreal either, even if many contracts are not drafted by lawyers or maybe not drafted at all in paper.

A good example of the internalized image of contracts is the following quote: "It's important to note that Project Alliancing is more than just a contract; it's a new approach to conducting business and constructing projects that's a dramatic departure from traditional contracting practices where trust is in short supply and antagonism runs rampant."[27] Even if project alliancing is presented in the title as a contracting mechanism, it is emphasized that it is not just a contract i.e. representative of the notorious legal contract. Very often the actual substances of the contract, like technical and working plans, are not considered parts of the contract. 'Contract' is understood to mean only the collection of legal clauses.

The view point of jurisprudence to contracting is application of legal rules in court decisions. This kind of attitude leads to concern for one's own interests: winning a case, even trying to get a contract which allows hidden benefits. From the judge´s standpoint, the business reality is *possibly* taken into consideration as one factor in evaluating the situation and the justness of the decision. Instead, lawyers, who prepare legal contracts, should try to understand enough of the business practice to be able to draft contracts which work in that particular environment and promote functioning cooperation. This is not always the case. Lawyers may draft contracts which may be good "law school documents" but are not useful in the particular case and/or branch of business. If one doesn't know the business reality in question one doesn't know either which are the relevant risks and problems to be prepared for. Preparation for risks and winning cases (influenced by the blind-folded goddess) does not lead to pondering how to enable success (influenced by the seeing goddess).

Frequently, the word 'law' refers to legal rules like legislation and precedents. However, modern law as a discipline (jurisprudence) and as professional expertise is about the art of legal interpretation: finding law and drawing decisions from existing legal rules according to legal

27. Matthew W. Sakal, *Project Alliancing: A Relational Contracting Mechanism for Dynamic Projects,* Lean Construction Journal vol. 2, 2005, April, 67-79.

logic and principles.[28] A reigning ideal is that modern law is a neutral channel through which different values and goals can be realized. As a research object, law is still often seen as an autonomous system of norms separate from society. Modern Civil Law jurisprudence has even been seen as being based on this separation. In real life, law as legal logic is not an isolated silo. It has indirect influence over most functions in modern society. In theory legislation and administration are as the main rule outside of the interest and responsibility area of law as social practices, even if in real life legal language and legal interpretation logic dominate legislation and administration. The main aim of legislation should be to co-create rules which together with other methods would realize the co-created social goals. The main objective of administration should be to realize targets of legislation. These main tasks have become secondary compared with adapting to legal interpretation logic.

Likewise, co-creating contracts and contracting processes as well as realizing and implementing the desired goals should be the main aims in business contracting instead of adapting to legal interpretation logic - but that is not how it is. Proactive attitude means co-creating the kind of documents and processes which forward collaboration towards the goals desired and in the real life circumstances in question. This attitude is usually considered concerning practical skills which are not included in law as legal expertise. Against the described background, it is not amazing that proactive attitude towards contracting is not taught in law schools.[29] From a viewpoint of a successful process, one needs to look at the whole picture and how the different phases work together: Creating the working methods and frames (compare contract drafting and legislation) and implementing them (compare contract implementation and administration) are parts of the same whole which interact continuously. Interpretation of the created rules and solving disputes (compare courts) would work best as parts of implementation, in checking point

28. Adapted from Montesquieu, the idea that legislation, court practice and administration should be separate areas – separation of power – has had an unquestioned black-and-white social influence and has also influenced the separation of jurisprudence. However, even legal security is more real in a self-reflexive and holistic system.
29. See also Soile Pohjonen, Sari Lindblom-Ylänne, *Challenges for Teaching Interaction Skills for Law Students*, The Law Teacher, Vol. 36, 2002, 294-306.

meetings, mediation-like problem solving and so forth. Realization of social goals demands perception of the whole process and the cooperation of different spheres or in contracting realization of the goals of the parties. Even if promotion of goals has been emphasized in many legal discussions and practices – it is essential for example in target-oriented welfare-state law and European law – the viewpoint of law is mainly that of legal decision making (for courts).

Turning the bad guy into a good guy

When focus is on preparing for disputes, the attitude appears mistrusting: aiming at protecting one's own interest and avoiding being exploited. It is, thus, no wonder that contracts are often seen as opposites of trust as for which is considered as an essential element of cooperation. In trusting cooperation, contracts are not considered needed, because partners trust each other and work for the common good. It may thus be dangerous to emphasize the c-word because it may signal to the partner that she is not trusted.[30]

The image of contracts and law vary in different discussions. Law may be seen as a protector of values and freedom or as a formal system creating irresponsibility, to name a few alternatives. Modern, formal-rational law has been considered to be based on autonomy and value neutrality concerning people's targets and moral ideas. Formal law has been seen to secure legal safety by creating clear rules, which diminish the administrators' responsibility.[31] In a formal attitude of following rules, individual responsibility is veiled. Law is seen as a system with its own logic separated from other realities. Contract law as a protector of a rational free will is in the core of modern legal thinking.

Compared to market, law is often seen as a value system and market as an unscrupulous seeking for own benefit. In legal thinking the traditional attitude towards contracts has been congruent with that: the image of a contract relationship is formal and people in it are consid-

30. The contradiction between legal and business attitudes has been recognized for a long time also in theoretical discussions, see already the classic article of Stewart Macaulay, *Non-Contractual Relations in Business: A Preliminary Study*, American Sociological Review V/28 1963, 55-67.
31. See more largely on law and responsibility Scott Veitch, *Law and Irresponsibility, On the legitimation of human suffering* (Routledge-Cavendish: Oxon 2007).

ered selfish and rational in comparison with "partnership in love" like marriage and cohabitation where people are seen as unselfish and emotional in a personal relationship. Another counterpoint to contract is gift: own interest versus altruism. On the other hand, in business practice, contracts represent lack of trust while business partners are supposed to trust each other in a loyal cooperation. Thinking in binary terms has been widely questioned: human beings are many-sided and function in human cooperation, whatever its title, according to "mixed" logics[32], gifts have many faces and may necessitate even harder obligations for the receiver than contracts[33], contract and trust may be conflicting or mutually reinforcing, substitutes or complements depending on the individual commercial relationship[34]. Anyway, whatever the discussion, contracts have often had the role of the "bad guy" which has had its effects in people's mind.

However, if the contracting logic is that of Proactive Law the image changes. When the idea is to promote successful business cooperation, the goal of contracting is to make sure that both parties understand the contract more or less in the same way instead of ensnaring each other. This is also the best way to prevent disputes and promote success. It is also the best way to enhance trust. Proactive contracts further trust because they facilitate reaching the business ends. Trust crumples quickly when vague agreements begin to cause misunderstandings and halting cooperation. It is not amazing that contracts are not usually seen as proactive instruments when they are drafted as legal documents by lawyers who are trained in legal neutrality and not to pursue contextual aims. The notion of 'contract' would need to be given back its pure meaning and not let it remain colored according to a particular

32. Soile Pohjonen, *Partnership in love and in business,* Feminist Legal Studies 8/2000, 47-63.
33. Marcel Mauss, *Essai sur le don,* in Sociologie et antropologie, Quadrige (Presses Universitaires de France 1950) and Mary Douglas, *No Free Gifts* (Routledge 1990).
34. Catherine Mitchell, *Contracts and Contract Law: Challenging the Distinction Between the "Real" and "Paper" Deal,* Oxford Journal of Legal Studies vol. 29 4/2009, 675-704. In her article she questions the real/paper distinction and explores for example the relationship between contract and trust in business dealings (684-687). She also points out how differently both terms "contract" and "trust" may be defined and understood.

i.e. legal perception. To convince anyone to further their contracting competence, they first have to be convinced that contracting in itself is a useful function for business. Above, we hope to have assured the reader that proactive contracting competence is worth developing for lawyers and for other professionals so that all actors involved are able to take back their own contracts.

7. Proactive contracting competence and public procurers

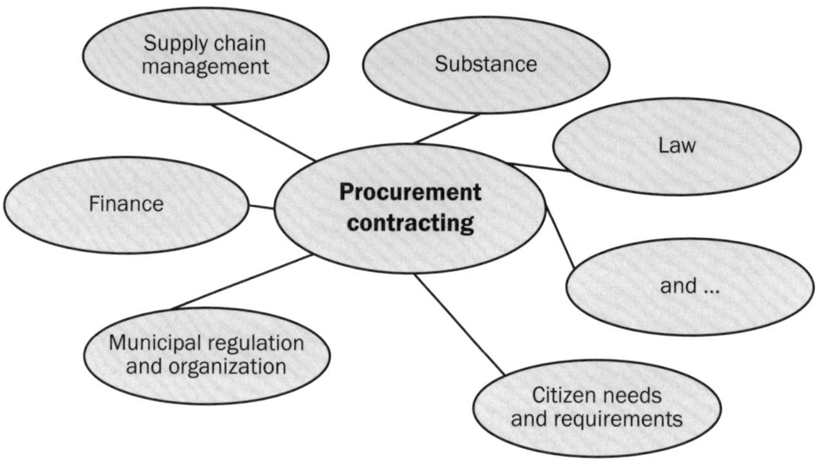

Picture 3: Procurement contracting expertise areas

Generally speaking, contracting and contracts are seen as highly legal activity and documents which are of marginal relevance to other professions. Contracts are perceived to be owned by the legal profession and they are left to the lawyers to deal with. How often do we face the cliché "a good contract is one that needs not to be referred to"? Unfortunately, the above illustrated approach to contracting loses wide potential of contracting processes and contracts as management tools and undermines the importance of legal competence. The same applies to procurement. Procurement is often seen as competitive tendering, although it is only one phase in the process.

By adopting a proactive contracting approach, the ownership of contracts is collective, i.e. all relevant actors and stakeholders are responsible for the contract and have a say on contractual issues. Contracting is perceived as a collective effort. All actors and stakeholders should be engaged throughout the entire contracting process. We perceive the public procurement contracting process to start from the contracting planning phase including the preparation of tendering/contract documentation. It continues through the tendering phase to the implementation and follow-up of the contract, as well as on demand contract portfolio management.

Below, knowledge sharing is discussed in two procurement contracting phases. We start with procurement preparation and how procurement documentation is built by the procurer through collaborative knowledge sharing. Then we move to discuss contract follow-up and what kind of knowledge sharing mechanisms our case procurer has utilized to enhance collaborative interaction between buyer and seller. Finally a short example is illustrated to show how deeper collaboration between contracting parties can be promoted with contractual arrangements.

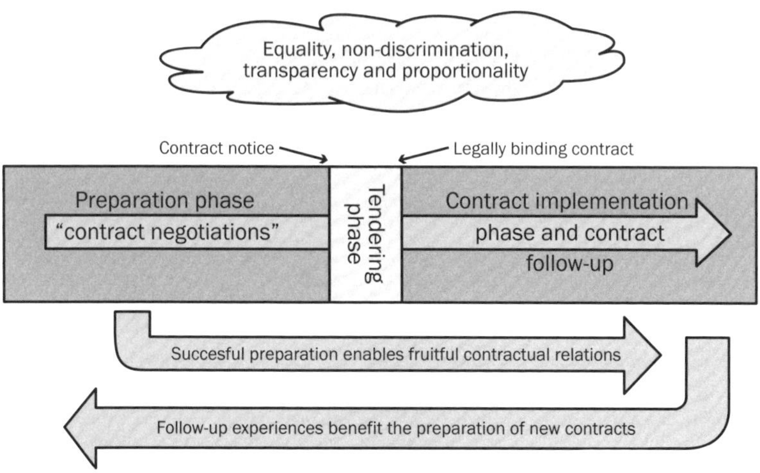

Picture 4: Public procurement contracting

Building a contract through knowledge sharing

First, procurement planning is viewed as how tendering documentation and an initial procurement contract template is built by taking advantage of cross-professional knowledge sharing. Proactive contracting competence includes the ability to acquire and combine necessary knowledge to build a contract into a well-functioning entity that fulfills the procurement needs. Substance issues of the procurement at hand need to be truly understood and considered in contracting. The procurement unit of a public procurer commonly does not have all necessary professional knowledge available within itself. Therefore the ability to acquire relevant knowledge from cross-professional networks to be utilized in contract preparation is an important required skill. A coordinator is responsible for the wholeness. In our cases, a procurement expert functions as the coordinator. This is true in many large public procurement units.

In our case organizations, procurement expertise is mainly centralized. This results in a natural and unavoidable separation of procurement expertise and substance expertise in the organization. This gap between varying expertise knowledge requires to be dealt with. Procurement professionals possess procurement expertise, which is largely legal skills regarding competitive tendering and contracting. Substance expertise is often dispersed in the organization. A procurement professional often lacks the substance knowledge by which the core of the procurement, product or service to be procured and related operations models, is defined. Therefore it is essential that substance experts commit to the preparation of procurement so that scope and quality can be defined to meet the practical needs of the end users.

Since resources are often scarce, an efficient process is required to motivate individuals to participate in and contribute to the process. Professionals are more willing to commit and participate in procurement work, if procurement preparation and contracting are seen as an efficient collaborative process, which benefits their own work. On the other hand, the coordinator needs to know whom to contact to acquire necessary information. Case organizations faced commitment challenges. Individuals were not motivated to participate in procurement preparation that reflected as retarded procurement process and dissatisfaction. The opening up of the procurement process and clearer definition of roles and responsibilities helped to arouse motivation to participate and contribute to the process. Case procurement units use various knowledge sharing instruments. Examples of inter-organizational knowledge sharing are weekly procurement meetings, work group meetings, joint planning meetings, ongoing co-working of procurement and substance professionals, commenting tender documentation from different viewpoints and continuous provision of knowledge on prior experiences which can be documented for future use.

The procurer may fall short of some knowledge. A self-reflexive procurer has a relatively clear picture of what knowledge it is able to gather from its own organization and what it is required to search for externally. Then it should turn to external sources of knowledge to ensure a successful and appropriate procurement. In many cases the market may provide the needed knowledge. An 'intelligent procurer' utilizes all sources of knowledge to define the scope of the contract through technical specifications which is comprised of characteristics required of a product, service or materials subject to tender.

Public sector procurers often do not have the newest knowledge as to what is available on the market. Naturally the best source of information is situated in the firms providing services and products. Contrary to common belief, procurement regulation does not prohibit a public procurer from interacting with the market. Consultation of the market is a general concept which consists of all possible methods and means of communicating and sharing knowledge between public procurer and the market, i.e. individual firms. The law requires that equal opportunity to participate in dialog has to be provided to all inclined to consider participating in the competitive tender.

There is a general sensitivity of public procurers on opening up the communication channels with the market as for sharing knowledge. However there is tentative change detectable in attitudes. Public procurers are increasingly opening up the dialogue with the market. Dialogue between procurer and firms has taken various forms. The most promising results have originated from dialogue outside the official tendering procedure. In those cases the dialogue resembles "normal" commerce or business negotiations and provides opportunities to discuss what solutions would best fulfill the procurement need. The public procurer is able to acquire knowledge which it can use while deciding what to procure and how to arrange associated operations models.

Much work has been done in case organizations to improve relations with firms and develop new interaction methods. The procurer balances constantly between the efficient use of its resources and participating in time consuming knowledge sharing activities. Internet serves as a practical instrument for acquiring knowledge fast and efficiently. It has proved to be a workable channel to find preliminary knowledge of what is available on the market. Limitations of this one-way information channel have been recognized and complementary channels are used.

Active procurers obtain information about new products and services available on the market continuously. Good sources of information are current suppliers and service providers. For instance, daily communication, contract follow-up meetings and even claims provide information that can be utilized in forthcoming competitive procedures to improve the quality of product and service specifications and defining of collaboration processes. However this may prove to be problematic concerning equality and non-discrimination principles. A responsible procurer uses acquired knowledge in an objective manner and retains in mind that other companies are provided with equal opportunity to present their solutions. Procurers invite firms to introduce their solutions. This is done either as a joint event or in private with one firm at a time. Firms prefer private face-to-face meetings to open joint sessions. Firms are not willing to expose their business secrets to competitors and therefore general, open events have not produced sufficient knowledge for the procurer. After contract award tenderers which have been rejected, lost the competition or which have been presumed to tender, but did not, are offered a possibility to come and discuss the procurement. This arrangement is appreciated and taken advantage of by many firms.

Another direction of knowledge sharing has been adopted by public procurers, i.e. opening up dialogue with the market in order to proactively inform the market what the procurer is searching for and what kind of experiences the procurer has acquired. However, to our knowledge these events have not been utilized to discuss how contractual relationships could be developed into a more collaborative form. Some public procurers have become active informants about their forth coming procurements, usually through their web-pages.

During the official competitive tendering phase, the nature of communication alters into a more strict form. However some interaction is possible also during that phase. A commonly used method provided by law is to allow clarifying questions. These questions are collected and answered simultaneously, usually via internet so that both the questions and answers are available to all interested. In service procurements, grand tours have been organized after the publication of a contract notice to provide potential tenderers with a possibility to become acquainted with the site where the service is to be provided. Procurement specific info events are another means of covering and discussing questions about the procurement. In these cases, the direction of the knowledge flow is from the procurer to the market, as the focus of these events is on clarifying information provided in an invitation to tender. Due to equality objective, new knowledge should not be provided, as it may not be open to all potential tenderers.

When procurement is prepared, acquired new knowledge should be utilized to define - or even redefine if necessary - the procurement need. Based on existent knowledge, the procuring unit selects the solution to be procured. At the same time related operations models must be decided on and specified in the invitation to tender. This requires going back and forth with legal, economic and substance issues to be able to achieve a tempting and lawful invitation to tender which in practice is often equivalent to the forthcoming contract. In addition to defining the scope of the contract, acquired knowledge may be utilized in defining collaborative operations models. If the procurer is sensitive to signals from the market, it may consider the use of certain contractual arrangements that may result in potential tenderers to refrain from tendering, e.g. too strict damage or liability clauses have led to firms opting out of competitive procedure.

Contract implementation and follow-up

People implementing contracts need to know what to do and how to do it. Contract documentation that supports practical activities provides clear instructions and working methods that different actors can follow. A well-structured contract is an approachable tool for different users. Procurement units have taken first steps to improve the visual structure of contract documentation to ease legibility and usability of the documentation. They have also taken notice of language used in contracts. The objective is to improve understandability and avoid misunderstandings on what the procurer desires to achieve with the contractual relationship.

Follow-up of contract implementation and contract management have an important role in ensuring that procurement objectives are met. However, contract follow-up has been the phase least taken account of in procurement contracting. As far as we know, procurement units have not been highly active, with some exceptions, to demand for rights secured by their contracts. Development of contract follow-up is quite new in public procurement contracting. Our case organizations have taken first steps to develop claims management and contract follow-up.

Contact literacy is an essential skill in contract follow-up, i.e. being aware of what rights the contract presents. Often users receive only price information, but may not be aware of other specific contractual arrangements. Contract follow-up meetings are the most used form of contract follow-up. In these meetings contracting parties assemble to discuss how the contract has been fulfilled and deal together with possible problems. They have been utilized to collaboratively discuss how both parties can together improve cooperation. Many implementation problems are due to lack of knowledge on the grass roots level when people do not know what has been agreed upon, what they need to inform and to whom, how things are experienced by others and so forth.

Towards deeper collaboration

An essential part of proactive contracting competence is to be able to create contracting instruments which promote the aims. If deeper collaboration is desired, decisions about: which competitive tendering procedure is selected, how long is the contract period, what is the coverage of the contract, all have implications on the contractual relationship. Different competitive procedures include different options and the contract period effects potential tenderers' willingness to invest money and effort. Individual contract relations may suffer if they have to compete as part of a larger whole when their special features and value may not be taken into consideration. Deeper commitment in one relationship may not be allowed to continue if its contents and price do not fit in the standard requirements of the invitation to tender as a whole.

A wish often expressed for contractual relationships is cooperation where problems and solutions are experienced as common. Project Alliance and Integrated Project Delivery (IPD) are examples of enhancing collaboration where risks and rewards are shared and different parties work closely together, sometimes even forming a joint company to realize the project. These kinds of ideas have been applied in a case presented by Scarbrough et al[35] even if Alliance or IPD approaches have not been mentioned. In the presented case, a contractual arrangement which promoted the realization of the collaboration wishes had been developed. In this "shared gain, shared pain" set-up, the contract was based on a lump-sum payment for an outline design instead of a detailed design and the parties shared the difference between the actual cost and the tendered cost. Besides the contractual change, working conditions were reorganized to support the sharing mentality: the parties relocated project team members onto the site which gave them greater autonomy. Problems were freely discussed and solutions developed jointly between the teams.

8. Sharing knowledge in collaboration

The European Economic and Social Committee (EESC) has given an opinion on the proactive law approach.[36] The EESC urges a paradigm shift: giving up the centuries-old reactive approach to law and adopting a proactive approach. It is time to focus on "*how the law is used and operates* in everyday life and how it is received in the community it seeks to regulate" (page 1). The EESC points out that Proactive Law is about enabling and empowering and that the Community legal system is by its very nature the type of system in which the proactive approach should be adopted. As EU law is specifically target-oriented, it would seem

35. Harry Scarbrough, Jacky Swan, Stéphane Laurent, Mike Bresnen, Linda Edelman and Sue Newell, *Project-Based Learning and the Role of Learning Boundaries*, Organization Studies 25(9) 2004, 1579-1600, 1589-1591.
36. European Economic and Social Committee (EESC), Opinion on The proactive law approach: a further step towards better regulation at EU level (own-initiative opinion), (INT/415-CESE 1905/2008 EN/o), available at http://www.eesc.europa.eu.

natural that a factual reaching of the targets would be taken seriously. In the EESC opinion it is believed that it would be beneficial if EU law and its makers would shift their focus from inside the legal system "to outward, to the users of the law: to society, citizens and businesses that the legal system is intended to serve" (page 2). At the end of the opinion, research projects and wide dialogue are wished for.

Clarity and plain language have become topics of interest in legal discussions and in contracting. Rabeea Assy[37] defines plain language as follows: "Typically, this means avoiding archaic and foreign expressions, using common and familiar vocabulary, simpler grammatical structures, shorter and simpler sentences, substituting active for passive voice, favouring verbs over nouns, and providing a better organized outlook – the latter entailing such features as wider spaces and margins, division into sections and subtitles, definition of technical terms, use of examples, provision of tables of contents, highlighting techniques, and the like." Assy argues (383-384) that drafting laws in plain English does not make legally untrained people into their own lawyers, but she admits that plain language could help people understand their rights and obligations sufficiently for everyday situations. Implementation of contracts belongs to this kind of situations. In contracting, people usually do not need to become their own lawyers or their own engineers, but they need to know enough to understand the effect of other branches of expertize to their own tasks which plain language can enhance. In contracting, non-lawyers should understand enough to know for example when to consult a lawyer and what kind of invisible fillings law provides for the gaps in contracts.[38] Layout solutions may help to fathom the idea of the contract and tailored versions for different users may help different professionals to find the information they need.

Assy points out that the contextual nature of legal concepts makes it difficult for laymen to understand laws even if plain language had been used and even if it had helped understanding to some degree. Similar logic applies to contracting; however, the logic to be adopted here is not

37. Rabeea Assy, *Can the Law Speak Directly to its Subjects? The Limitation of Plain Language* 379, Journal of Law and Society, Vol. 38, September 3/2011, 376-404.
38. Helena Haapio, *Invisible Terms in International Contracts and What to Do about Them*, Contract Management, July 2004, 32.

that of law, but of collaboration. The meanings have to be understood in the context of the particular contract. Various professional argots should form a whole which corresponds to the perception of the parties and shares knowledge with people whose task it is to implement the contract. Not everybody needs to understand technical plans, legal clauses and financial arrangements to name a few, but some of them should understand what kind of wholeness they form and people who implement the contract would need to know what is expected from them and why.

Ideas to improve usability of contracts and how they enable aims of contracting have been developed as a part of business and project management. Lean and agile thinking are two examples. They emphasize concentrating on the essentials and creating fluent processes. Contracting has adopted ideas from these other professional discourses. Lean and agile contracting means drafting clear and short contracts, evaluating the real needs and eliminating unnecessary clauses. Especially the need for long and complex contracts has been questioned. Contracts should be understood by people who are supposed to realize them and who usually have not drafted them. Even if many contracts need to be stripped out of text to become leaner that is not the sole solution. Lean i.e. short contracts may look clear and easy to understand, but they may not always be informative enough. In addition, common, easy to understand words may cause even more misunderstandings than concepts which are clearly unfamiliar. People believe they know what is meant with ordinary words and do not ask if their perception corresponds to others' personal or professional understandings.

Based on the Cartesian influence main stream science is still much embedded in dualism: the rational mind has been emphasized at the expense of embodied emotions as well as rational knowledge at the expense of practical skills. Accordingly, law is textual interpretation created by legal professionals in a dialectic and rational process. But if we, instead, see law as an actor in a target-oriented process, contextual knowledge sharing and knowledge co-creation become more relevant than text interpretation. Public procurement is a good example of a complex and many-sided whole where most of the problems may be referred to lack of clarity. Often, actors in these complex processes are not able or motivated to find the information needed or have not even realized the need. They should be tempted towards the information.

Public procurement contracting documents like invitations to tender should attract a sufficient number of suitable tenderers. Building collaboration is a dialogic process where participants need to attract interest and listen actively. When the Cartesian emphasis is on rational mind, the proactive significance of embodied emotions is neglected. Emotion is critical for the appropriate direction of attention, because it provides an automated signal about the organism's past experience with given objects, and thus provides a basis for assigning or withholding attention relative to a given object.[39] Neurologist Antonio Damasio has pointed out that consciousness begins as a feeling.

Business competence includes the ability to arouse interest. Contracts are increasingly seen as a part of productization and marketing. They are more and more often well thought out module contracts offering particular alternatives and including parts which are regularly updated. They are thus kind of products themselves. Service contracts may not sell anything tangible at all. The customer is actually buying a service contract.[40] The value of contracts should be considered also from the aspect of their selling capacity: How they promote or hinder sales? How they enhance the good reputation, the image and brand of the company?

The more dialogic and co-creating we attempt to be, the more sophisticated methods for knowledge sharing and knowledge co-creation we need. In contracting processes, boundary objects[41] need to be developed to cross the boundaries between human minds while co-creating the common will and building contracts to plan the realization of this will as well as in implementing it. Rational and impersonal writing is seldom the best method of reaching this aim. In our scientific traditions, concepts have often been understood as conscious, literal and disembodied. Like seeds, words and thoughts have been seen as something which may be transferred in containers, as more or less unchanged. Legal language and its ideal of clarity are largely based on this understanding. It has, though,

39. Antonio Damasio, *A Feeling of What Happens* (Vintage: London 2000), 273, 312.
40. See more Katri Rekola, Helena Haapio, *Industrial services and Service Contracts, A Proactive Approach* (The federation of Finnish Technology Industries: Helsinki 2009).
41. See Paul Carlile, *A Pargmatic View of Knowledge and Boundaries: Boundary Objects in New Product Development,* Organization Science, Vol. 13, No. 4, July-August 2002, 442-455.

been argued that human thought processes are largely metaphorical and that our conceptual system is mostly metaphorically structured.[42] Metaphors are imaginative rationality, uniting reason and imagination. Besides being linguistic and conceptual, metaphorical thought is embodied.[43] Metaphors are open-ended and thus more holistic than definitions. When metaphors are understood as our way of having a reality, the question will not be what they mean, but how they *work*. A metaphor is not asked to validate a rule of logic; the question is what logic and reality it constitutes and *enables* (Winter 2001, 58, 65-66).

Contracts should act as boundary objects to enable successful collaboration in business relations. Visualization is a strongly emerging answer. Visualization may mean anything from infographics to films. The former are comparable to plain language in the world of words and the latter nearer narratives. Messages of the latter category are received more spontaneously and holistically than more rational presentations. In a dialog it is not enough – or even possible - to transfer one-sidedly already existing information but to create new understanding together. The more narrative and poetic visual presentations are, the more effective they are and the more difficult their influence is to realize. Visual literacy and competence are needed to increase our ability to send and receive visual messages more consciously.[44]

In public procurement contracting, infographics and illustrative pictures might usually be a sufficient visualizing tool to clarify agreed obligations and the whole picture: how different regulations, different operational spheres and different working phases are connected to each other and how actors can easily find the information which is relevant to

42. On metaphors see George Lakoff & Mark Johnson, *Metaphors we live by* (The University of Chicago Press: Chicago and London 2003). The conduit metaphor originates from Michael Reddy.
43. See on design as embodied activity Juha Kronqvist & Anna Salmi, *Co-Designing (with) Organizations – Human-Centeredness, Participation and Embodiment in Organizational Development,* in Proceedings of Designing Pleasurable Products and Interfaces DPPI 287-294(Politecnico di Milano: Milan 2011).
44. On visualization, visual literary and visual jurisprudence see Richard K. Sherwin, *Visualizing Law in the Age of the Digital Baroque, Arabesques and entanglements, supra* note 3.

them.[45] This would further compliance as well as ability and possibilities to develop functioning working methods and collaboration. Innovative solutions can already be found[46] but there is no lack of opportunities for developers.

Picture 5: An example of the illustrated working instructions for cleaning used by the city of Espoo. Colored boxes signify how often the objects pointed with similar colors have to be cleaned.

45. At present our research project is scheduled to have developed infographics to clarify change management mechanisms concerning price in public procurement contracts in relation to Finnish General Terms of Public Procurement and other regulation. The intention is to widen the scope of this work after the first experiment.
46. See for example Procurement Journey toolkit of the Scottish government, available at http://www.scotland.gov.uk/Topics/Government/Procurement/buyer-information/spdlowlevel/routetwotoolkit.

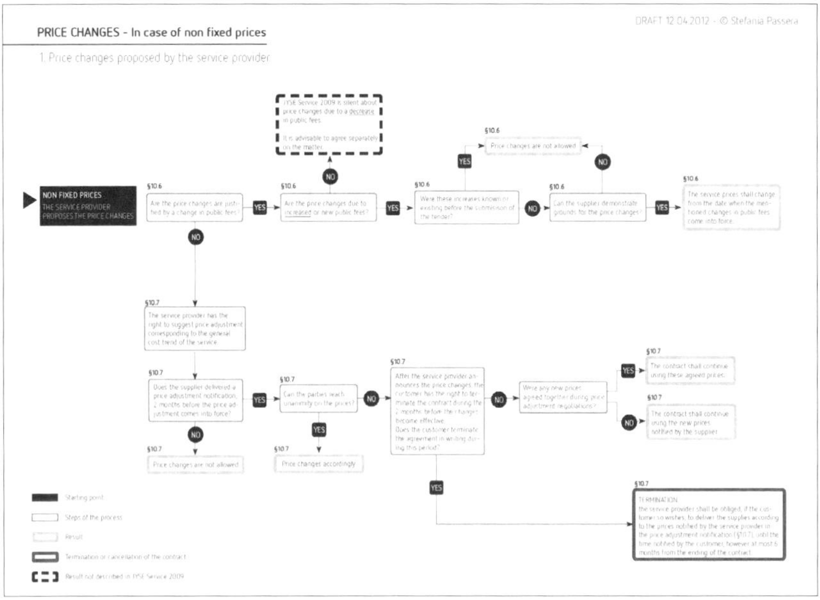

Picture 6: Visualization of the term concerning prices in the General Terms of Public Procurement in service contracts (JYSE 2009) designed for our research project by designer Stefania Passera, a draft to be modified.

9. Conclusions

Both public procurement regulation and contracting reflect the logic of law, an interpretation system which has succeeded in making the procurement documents serve its own purposes and not those of target-oriented operations what social and contractual processes actually are. The EU public procurement regulation is based on the legal formalistic logic, to protect procurement against favoritism and corruption. The substance goals: enhancement of competition capabilities of European companies and good procurement for the public sector, here municipalities, are not very well reached with the emphasis on legal formalities. When the main focus of the authorities is on managing the competitive tendering process without appeals, the reasonability of the procurement is overshadowed. When companies usually have to offer exactly what they were asked for so that the transparency of the competition would be ensured, their normal offering capabilities have to be abolished rather than ameliorated. Fear for the court proceedings spreads formalistic attitudes which rather harm than develop procurement. Changing the EU regulation and national legislation based on it, is a long-term goal. Contracting may, instead, be developed immediately. The legal formalistic or nonchalant attitude towards contracts and contracting may be altered to suit the demands of target-oriented collaboration.

When invitations to tender are really seen as invitations they should tempt a sufficient number of good quality tenderers. That could be achieved by well-functioning information, clear guidelines, documents with plain language and infographics, functional product or service descriptions made with the help of the market, invitations which describe more the target and purpose than all the demanded details to leave room for amelioration and change and so forth. Similar demands apply to contracts, their implementation and follow-up. Contracting is implemented by people who need to know what they are supposed to do and why. It is challenging in all organizations to deliver information and create collaboration. In the public sector that is even more so. Different units may be functionally detached from each other and their standing orders and strategies concerning procurement may even be contradictory. Authorities who will be using the products or services to be procured do not always perceive it as their task to participate in defining the products, but see it as the task of procurement experts. Those are, however, usually not able to do that properly without the help of substance experts. Procurement is often considered a dull formality. The whole picture is not realized and motivation to learn and participate often lack. Even public decision makers are often quite vaguely aware of the procurement system and may make for contradictory policy. Neither the public media always understands the logic of the system, delivering thus erroneous information to end users, i.e. citizens, which may cause unnecessary problems to procurement authorities.

Knowledge sharing between and within the organizations is the most important element for successful procurement contracting. Instead of the effort to please legal interpretation the focus should be in cross-professional collaboration to plan what is desired and how the expertise of different actors and their viewpoints can together contribute to the whole. The planning phase and the implementation, follow-up phase are emerging from the shadows of the competitive tendering process as the relevant ones. Procurement centers are waking up to the importance of contracting as a knowledge sharing process. After our research report it may have first come as a shock to a procurement center how many gaps there are in knowledge sharing in their organization and in their contracting processes. Sometimes this awareness has already been an important research result but the self-reflection has also inspired to develop the systems further. The usefulness of infographics has been realized.

Separation of operational spheres is not the fault and consequence of only legal thinking. Segregation of branches of science and sectors of organizations manifest similar attitude. The differentiated logic, language and working methods often make it very difficult to develop cross-disciplinary and cross-professional collaboration. It is worth the effort, because without dialogic thinking and good quality boundary objects it is impossible to develop intelligent and functioning systems.

Acknowledgements
This article has been written in the research project PRO2ACT (Proactive contracting processes in public procurement) at Aalto University, SimLab. The authors are grateful for the fruitful collaboration in SimLab and with Helena Haapio on visualization. PRO2ACT is financed by the Finnish Funding Agency for Technology and Innovation (Tekes) and partner organizations.